# MARK HIX

## THE COLLECTION

Photography by Jason Lowe

# MARK HIX
## THE COLLECTION

Quadrille
PUBLISHING

## Notes

All spoon measures are level unless otherwise stated:

1 tsp = 5ml spoon; 1 tbsp = 15ml spoon.

Egg sizes are given where they are critical, otherwise use medium eggs, preferably organic or free-range. Anyone who is pregnant or in a vulnerable health group should avoid sauces that use raw egg whites or lightly cooked eggs.

Use fresh herbs, sea salt and freshly ground black pepper unless otherwise suggested.

Timings are for conventional ovens. If using a fan-assisted oven, decrease the temperature by 15°C (1 Gas mark). Use an oven thermometer to check the temperature.

EDITORIAL DIRECTOR Jane O'Shea
CREATIVE DIRECTOR Helen Lewis
PROJECT EDITOR Simon Davis
EDITOR Louise McKeever
DESIGNER Liz Hallam
PHOTOGRAPHER Jason Lowe
PRODUCTION Sasha Taylor, Vincent Smith

First published in 2013 by
Quadrille Publishing Limited
Alhambra House
27–31 Charing Cross Road
London WC2H 0LS
www.quadrille.co.uk

Text © 2013 Mark Hix
Photography © 2005–2013 Jason Lowe
Artwork © Tracey Emin (page 2); Caragh Thuring (pages 8 & 9); Michael Landy (pages 58 & 59); Michael Craig-Martin (pages 86 & 87); Polly Morgan (page 117); Tracey Emin (pages 150); Sarah Lucas (pages 178–179); Laura Quick (page 217); Gary Webb (page 249); Mat Collishaw (page 291); Tim Noble and Sue Webster (page 303)
Design and layout © 2012 Quadrille Publishing Limited

The recipes in this compilation have been previously published in Mark Hix's earlier books: *British Food*, *British Regional Food*, *British Seasonal Food*, *Fish Etc.*, *Hix Oyster & Chop House*.

The rights of the author have been asserted.

ISBN 978 1 84949 317 8

Printed in China

# CONTENTS

# INTRODUCTION

Over the years I've often been asked when I'm going to get around to putting together a collection of my best recipes. Well, here it is!

I've really enjoyed putting this book together – the process of trawling back through my recipe archive and picking out my favourites has been a lot of fun. But it's also been great to have had the chance to mull over how much things have changed in the food world over the years, and it's given me the chance to tweak and revise certain recipes where necessary to show this. For example, things have changed so much in our oceans in terms of fish stocks that I've tweaked a number of the fish recipes here to use what are now more sustainable options (though who knows what will happen to even these stocks over the coming years if our fishing policies don't change!).

Since I started cooking so much to do with our food has changed for the better. People now are genuinely interested in the provenance of the food they are buying, sometimes to the point that they are getting out there and foraging some of it for free (something which always makes cooking at home a little more interesting and certainly prompts dinner party conversation!). British farming has certainly moved on in the last few decades and there's now little excuse for putting anything into your shopping basket that isn't British, while food and farmers markets are cropping up all over the country – offering great support for local producers by providing an opportunity to educate the general public about the great food that is available on their doorsteps.

Similarly the many food festivals that have started across the country, including my own down in Lyme Regis, give the public a great chance to meet to chat about food and watch the chefs perform. This is something I love, as I truly believe that food should be about fun. It's a huge part of our lives and a gathering around the table, whether it be at a festival, in a restaurant or at home, should be a lively occasion with ingredients that celebrate their season, obviously with good wines or beer or cider to match. Hopefully the food you'll see in this book reflects this, and will give you a bit of inspiration to get in the kitchen and get cooking.

**MARK HIX**

# STARTERS AND SNACKS

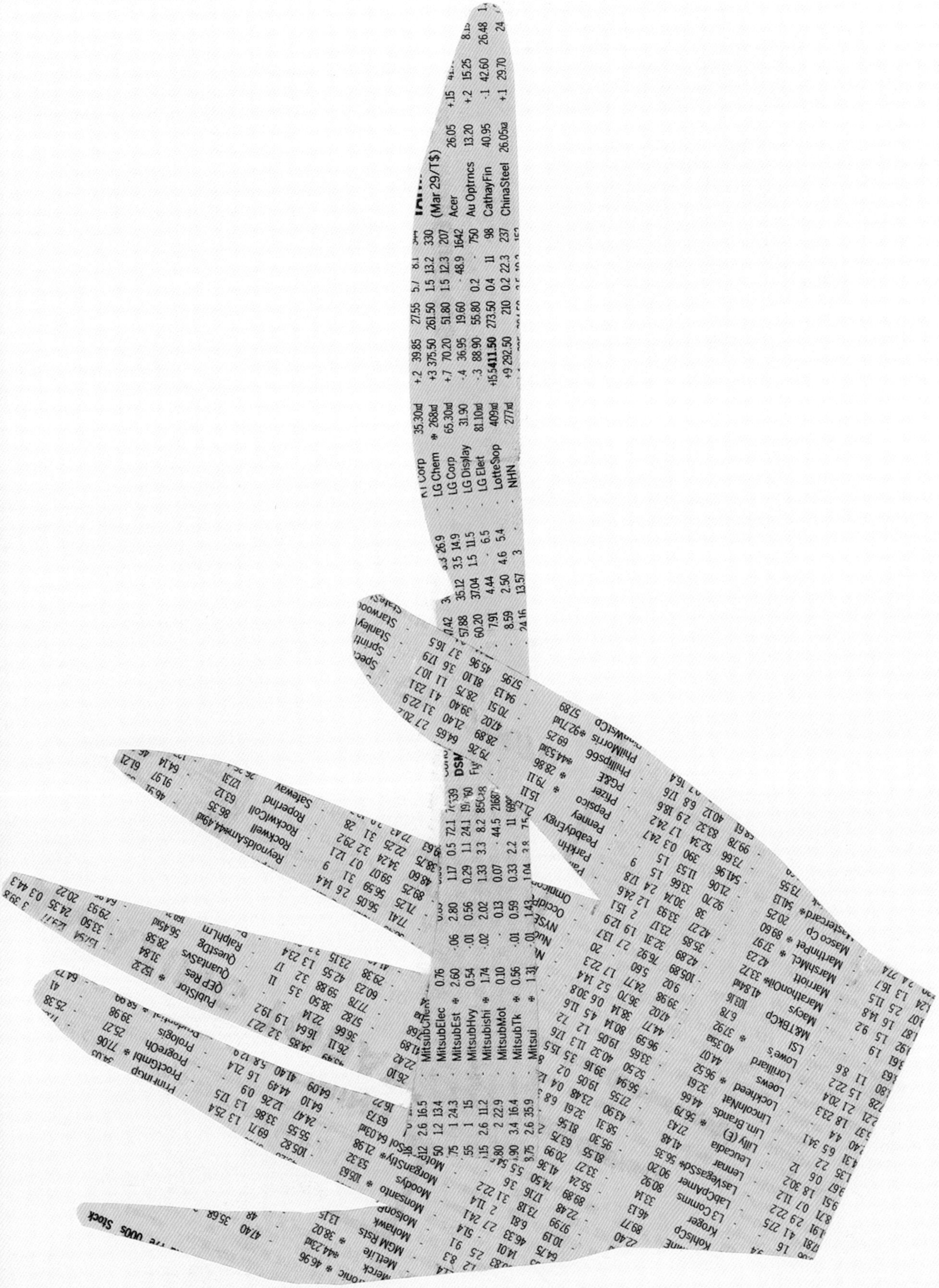

**66** These are worth the effort even if they do take a little time to prepare. My favourites are celeriac and parsnip crisps. Beetroot crisps look spectacular, though they are trickier to get really crisp. A combination of all three makes a great snack. **99**

# VEGETABLE CRISPS

1 small head of celeriac, peeled
1 large parsnip, scrubbed clean
1 large beetroot, peeled
vegetable or corn oil, for deep-frying
sea salt

SERVES 8

Using a mandolin or swivel vegetable peeler, cut the celeriac, parsnip and beetroot into wafer-thin slices, then pat the vegetable strips dry on kitchen paper.

Heat approximately an 8cm depth of oil in a deep-fat fryer or other suitable deep, heavy pan to 180°C. (Check the temperature with a thermometer.)

Deep-fry the vegetable slices, a handful at a time, for 2–3 minutes until lightly coloured and just starting to crisp; stir them around in the oil to ensure that they cook evenly and that they don't stick together.

Using a slotted spoon, transfer the crisps to a rack lined with kitchen paper and immediately sprinkle with sea salt. Leave them to dry somewhere warm but not hot – they will continue to crisp up as they dry – while you deep-fry the rest. Serve the crisps as soon as possible.

# HERITAGE RADISHES WITH MAYONNAISE

2–3 bunches of radishes, preferably with leaves
mayonnaise (see page 295)

SERVES 6–8

To prepare the radishes, remove any dead leaves and give them a good wash in cold water. Drain well and pat dry on kitchen paper.

Serve the radishes on a platter, with the mayonnaise in a bowl alongside, for dipping.

66 There are several interesting varieties of radishes on the market these days, so buy a couple of different types if possible. If you are a gardener you can, of course, easily grow your own. 99

# FRIED GREEN TOMATOES IN BEER BATTER

4 green tomatoes
vegetable or corn oil, for deep-frying
plain flour, for dusting
sea salt

FOR THE BATTER
8 tbsp gluten-free self-raising flour
about 200–225ml light beer, such as pale ale
a good pinch cayenne pepper

SERVES 4

First make the batter. Put the self-raising flour into a bowl and whisk in enough beer to make a smooth, coating batter. Season with salt and cayenne pepper.

Cut the green tomatoes into even slices, about 1cm thick, using a sharp knife.

Heat about an 8cm depth of oil in a deep-fat fryer or other suitable heavy pan to 160–180°C. (Check the temperature with a thermometer.)

You'll need to fry the tomato slices in batches. Dust them with flour, then dip into the batter to coat, lower into the hot oil and fry for 3–4 minutes until golden. Drain on kitchen paper and lightly season with salt. Keep warm while you fry the rest. Serve piping hot.

When making a batter with self-raising flour I now use gluten-free flour instead of wheat flour. I find that it makes for a much lighter batter that stays crisp for longer.

# ROASTED GARLIC-STUDDED CEPS

1kg firm medium ceps
6–8 garlic cloves, peeled and sliced
200g butter
sea salt and freshly ground black pepper
2 tbsp chopped flat-leaf parsley

SERVES 4

Preheat the oven to 220°C/gas mark 7. Clean the ceps with a cloth and make about 5 incisions in each one with the point of a knife. Push a slice of garlic into each incision.

Melt half of the butter in a roasting tray. Add the ceps, turn to coat them in the butter and season generously with salt and pepper. Roast in the oven for 20–30 minutes until the ceps are just tender, turning them every so often to ensure they cook and colour evenly.

Add the rest of the butter and the chopped parsley, stir well and return to the oven for 2–3 minutes. Serve at once.

"When ceps are in season during the autumn, there is nothing better than a plate of them simply roasted as a starter – or even as a side or vegetarian main course. I served this dish as a main course for everyone at dinner when a couple of my guests were vegetarian and I wanted a dish that would satisfy everyone. It went down a treat."

## ASPARAGUS ON TOAST WITH DORSET DRUM CHEDDAR

300–350g medium asparagus spears
sea salt and freshly ground black pepper
a couple of generous knobs of butter
4 slices of brown or white bloomer-type bread
100g mature Dorset Drum Cheddar cheese
3–4 tbsp cold-pressed rapeseed oil

SERVES 4

To cook the asparagus, bring a pan of well-salted water to the boil. Cut off and discard the woody ends of the asparagus, then add to the pan. Simmer for 4-5 minutes or until just tender. Drain and trim the base of the spears so they are roughly the same length as the bread slices.

Put the asparagus trimmings into a blender and process briefly to a rough purée. Reheat in a pan with the butter and season to taste.

Toast the bread on both sides. Spread generously with the asparagus purée and lay the hot or warm asparagus on top. Using a peeler or sharp knife, shave the cheese over the top and drizzle with the rapeseed oil.

## TOMATOES ON TOAST WITH AGED LANCASHIRE CHEESE

4 large ripe tomatoes
1 tbsp cold-pressed rapeseed oil, plus extra to drizzle
1 garlic clove, peeled and roughly crushed
a few sprigs of thyme, leaves only
sea salt and freshly ground black pepper
4 slices of sourdough bread, 1cm thick
100–120g mature Lancashire cheese
wood sorrel leaves or chives, to garnish

SERVES 4

Cut about 6 slices from the centre of each tomato, around 0.5cm thick, and put to one side.

Chop up the rest of the tomatoes and place in a saucepan with the rapeseed oil, garlic and thyme leaves. Season with salt and pepper and cook, stirring, over a low heat for 2-3 minutes until the tomatoes disintegrate into a pulp.

Toast the sourdough bread on both sides, then spread with the tomato mixture and arrange the slices of tomato on top.

With a swivel vegetable peeler or sharp knife, cut the cheese into shavings and arrange on the tomatoes. Drizzle with a little rapeseed oil, top with a little pepper and scatter with wood sorrel leaves or chives to serve.

"During its relatively short season I like to serve home-grown asparagus in as many ways as possible. Serving it on toast turns it into a sophisticated snack. I've topped this with one of my favourite cheeses, Dorset Drum Cheddar, which comes from Denhay Farm, just outside Bridport in west Dorset."

This simple snack is delicious, particularly if you use one of the sweet, tasty heritage varieties or a large juicy beefsteak tomato, though any flavourful tomatoes will do. Use a sourdough base and a great cheese, such as the one produced by the Kirkhams in Lancashire.

## ST GEORGE'S MUSHROOMS ON TOAST

2 tbsp cold-pressed rapeseed or vegetable oil
400–500g St George's, or other wild mushrooms,
     cleaned
sea salt and freshly ground black pepper
2 garlic cloves, peeled and crushed, or a handful of
     wild garlic leaves, roughly chopped
60–70g butter
2 tbsp chopped flat-leaf parsley
4 slices from a bloomer or similar-style loaf,
     about 1.5cm thick

SERVES 4

Heat the oil in a large heavy-based frying pan and
cook the mushrooms over a medium heat for 3–4
minutes, adding a little seasoning and the garlic
halfway through cooking. Stir them every so often.
You may need to do this either in 2 large pans or
in 2 batches.

Add the butter and parsley to the pan(s) and cook
for another minute, stirring well.

Toast the bread on both sides and serve with the
mushrooms and the cooking juices spooned over
the top.

Try to avoid washing wild mushrooms,
unless it is absolutely necessary, as
they tend to soak up the water like
a sponge and you will end up with a
pan full of water when you try to sauté
them. Instead, brush or wipe off any
soil or grit with a cloth or kitchen paper.

## POTTED SHRIMPS ON TOAST

175g unsalted butter
juice of ½ lemon
a good pinch of freshly grated mace or nutmeg
a pinch of cayenne pepper
1 small bay leaf
1 tsp anchovy essence or paste
200g peeled brown shrimps
sea salt and freshly ground white pepper

TO SERVE
good-quality brown bread
2 lemons, halved

SERVES 4

Melt the butter in a pan, add the lemon juice,
mace or nutmeg, cayenne pepper, bay leaf and
anchovy essence or paste, and simmer gently on a
very low heat for 2 minutes to allow the spices to
infuse. Remove from the heat and leave the mixture
to cool until it is just warm.

Add the shrimps and stir well, then season with
salt and pepper. Put the mixture into the fridge and
stir every so often. When the butter starts to set, fill
4 ramekins with the mixture.

If you are not serving the shrimps that day, cover
the ramekins with cling film and store them in the
fridge. It is important, though, not to serve them
straight from the fridge, as the butter will be too
hard to spread nicely on to the toast and won't taste
as good. Serve on or with toasted brown bread and
lemon halves.

Ask your fishmonger to order you
some peeled brown shrimps, because
it could take you the best part of a day
to peel enough for four. They will be
expensive but well worth it. If you can't
find these, use cooked and peeled
prawns or even crab meat.

"This is a nice simple starter that can be made the day – or even a few days – before and just brought out of the fridge an hour or so ahead of time to allow it to soften up slightly. Morecambe Bay, on the Lancashire coast, is the home of shrimping in Britain and many commercial potted shrimps come from there."

# RED MULLET ON TOAST WITH CRUSHED BROAD BEANS AND PEAS

250g podded young broad beans
sea salt and freshly ground black pepper
a couple of generous knobs of butter
60g podded peas
4 small red mullet fillets, each about 80g, or 2 halved
    fillets from a larger fish
4 slices of brown or white bloomer-type bread
½ tbsp cider vinegar
1½ tbsp cold-pressed rapeseed oil
a handful of pea shoots (optional)

SERVES 4

Cook the broad beans in boiling salted water for 3–4 minutes (or a little longer if they are large) until tender. Drain them and blend to a coarse purée in a food processor, adding a knob of the butter and seasoning to taste; keep warm.

Cook the peas in boiling salted water for a couple of minutes until tender. Drain and set aside.

Melt the rest of the butter in a heavy or non-stick frying pan. Season the red mullet fillets and fry them, skin side down first, over a medium heat for a couple of minutes on each side.

Toast the bread on both sides. Meanwhile, whisk the vinegar and oil together to make a dressing and season with salt and pepper.

Spread the broad bean purée generously on the toasts and top with the red mullet. Arrange the peas and pea shoots, if using, around the toasts and spoon the dressing over them to serve.

66 This is a popular dish at the Hix Oyster & Fish House in Lyme Regis. It really says summer when it arrives at the table, especially when you have a great sea view. You could use red gurnard or even mackerel fillets instead of red mullet. 99

# HERRING ROES ON TOAST

400–450g soft herring roes
150g butter
sea salt and freshly ground white pepper
4 slices of a bloomer-style loaf, about 1.5cm thick
60g capers, drained and rinsed
1 tbsp finely chopped flat-leaf parsley

**SERVES 4**

Pat the herring roes dry on some kitchen paper. Heat 50g of the butter in a trusty heavy frying pan (or, better still, a non-stick one). Season the roes with salt and pepper and cook them on a medium heat until they are golden brown – they will curl up during cooking.

Meanwhile, toast the slices of bread on both sides. When the roes are ready, pile them on the toast. Melt the rest of the butter in the pan, add the capers and parsley and spoon it over the roes.

# PILCHARDS ON TOAST

6 tbsp cold-pressed rapeseed or olive oil, plus more
    for brushing
2 shallots, finely chopped
3 ripe tomatoes, skinned, deseeded and cut into
    rough 1cm cubes
2 tsp white wine vinegar
1 tbsp chopped flat-leaf parsley
sea salt and freshly ground black pepper
8 pilchards, scaled, filleted and any residual small
    bones removed
4 slices of bread, about 1cm thick

SERVES 4

Heat the oil in a pan and gently cook the shallots in the oil for 2–3
minutes without allowing them to colour. Add the tomatoes, vinegar,
parsley and season with salt and pepper, then simmer for another
couple of minutes. Take off the heat and set aside.

Meanwhile, preheat the grill to its hottest temperature. Make a
couple of diagonal slashes across the skin side of each pilchard fillet,
then brush them with olive oil, season with some salt and pepper,
and grill for about 3–4 minutes with the skin side up.

Toast both sides of the bread and serve with the tomato sauce and
pilchards piled on top.

"This dish does bear an obvious resemblance to those
rather grim canned pilchards in tomato sauce, but
the combination is a good one, and the acidity of the
tomato cuts the oiliness of the fish to produce a snack
or supper dish that is both satisfying and healthy."

"You can't beat a good crab sandwich. I've had some pretty appalling ones in the past, so now I won't order one unless I know the establishment. I suppose I was spoilt in my childhood – crab straight off the boat, into the pot, into a sandwich and eaten within 24 hours."

# CRAB SANDWICH

2 cooked crabs, each about 500–600g, or 1 cooked
    crab, about 1kg, white and brown meat picked
2–3 tbsp mayonnaise (see page 295)
sea salt and freshly ground white pepper
a squeeze of lemon juice, to taste (optional)
8 slices of wholemeal bread, about 1cm thick
softened butter, for spreading
lemon wedges, to serve

SERVES 4

Check the crab meat for any tiny fragments of shell
and keep the brown and white meat separate.

Put the brown crab meat into a bowl and mix with
1–2 tablespoons of the mayonnaise. Season with
salt and pepper to taste and add a little lemon juice
if you wish. Butter the bread and spread a couple of
tablespoonfuls of the brown meat mix onto half
of the slices.

Spread a little mayonnaise onto the other slices
of bread. Lightly season the white meat and pile it
on to these slices. Ideally, you want to use about
double the quantity of white meat to brown meat,
although it depends on your taste and how much
brown meat you can get out of your crab(s).

Sandwich the slices together and cut in half or into
quarters. Serve with lemon wedges, for squeezing.

Any leftover crab can be mixed together and spread
onto hot buttered toast.

For a good crab sandwich, you
need very fresh crab – and plenty of
white claw meat in particular. Good
wholemeal bread and homemade
mayonnaise are also essential. I've
known breadcrumbs to be mixed into
the brown meat along with the mayo.
That's understandable if the meat is
wet, but otherwise I wouldn't advocate
this as it will weaken the flavour.

# SMOKED HADDOCK RABBIT

150–200g undyed smoked haddock
about 160ml milk, for poaching
5 tbsp stout
5 tbsp double cream
75g Caerphilly cheese, grated
75g Cheddar cheese, grated
2 egg yolks
2 tsp Worcestershire sauce, or more to taste
1 tsp English mustard
sea salt and freshly ground black pepper
4 slices of brown or white bloomer-type bread

SERVES 4

Poach the smoked haddock in gently simmering
milk to cover for 3–4 minutes, then drain. Leave to
cool a little, then remove the skin and any bones
and flake the haddock flesh into a bowl.

In a small heavy-based pan, simmer the stout
until it has reduced by half. Add the cream and
again reduce this by half until it is really thick.
Leave to cool a little, then mix in the grated cheese,
followed by the egg yolks, the Worcestershire sauce
and the mustard. Stir in the flaked haddock and
season with salt and pepper to taste.

Preheat the grill to medium. Toast the bread on
both sides. Spread the haddock mixture thickly on
top of the toasts, about 1cm thick and right to the
edges to avoid them burning under the grill. Place
under the grill until the topping is nicely browned,
then serve.

"This fishy variation on a classic Welsh rabbit makes
an excellent brunch dish or teatime snack. Use either
Arbroath smokies or undyed smoked haddock."

## GROUSE ON TOAST WITH DANDELION

2 oven-ready grouse, livers reserved
a few generous knobs of butter
2 shallots, peeled and finely chopped
1 garlic clove, peeled and crushed
sea salt and freshly ground black pepper
2 tbsp sherry
4 slices of white or brown bread from a small bloomer
    loaf, about 1cm thick
a handful of dandelion or other small salad leaves

FOR THE DRESSING
1 tbsp sherry vinegar
3 tbsp walnut oil

SERVES 4

Preheat the oven to 220°C/gas mark 7. Clean the livers, cut them into even-sized pieces and pat dry with kitchen paper. Heat a knob of the butter in a frying pan and briefly fry the shallots and garlic for a minute or so without colouring. Season the livers and add them to the pan. Fry over a medium heat for 2–3 minutes, stirring every so often. Stir in the sherry, then remove the pan from the heat.

Rub the grouse breasts with butter, season with salt and pepper and place in a roasting pan. Roast for 10–15 minutes, keeping them nice and pink.

Meanwhile, for the dressing, whisk the sherry vinegar and walnut oil together and season to taste.

Chop the liver mixture by hand or in a food processor, as finely or coarsely as you wish, tasting and seasoning again if necessary. Toast the bread on both sides, then spread with the liver mixture.

Remove the breasts from the grouse, slice and arrange on top of the toasts. Shred any leg meat from the birds and mix with the dandelion leaves and dressing. Season and arrange on plates, placing the warm liver toasts in the centre. Serve at once.

You can, of course, serve other game, like wild duck, teal, widgeon or snipe, in this way. If the grouse giblets have been removed, buy 120g chicken or duck livers to use instead.

## CHOPPED LIVERS ON TOAST

250g fresh chicken or duck livers, cleaned
100g butter
2 large shallots, peeled and finely chopped
1 garlic clove, peeled and crushed
sea salt and freshly ground black pepper
4 slices of brown or white bloomer-type bread
a handful of landcress, young watercress or other
    small salad leaves

SERVES 4

Cut the livers into small, even-sized chunks. Melt half the butter in a saucepan and gently cook the shallots and garlic for 3–4 minutes, stirring every so often, until soft. Take off the heat.

Pat the chicken livers dry with kitchen paper and season with salt and pepper. Melt the rest of the butter in a frying pan until it begins to foam. Add the livers and cook them for a couple of minutes on each side. Transfer to a board and chop finely, or give them just a few seconds in a food processor.

Toast the bread on both sides. Mix the livers with the shallots and garlic. Re-season if necessary and spoon generously on to the toasts. Top with the cress and serve.

"This is such a simple, inexpensive dish to knock up quickly at home. You can use either chicken or duck livers, preferably fresh rather than frozen though the latter will do."

## COBB EGG

200g white fish fillets, such as whiting, pollack
   or haddock, boned and skinned
150g sea salt flakes or rock salt crystals
4 duck's eggs
100g smoked white fish fillet, such as pollack, haddock,
   etc., boned and skinned
freshly ground white pepper
2–3 tbsp plain flour, plus extra for dusting
1 egg, beaten
60–70g fresh white breadcrumbs
vegetable or corn oil, for deep-frying

MAKES 4

Lay the white fish on a non-reactive tray, scatter over the salt and let stand for 1 hour. Rinse well under cold water, drain and pat dry.

Bring a pan of water to the boil and carefully drop in the duck's eggs, using a slotted spoon. Simmer for 5 minutes, then drain and refresh under the cold tap for several minutes to stop them cooking.

Meanwhile, check the white and smoked fish for small bones, removing any with tweezers, then put into a food processor. Pulse together to a coarse texture and season with pepper. Divide the fish mixture into 4 portions, shape into balls and flatten them on a lightly floured surface.

Carefully shell the duck's eggs, then mould the fish mixture around them ensuring they are well sealed.

Have 3 shallow bowls ready, one containing the flour, one with the beaten egg and the third with the breadcrumbs. One at a time, coat the duck's eggs with the flour first, shaking off any excess, then put through the beaten egg and finally into the breadcrumbs, turning them to coat all over and re-moulding as necessary.

Heat an 8cm depth of oil in a deep-fat fryer or other suitable deep, heavy pan to 140–150°C. Deep-fry the eggs for 4–5 minutes, turning them every so often to colour evenly. Remove with a slotted spoon and drain on kitchen paper.

Serve hot or warm, with salad and a herb mayonnaise or tartare sauce (see page 295).

## QUAIL'S EGG SHOOTERS

2 rashers of smoked streaky bacon, rind removed
2 tsp finely chopped chives
12 quail's eggs
coarse sea salt, to sit the eggs in

SERVES 4

Grill or fry the bacon rashers until crisp, let cool and then chop as finely as you can. Mix with the chives.

Bring a pan of water to the boil and lower the quail's eggs in carefully. Simmer for 20 seconds, then drain and run under the cold tap briefly.

Spoon a good layer of sea salt onto a serving dish. Cut the tops off the quail's eggs to expose the yolk and stand them in the salt. Spoon the bacon mixture on top of each one and serve immediately.

To eat, knock them back like a shot, squeezing the shell slightly to release the egg.

"One of my chefs at the Hix Oyster & Fish House in Lyme Regis developed this Cobb egg as a fishy take on a Scotch egg. Customers really took to it, as the soft yolk ran down their chins while they were overlooking the Cobb. You could make little ones with quail's eggs for bar snacks or pre-dinner drinks."

"One of my favourite restaurants in New York, the Fatty Crab, offers these with Southeast Asian flavourings, but they work equally well with British flavours – like crisp bacon and chives. Vary the toppings as the mood takes you. For the restaurants I've had some wooden boards made with cavities to hold the eggs, but you can just sit them in coarse sea salt."

# BOILED DUCK'S EGG WITH ASPARAGUS SOLDIERS

900g medium to thick asparagus spears
4 large duck's eggs (or ordinary hen's eggs)
coarse sea salt

SERVES 4

To prepare the asparagus, cut or break off the woody ends. Peel the stalks with a fine swivel vegetable peeler, starting about 5cm (2 inches) down from the tips. Set aside.

Carefully lower the eggs into a pan of boiling water and boil for 6 minutes for duck's eggs (or 4–5 minutes for ordinary hen's eggs).

Meanwhile, add the asparagus to a pan of boiling salted water and cook for 4–5 minutes until tender.

Sit the eggs in the egg cups and cut off the tops. Drain the asparagus and arrange in bundles next to the eggs, for dipping. Serve with a little pile of coarse sea salt.

66 Fresh asparagus is an excellent accompaniment for rich, soft-boiled duck's eggs. Serve as an elegant starter, brunch or snack. 99

# OMELETTE WITH ST GEORGE'S MUSHROOMS AND WILD GARLIC

90g butter
700–800g St George's mushrooms, cleaned and
   sliced (or left whole if small)
sea salt and freshly ground black pepper
a handful of wild garlic leaves, stalks removed
   and chopped
12 medium eggs

SERVES 4

Melt about half of the butter in a hot frying pan. Add the St George's mushrooms, season and cook gently over a medium heat for 3-4 minutes or until they soften. Stir in the wild garlic leaves, then take the pan off the heat and set aside; keep warm. Preheat the oven to 180°C/gas mark 4.

Beat the eggs in a bowl and season with salt and pepper. Rub a little butter over the bottom of a non-stick frying pan and heat gently, then add a quarter of the egg mixture. Stir with a rubber spatula or wooden spoon until the egg begins to set. Remove from the heat and slide the omelette flat onto a cold heatproof plate to prevent it cooking any further; set aside. Keep the omelettes a little undercooked to allow for reheating later. Repeat to make another 3 omelettes.

When all the omelettes are cooked, warm them through in the oven for a couple of minutes, then scatter the mushrooms and wild garlic on top. Serve at once.

A good non-stick frying pan is essential for successful omelettes. Gone are the days of proving your pan for hours on end with salt and oil.

# OMELETTE ARNOLD BENNETT

200g undyed smoked haddock fillet
1 large shallot, peeled and finely chopped
200ml double cream
1 tsp Dijon mustard
1 tbsp chopped dill
sea salt and freshly ground white pepper
8 large eggs, beaten, plus 1 extra egg yolk
a good knob of butter

**SERVES 4**

" This is one of those old classics that was created by the customer and not the chef. It was, in fact, requested at the Savoy Hotel for the writer and critic whose name has been well stamped on the dish. It doesn't appear on too many restaurant menus, which is a shame because, made well, it's a delight. "

Put the fish and shallot in a pan and just cover with water. Bring to the boil, cover and simmer for 2 minutes. Remove the fish with a slotted spoon and drain on kitchen paper. Carefully remove the skin and any bones.

Continue to simmer the cooking liquid until almost completely reduced, then add 150ml of the cream and the mustard. Bring back to the boil and continue to simmer until it has reduced by two-thirds and has thickened. Remove from the heat and leave to cool a little.

Flake the haddock into the sauce, stir in the dill and season with salt and pepper. Preheat the grill to its maximum setting.

In a bowl set over a pan of simmering water, whisk the egg yolk and remaining cream until light and frothy but not starting to cook, then remove the bowl from the pan and set aside.

Heat the butter in a small non-stick frying or blini pan over a low heat. Season the beaten eggs and pour a quarter of the mix into the pan, or enough to fill it until two-thirds full. Over a low heat, stir the eggs with a wooden spoon or plastic spatula, until the mixture begins to set but the eggs are still soft. Stop stirring to allow the bottom to set slightly.

Turn a plate a little larger than the pan upside down on top of it. Invert the omelette on to the plate and transfer to a heatproof plate or serving dish. Repeat with the remaining mixture to make 3 more.

Mix the whisked egg yolk and cream into the haddock mixture and pour over the omelettes, spreading it evenly with the back of the spoon until covered. Put under the grill for a minute or two until evenly browned.

Try to buy good-quality undyed smoked haddock, as God alone knows what's in the bright yellow stuff.

# FRIED DUCK'S EGG WITH BROWN SHRIMPS AND SPRUE ASPARAGUS

250g sprue or extra fine asparagus
sea salt and freshly ground black pepper
1 tbsp olive oil
4 duck's eggs
a couple of generous knobs of butter
50g brown shrimps or tub of potted shrimps

SERVES 2

**❝**If you like the idea of the brown shrimps and can't find them, cheat by buying a tub of potted shrimps.**❞**

Trim off the woody ends from the asparagus and cut the spears in half if they are long. Cook in boiling salted water for 2–3 minutes or until tender, then drain.

Heat the oil in a frying pan and lightly fry the eggs for a couple of minutes until the white has just set.

Meanwhile, melt the butter in a pan and add the shrimps. Add the asparagus, season and warm for a minute or so until hot. Transfer the eggs to warm plates and season with salt and pepper. Spoon the asparagus, shrimps and butter on top and serve.

# LEEK AND POTATO STOVIES WITH ARBROATH SMOKIES

2 medium leeks, halved lengthways, well rinsed and
  coarsely chopped
sea salt and freshly ground black pepper
2 large baking potatoes, boiled in their skins until
  cooked but still firm, then peeled
1 Arbroath smokie, weighing around 250g, skinned and
  boned, or undyed smoked haddock fillet
2 tsp freshly grated horseradish
2 tbsp chopped flat-leaf parsley
vegetable oil, for frying
4 medium eggs
a good knob of butter

SERVES 4

Cook the leeks in some boiling salted water for
5–6 minutes, or until tender. Drain well, then
transfer to a bowl.

Coarsely chop the potatoes and flake the smokie
flesh. Add both to the leeks along with the
horseradish and parsley, season and then mix well.

Heat a tablespoon of oil in one or two frying pans,
preferably non-stick. Divide the mixture into 4
and shape each into a cake with a spatula. Let the
cakes cook for 4–5 minutes, until they begin to
colour nicely underneath, then flip them over like
a pancake. Alternatively, you can turn them out by
inverting them on to a plate, then heating a little
more oil in the pan and sliding the cake back into
the pan(s). Cook for another 4–5 minutes.

While the stovies are cooking, fry the eggs in some
oil and butter, and serve on top of the stovies.

Stovies are traditionally made with
leftovers on the stove, rather like
English bubble and squeak. You can
make individual stovies if you have one
of those tiny non-stick egg (or blini)
pans, or make one large one and cut it
into portions afterwards.

# SCRAMBLED EGGS WITH SEA URCHINS

4 fresh sea urchins
50g butter
6 medium eggs, beaten
sea salt and freshly ground white pepper
2 tbsp double cream

SERVES 4

Wearing a sturdy pair of gloves and using a kitchen
knife, scrape away all the spines from the sea
urchins and give the urchins a good wash. With a
pair of scissors, make a hole just above the middle
line of the sea urchin and carefully snip around so
you have 2 halves. One half will be empty and the
other will have orange eggs in segments.

With a teaspoon, carefully remove just the orange
eggs and put them into a bowl. Discard the rest of
the sea urchin from inside the shells and give the
shells a good wash and scrub. Put the shells into
a saucepan, cover with water, bring to the boil and
simmer for a couple of minutes to sterilise them.
Drain and give them a final wash, removing any
membrane, then dry them off.

Melt the butter in a pan, add the eggs, season with
salt and pepper and cook over a low heat, stirring,
until the eggs begin to set. Stir in the double cream
and cook for another 30 seconds. Stir in the sea
urchin eggs, remove from the heat and spoon into
the warmed shells. Serve immediately.

**“** You will probably need to order the
sea urchins in advance from your
fishmonger, as they are not as common
on the fishmonger's slab in this country
as they are abroad – unless you know a
friendly diver, that is. **”**

# DEEP-FRIED WHITEBAIT

vegetable oil, for deep-frying
100g gluten-free self-raising flour
sea salt
a good pinch of cayenne pepper
400g frozen whitebait, defrosted
100ml milk

TO SERVE
lemon wedges
tartare sauce (see page 295)

SERVES 4

Preheat about 8cm of oil to 160-180°C (use a thermometer) in a large heavy-based saucepan or electric deep-fat fryer.

Mix the flour with a pinch of salt and the cayenne pepper. Dust the whitebait in the flour, shake off the excess and dip briefly in the milk, then back into the flour. Ensure they are all well coated and shake off the excess flour again.

Fry the fish in 2 or 3 batches, depending on how many you're cooking, for 3-4 minutes each batch, until crisp. Drain on some kitchen paper and season with sea salt.

Serve immediately with lemon wedges and tartare sauce.

Whitebait are usually sold frozen or recently defrosted and rarely fresh, as they are so perishable. As a young man, working in a pub kitchen in West Bay, I was brought whitebait freshly landed by local fishermen, which I ended up freezing anyway. We've come to live with frozen whitebait, and they still make a perfect comforting starter and snack.

# DEEP-FRIED SALMON SKIN

vegetable or corn oil, for deep-frying
skin from 1–2 sides of smoked or fresh salmon

SERVES 6–8

Heat an 8cm depth of oil in a deep-fat fryer or other suitable deep, heavy pan to 160–180°C. Cut the salmon skins into rough strips, about 2–3cm long and 1cm wide.

Deep-fry the skins a handful or so at a time, stirring them every so often, for 2–3 minutes until crisp. Drain on kitchen paper and serve just warm or cold.

❝Many years ago at The Dorchester we used to fry up the skins of gravadlax and smoked salmon to serve as bar snacks. Since then I've always saved skins from smoked salmon, or even fresh salmon. They really are delicious little snacks, made from something you would usually just throw away.❞

# DEEP-FRIED SCALLOP FRILLS

200–250g scallop frills, black sac removed and well washed
sea salt and freshly ground black pepper
150g gluten-free self-raising flour
200ml milk
vegetable or corn oil, for deep-frying

SERVES 6–8

Check that the scallop frills are clean and that all of the sand has been washed away, then place them in a pan, cover with water and add 1–2 tsp salt. Bring to the boil, lower the heat and simmer for 3–4 minutes, then drain in a colander and dry the frills on kitchen paper.

Season the flour well. Have 3 bowls ready, one containing the seasoned flour, one for the milk and the third for the finished scallop frills.

Heat an 8cm depth of oil in a deep-fat fryer or other suitable deep, heavy pan to 160–180°C (use a thermometer). Coat the scallop frills in the flour, shaking off any excess, then pass them through the milk and again through the flour. Deep-fry the frills in batches, moving them around in the oil, for 2–3 minutes until golden.

Remove the scallop frills with a slotted spoon and drain on kitchen paper. Sprinkle with salt and serve.

Scallop frills! You may wonder what the hell I'm on about but as usual I don't like to see good things going to waste. These are the frills surrounding the white nugget of scallop meat and they normally end up in the bin. To accumulate enough, ask your fishmonger to keep them for you, or save them up in the freezer.

## OYSTERS MARY

12 rock oysters, shucked, juices reserved and left
   in the half-shell
seaweed or rock salt, to serve

FOR THE BLOODY MARY
200ml tomato juice
30–50ml vodka, or less if you wish
1 tbsp Worcestershire sauce, or less if you wish
juice of ½ lemon
a couple of drops of Tabasco, or to taste
1 tbsp freshly grated horseradish, or to taste
a pinch of celery salt

SERVES 4

First mix all of the ingredients for the Bloody
Mary together in a bowl, adjusting the seasoning
and spiciness to taste. Transfer to a freezerproof
container and place in the freezer for 2–3 hours,
stirring every 45 minutes or so as it freezes. Once
frozen, break it up into small crystals with a spoon
then return to the freezer until required.

To serve, place the oysters in their half-shell on
a bed of seaweed or rock salt on serving plates.
Equally spoon the frozen Bloody Mary on top of the
oysters to serve.

## MANX QUEENIES WITH CUCUMBER AND WILD FENNEL

24–32 very fresh queenies, prepared and left in
   the half-shell

FOR THE DRESSING
2 shallots, peeled and finely chopped
2 tbsp cider vinegar
⅓ cucumber
1 tbsp cold-pressed rapeseed oil
½ tbsp chopped wild fennel
juice of ½ lemon
sea salt and freshly ground black pepper

SERVES 4

For the dressing, place the shallots and cider
vinegar in a small pan, bring to the boil, then tip
into a bowl.

Cut the cucumber in half lengthways and scoop
out the seeds with a teaspoon. Finely chop the
cucumber into 5mm dice, then add to the shallots.
Add the rapeseed oil, fennel and lemon juice, toss
to combine and season well. Leave to stand for
about 20 minutes.

Spoon the marinated cucumber onto the queenies
and serve.

There's something of a 'morning after'
trait about oysters and the idea of
sliding one down topped with frozen
Bloody Mary is a bit of a sobering
thought. You can make your Bloody
Mary mix as spicy as you wish, and
even use it with other raw shellfish like
queen scallops or clams.

"A few years ago I was invited to the first ever Isle of
Man Queenie Festival. As you might guess, fishing
for queen scallops is a pretty serious business on
the island. Given that it takes as long to prep a little
queenie as it does to clean a large scallop, you could
argue that it's not worthwhile, but they are delicious
and the possibilities are endless. Very fresh queenies
are excellent eaten raw – I rate them on a par with
oysters and they can be served in the same way."

# SCALLOPS WITH PURPLE-SPROUTING BROCCOLI

8–10 small tender stems of purple-sprouting broccoli
sea salt and freshly ground black pepper
100g butter
12 medium scallops, shelled and cleaned

SERVES 4

**"** Sprouting broccoli complements the firm, sweet scallops and makes a great seasonal starter. Ideally buy scallops in the shell and prepare them yourself, or at least buy them freshly shucked. I now keep the muscles on scallops, as it seems such a waste to trim it off. Likewise I don't discard the corals. **"**

Trim the nice purple heads and a few leaves from the broccoli and set aside. Chop the rest and cook in a pan of boiling salted water for 4–5 minutes until tender, then drain and whiz in a blender or food processor until smooth. Transfer to a clean pan, season with salt and pepper to taste and add a couple of knobs of the butter; keep warm.

Remove the corals from the scallops and cut in half if large. Heat about a third of the remaining butter in a heavy-based frying pan. Season the corals and fry for 4–5 minutes, turning them every so often until crisp.

Meanwhile, add the purple heads and leaves to a pan of boiling salted water and cook for about 3 minutes until tender, then drain.

When the corals are crisp, remove and set aside. Wipe out the pan, then rub some butter over the base and place over a medium-high heat. Season the scallops and cook for just 1 minute on each side, then add the rest of the butter, corals and broccoli heads and leaves.

Spoon the broccoli purée onto warm plates, arrange the scallops, corals and broccoli on top and serve at once.

# BAKED SEA SNAILS
# WITH GARLIC SHOOTS

2kg medium-to-large-sized live sea snails

about 500g sea salt

6–8 pieces of garlic shoots or chopped wild garlic
    leaves or garlic chives, trimmed and finely chopped

150g butter, softened

juice of 1 lemon

sea salt and freshly ground black pepper

crusty bread, to serve

FOR THE COOKING LIQUID

1 onion, peeled and roughly chopped

12 white peppercorns

1 tsp fennel seeds

a few sprigs of thyme

1 bay leaf

juice of 1 lemon

100ml white wine

SERVES 4

Wash the sea snails well in cold water, then drain them and put them into a bowl with 300g of the sea salt. Leave for 2 hours, then leave them to wash under a trickle of running water for 30 minutes, giving them a good stir every so often.

Drain them well and then put them in a pan with the cooking liquid ingredients. Cover them with water and add a tablespoon of salt. Bring to the boil and then lower the heat and simmer gently for 45 minutes. Remove the pan from the heat and leave the sea snails to cool in the liquid for about an hour or so.

When the sea snails are cool enough to handle, remove them from the shell with a small skewer or lobster pick and discard the small disc-like piece of shell attached to the body, as well as the dark grey sac. Rinse and dry the shells on some kitchen paper.

Chop each piece of meat into 3 or 4 pieces and put them in a bowl with the garlic shoots, butter and lemon juice. Season with salt and pepper. Mix well and then push the mixture back into the shells.

Preheat the oven to 200°C/gas mark 6. Scatter the remaining sea salt about 1cm deep on one large, or 4 individual, ovenproof serving dish(es) and embed the sea snails in the salt (you may need more salt, depending on the size of your dishes) so that they don't fall over during cooking and most of the butter stays in the shells.

Bake for 12–15 minutes and serve with some crusty bread.

This recipe makes good use of garlic shoots – they look like spring onions and are the part of the plant that grows above the ground. They're hard to find, but if you grow garlic, you could harvest your own, or use garlic chives or finely chopped wild garlic instead.

"Sea snails, or whelks, are associated with the seaside or East End seafood stalls, where they are sold in little tubs with malt vinegar, and are generally as edible as rubber bands. However, I find whelks much tastier than their landlubber snail cousins, and this dish is like a marine version of that bistro staple, *escargots à l'ail*. Fishmongers may be able to order live whelks for you, or you could use large mussels or queen scallops in the shell."

# STEAMED COCKLES WITH BACCHUS AND SAMPHIRE

1.5kg plump, fresh cockles
a handful (or more) of samphire, washed
a few generous knobs of butter
4 shallots, peeled and thinly sliced
2 garlic cloves, peeled and crushed
sea salt and freshly ground black pepper
100ml white wine (preferably English Bacchus)

SERVES 4

Wash the cockles (as described below) and drain. Trim any woody stalks from the samphire and set aside.

Heat the butter in a large pan and gently cook the shallots and garlic for 2–3 minutes until softened. Add the drained cockles, season with salt and pepper, then pour in the wine and 100ml water. Cover with a tight-fitting lid and cook over a medium-high heat for about 2–3 minutes, shaking the pan frequently.

Add the samphire and cook for another 2–3 minutes until the cockle shells have opened; discard any that remain shut. Serve immediately.

"If you can find them, large fresh cockles are as good as any clams. Here I've cooked them in a British wine made from the Bacchus grape, which seems to cope well with our climate. I'd recommend the white wines from the Chapel Down Bacchus vineyard in Kent and Coddington vineyard up in Herefordshire. They are very good with seafood and, as here, adding a splash during cooking works a treat."

The problem with cockles is their gritty reputation, acquired from those little tubs of mass-produced cockles you can buy along with crabsticks and prawn shapes. To clean cockles properly, you need to leave them under running water for about 15 minutes, agitating them every so often with your hands to release any sand which tends to get trapped in the grooves of the shell.

# BRAISED CUTTLEFISH WITH WILD GARLIC

1kg cuttlefish, cleaned and ink reserved
sea salt and freshly ground black pepper
1 tbsp vegetable oil
a couple of good knobs of butter
2 shallots, peeled and finely chopped
2 garlic cloves, peeled and crushed
1 tbsp plain flour
100ml white wine
250ml fish stock (see page 293)
reserved cuttlefish ink (or 5 sachets from the
    fishmonger)
a handful of wild garlic leaves

SERVES 4

Wash the cuttlefish in cold water, then pat dry with some kitchen paper. Cut roughly into 3cm pieces and season with salt and pepper.

Heat the oil in a heavy-based frying pan. Fry the cuttlefish pieces over a high heat for a few minutes until golden, then drain and set aside.

Melt the butter in a clean pan and cook the shallots and garlic for 2–3 minutes until softened, then stir in the flour. Now gradually add the white wine and fish stock, stirring well to avoid lumps forming as you do so. Bring to the boil, season and add the cuttlefish and ink.

Simmer gently for about 30–40 minutes or until the cuttlefish is tender, then stir in the wild garlic leaves and simmer for a couple more minutes before serving.

# RAZOR CLAMS WITH WILD BOAR BACON AND HEDGEROW GARLIC

8 or 12 live razor clams
150g piece of wild boar bacon or normal bacon, cut
    roughly into 1cm cubes
100ml white wine
a few sprigs of thyme
a few parsley stalks
3 garlic cloves, peeled and roughly chopped
1 tsp sea salt
1 tbsp vegetable oil
50g butter
a handful of wild garlic, chopped

SERVES 4

66 Razor clams are the oddest of
shellfish and not commonly found in
fishmongers. They have a texture and
flavour somewhere between scallops
and squid and they'll turn rubbery if
you overcook them. 99

Preheat the oven to 150°C/gas mark 2. Wash the razor clams under cold running water for 10 minutes. Meanwhile, blanch the bacon in boiling water for 2 minutes, then drain and set aside.

Put the razor clams into a saucepan large enough to hold them comfortably and add the wine, thyme, parsley stalks, garlic and salt. Cover with a tight-fitting lid and cook over a high heat for a couple of minutes, giving the occasional stir, until the shells are just starting to open. Drain in a colander.

When cool enough to handle, carefully remove the clams from their shells, keeping the shells intact. Cut away the dark looking sac and discard, then cut each clam into two or three pieces. Lay the razor shells in a warm shallow baking dish.

Heat the oil in a pan and fry the bacon over a medium heat for a couple minutes until lightly coloured. Add the butter and wild garlic and stir.

Arrange the clams in their shells, then scatter over the bacon and wild garlic mixture. Warm through in the oven for a couple of minutes, then serve.

# LOBSTER AND ASPARAGUS COCKTAIL

1 small head of Cos lettuce

1 head of chicory

4 spring onions, finely shredded into strips

450–500g asparagus, woody ends trimmed off

sea salt and freshly ground black pepper

2 cooked lobsters, each about 500–600g,
    meat removed from the shell
    and sliced into bite-sized pieces

1 lemon or lime, quartered, to serve

FOR THE COCKTAIL SAUCE

5 tbsp thick mayonnaise (see page 295)

5 tbsp tomato ketchup

2 tsp Worcestershire sauce

a few drops of Tabasco sauce

1 tbsp orange juice

1 tbsp creamed or freshly grated horseradish

1 tbsp Pernod or Ricard

1 tbsp chopped dill

SERVES 4

Shred the lettuce and chicory as finely as you can and mix together with the spring onions.

Meanwhile, cook the asparagus in boiling salted water for 4–5 minutes, or until just tender. Drain well and leave to cool.

At the same time, make the sauce by mixing all of the ingredients together and seasoning with salt and pepper.

To serve, put the lettuce mixture into small bowls, large martini glasses or similar, arrange the lobster meat on top with the asparagus and spoon the sauce over the lobster (or spoon it over the lettuce before the lobster and asparagus). Serve with lemon or lime quarters.

❝As with prawns, when it comes to serving lobster, sometimes the good old classic dishes – smart or otherwise – work best. You may think it's a waste of lobster making it into a cocktail, but why? If it's prepared and cooked well, you just can't beat it; while even the best and most sophisticated of lobster dishes can be messed up by bad preparation and cooking.❞

## FRIED MONKFISH LIVER WITH SWEET AND SOUR ALEXANDERS

8 stems of alexanders, about 300–400g, trimmed,
    a handful of leaves reserved
sea salt and freshly ground black pepper
2 tbsp cold-pressed rapeseed oil
3 shallots, peeled and finely chopped
4 tbsp cider vinegar
2 tbsp caster sugar
1 tbsp tomato ketchup
1 tsp English mustard
300–400g monkfish liver
a couple of good knobs of butter

SERVES 4

Peel the alexander stems and cut them into rough batons, about 5 x 1cm. Cook in boiling salted water for 3–4 minutes or until tender, then drain and leave to cool. Chop the leaves and set aside.

Heat the oil in a pan and gently cook the shallots for a few minutes to soften. Add the vinegar, sugar, ketchup, mustard and 100ml water. Let bubble to reduce until there are just a few tablespoonfuls of liquor remaining. Stir in the alexander batons and another splash of water. Season and simmer for a couple of minutes, then remove from the heat.

Cut the monkfish liver into 1cm thick slices and season with salt and pepper. Heat the butter in a heavy-based frying pan until foaming and cook the liver for a couple of minutes on each side until nicely coloured. Add the reserved alexander leaves as you turn the liver to cook them briefly.

Spoon the alexanders and sauce onto warm plates and top with the monkfish liver and wilted alexander leaves. Serve at once.

*Alexanders grow along the roadsides and are prolific as you near the coastline. Somewhere between celery and cardoon, with a slightly perfumed taste, you'll need to peel the stems first, then simply blanch, boil or braise them. There is little demand for monkfish liver here, so you'll need to ask your fishmonger to source it for you. For me, it's the foie gras of the fish world.*

## SPICED BAKED SPIDER CRAB

1 large cooked spider crab or brown crab, about 1.5–2kg
200g brown crab meat
½ onion, peeled and finely chopped
1 garlic clove, peeled and crushed
10g knob of ginger, scraped and finely chopped
½ small mild chilli, deseeded and finely chopped
115ml olive oil
3 tbsp sherry
3 tbsp fish stock (see page 293)
50g fresh white breadcrumbs
juice of ½ lemon
sea salt and freshly ground black pepper
thin slices of toast, to serve

SERVES 4

To get the meat out of the crab, twist the legs and claws off, then crack them open and remove the white meat. Now turn the main body on its back and twist off the pointed flap. Push the tip of a table knife between the main shell and the bit to which the legs were attached, and twist the blade to separate the two, then push it up and remove. Scoop out the brown meat in the well of the shell and put with the leg and claw meat. On the other part of the body, remove the 'dead man's fingers' (the feathery grey gills attached to the body) and discard. Split the body in half with a heavy knife. Now patiently pick out the white meat from the little cavities in the body. Add to the rest of the meat. Clean and reserve the shell if you want to use it for serving.

Gently cook the onion, garlic, ginger and chilli in 2 teaspoons of the oil until soft. Add the sherry, fish stock and brown crab meat (to boost the flavour), stir well then add half the breadcrumbs (reserving the rest to scatter on top), half the lemon juice and seasoning to taste. Bring just to the boil and simmer for 15 minutes, stirring occasionally.

Preheat a hot grill. In a blender, process one-third of the mix with the rest of the olive oil, then stir it back into the mixture along with the crab meat. Add more lemon juice and seasoning if necessary.

Spoon into the shell or an ovenproof serving dish and scatter over the reserved breadcrumbs. Lightly brown under the grill. Serve with toast.

# COD'S TONGUES
# WITH SMOKED BACON

200–250g piece of smoked streaky bacon
a couple of good knobs of butter
1 onion, peeled and finely chopped
2 garlic cloves, peeled and crushed
1 tsp plain flour
100ml white wine
300ml fish stock (see page 293)
400g cod's tongues
sea salt and freshly ground black pepper
4 slices of sourdough or country-style bread, about
    1cm thick, to serve
1 tbsp chopped flat-leaf parsley

SERVES 4

Cut the bacon roughly into 1cm chunks. Heat half
of the butter in a pan and gently cook the onion,
garlic and bacon for 3-4 minutes, turning every so
often. Dust with the flour, stir well, then gradually
stir in the wine and stock. Simmer gently for about
45 minutes.

Season the cod's tongues lightly with salt and
pepper. Heat the rest of the butter in a frying pan
and fry the cod's tongues over a high heat for 3-4
minutes until lightly coloured. Meanwhile, toast or
griddle the bread on both sides.

Add the fried cod's tongues to the sauce, check the
seasoning and scatter over the parsley. Place a slice
of toast on a warmed plate, spoon over the cod's
tongues and sauce, then serve at once.

66 Ok, the idea of eating cod's tongues might not
appeal to everyone, but they have a delicious
gelatinous quality about them, and can take on
bold flavours, like smoked bacon. 99

# TREACLE-CURED SALMON

1 salmon fillet (with skin on), about 750g–1kg, trimmed
80g black treacle
1 tsp fennel seeds, crushed
grated zest of 1 lemon
50g sea salt
1 tbsp English mustard
2 tsp coarsely ground black pepper

SERVES 8–10

Lay the salmon fillet skin side down on a sheet of
cling film. Warm the treacle in a bowl over a pan
of simmering water until it is just runny. Mix the
fennel seeds, lemon zest, salt, mustard, pepper and
treacle together. Spread evenly over the salmon and
wrap well in more cling film. Place on a tray, still
skin side down, and leave at room temperature for
1 hour, then refrigerate for 48 hours.

When ready to serve, remove the cling film and
scrape away any excess liquid and marinade from
the salmon. Pat dry with kitchen paper.

Cut the salmon at a 90° angle to the skin into
even slices, about 3mm thick. Serve with pickled
cucumber or pickled samphire, or just some good
bread and a leafy salad.

66 This dish comes from chef and
restaurateur Nigel Haworth. He
served it up at one of his annual food
festivals, where he invites chefs from
around Britain and further afield to
cook for the evening. It can also be
made with sea trout. 99

"Mackerel is such a versatile fish, but it is rarely treated in an interesting way, which is a great shame. With this recipe, you can pack the mackerel immersed in the spiced oil in kilner jars and keep it in the fridge for a week or so to have as a quick, tasty snack. Here I'm serving it as a summery salad with artichokes."

# MACKEREL WITH BROAD BEANS AND ARTICHOKES

100ml cold-pressed rapeseed oil
2 large shallots, peeled and finely chopped
6 garlic cloves, peeled and sliced
1 small chilli, stalk removed and finely chopped
12 black peppercorns, lightly crushed
1 tsp fennel seeds, crushed
½ tsp ground cumin
1 tbsp cider vinegar
juice of ½ lemon
sea salt
6 medium mackerel, filleted
1 tbsp roughly chopped flat-leaf parsley, to serve

FOR THE ARTICHOKES AND BEANS
2 large globe artichokes
juice of ½ lemon
200g podded broad beans

SERVES 4

Heat 2 tbsp of oil in a pan and add the shallots, garlic, chilli, pepper and spices. Cook gently for 2–3 minutes until soft, without colouring. Add the vinegar, lemon and remaining oil. Bring to a gentle simmer and add some salt and the mackerel. Bring to a simmer, take off the heat, cover and let cool.

Meanwhile, prepare the artichokes one at a time. Have ready a bowl of cold water with the lemon juice added. Cut off the stem from the artichoke and carefully cut away the leaves with a serrated knife until the meaty heart is exposed; try to keep the circular shape. Using a spoon, scoop out the hairy choke, leaving the heart. Immerse the artichoke in the lemon water to prevent discoloration.

Put the hearts in a non-reactive saucepan with the lemon water, add a pinch of salt and bring to the boil. Lower the heat and simmer for 12–15 minutes until tender, then leave to cool in the liquid.

Bring a pan of salted water to the boil. Add the beans and cook for 3–4 minutes until tender. Drain and run under the cold tap. Remove the tough skins from larger beans; leave smaller ones as they are.

When ready to serve, cut each heart into 8 wedges. Remove the mackerel from the oil with a slotted spoon and break the fillets into 4 or 5 pieces. Mix the beans and artichokes with a few spoonfuls of the mackerel liquor and season. Divide among plates and arrange the mackerel on top. Spoon over some more dressing and scatter over the parsley.

# SOUSED GURNARD WITH SEA PURSLANE

4–6 small red gurnard, each about 140g–160g, scaled, filleted and gutted
120ml cider vinegar
1 medium carrot, peeled and thinly sliced at an angle
2 medium shallots, peeled and thinly sliced into rings
10 coriander seeds
a good pinch of cumin seeds
sea salt
a handful of sea purslane, trimmed of any thick stalks
1–2 tbsp cold-pressed rapeseed oil

SERVES 4–6

Preheat the oven to 200°C/gas mark 6. Check over the gurnard fillets for pin bones, removing any you find with tweezers. Cut any larger fillets in half. Lay the gurnard fillets in a shallow dish in which they fit snugly.

Put the cider vinegar, 120ml water, carrot and shallots in a saucepan. Add the spices and 1 teaspoon of salt, then bring to the boil. Allow to simmer for a minute, then pour over the fish. Cover with foil and cook in the oven for 10–15 minutes or until the fish is just cooked.

Set aside to cool for a couple of hours. Once cooled, you can refrigerate the dish overnight if preparing ahead, but bring back to room temperature to serve.

When ready to serve, blanch the sea purslane in lightly salted water for a couple of minutes, then drain and refresh under cold water.

Divide the soused gurnard and vegetables among individual serving plates, spooning over the liquor. Scatter over the sea purslane, drizzle lightly with the rapeseed oil and serve.

# SMOOTH WOODCOCK PATE

2–3 woodcock
100ml white wine
100ml red wine
50ml Madeira
50ml port
2 tbsp brandy
a little vegetable oil
3 large shallots, peeled and roughly chopped
1 litre chicken stock (see page 293)
2 garlic cloves, peeled and crushed
a few sprigs of thyme
4 juniper berries
sea salt and freshly ground black pepper
a couple of good knobs of butter
100g duck or chicken livers
100ml double cream
toast or salad leaves, to serve

SERVES 4–6

❝This is a nostalgic dish for me, as it takes me back to my early days at Grosvenor House in London, where a rich, silky smooth woodcock pâté – well, more of a mousse really – was on the menu. It was a bugger to make, involving lots of reductions of meat liquid, as well as forcing the mixture through a sieve. I thought I should share it with you, though I've shortened the laborious process so it won't drive you completely mad, although you will need to start a couple of days ahead.❞

Remove the legs from the woodcock, and then cut through the leg joint to separate the thigh from the drumstick. Put the drumsticks to one side. Remove the skin from the thighs and cut out the bone with the point of a sharp knife. Cut the breasts away from the carcass and remove the skin.

Cut the thigh and breast meat into rough 2cm chunks and place in a bowl with the wine, Madeira, port and brandy. Leave to marinate in the fridge for 24 hours.

Chop the drumsticks and carcass into small pieces using a heavy knife or cleaver. Heat a little oil in a heavy-based saucepan and fry the bones and shallots, stirring well, until they are nicely coloured. Add the chicken stock, garlic, thyme and juniper. Bring to the boil, lower the heat and simmer for an hour.

Strain the stock through a fine sieve into a clean pan. Add the marinating liquor from the woodcock and boil until reduced to about 2 or 3 spoonfuls of syrupy liquid.

Dry the pieces of meat on some kitchen paper and season with salt and pepper. Heat half of the butter in a frying pan and cook the meat over a medium heat for 3–4 minutes, stirring every so often and keeping it pink. Remove and put to one side.

Add the rest of the butter to the pan, season the livers and sauté them for 2–3 minutes, stirring and keeping them pink. Mix the woodcock, livers and reduced stock together. Now purée the mixture in a blender or food processor, in two or three batches to keep it as smooth as possible. You will need to stop every so often during blending to scrape down the sides with a spatula.

Whip the cream to a fairly stiff consistency and carefully fold into the mixture using a metal spoon. Transfer to a serving dish or container, cover with cling film and refrigerate overnight.

Serve the pâté with toast and a salad of small leaves on the side.

If you can't get your hands on a woodcock, you could use partridge, pigeon or pheasant – even a mixture of game birds will do. Sometimes good game dealers have birds that are not in perfect condition for roasting but are still fine to eat, and these would be ideal here.

# RABBIT BRAWN

1 pig's trotter, chopped or sawn into 4–5 pieces
1 onion, peeled and halved
2 garlic cloves, peeled
2 tsp sea salt
the carcass and back and front legs from 2 rabbits

FOR THE BOUQUET GARNI
1 bay leaf
a sprig of thyme
12 coriander seeds
12 white peppercorns
toast or salad leaves, to serve

SERVES 6–8

❝ This is a perfect dish for using the front and back legs and the carcass of a rabbit if you've just used the fillets. Piccalilli (see page 54) makes a great accompaniment, or you can thickly slice for a starter, or serve it on hot toast.❞

For the bouquet garni, tie the herbs and spices in a square of muslin to make a bag, securing with string. Put into a large saucepan with the pig's trotter, onion, garlic and salt. Pour in enough water to cover the trotter, then bring to a simmer. Skim off the scum from the surface and simmer for 1 hour, skimming every so often.

Add the rabbit to the pan and continue to simmer and skim for a further hour. By this time, the rabbit meat should be coming off the bone and the pig's trotter disintegrating. If not, continue simmering for another half an hour or so. Tip into a colander over a bowl to save the liquor, then strain the liquid through a fine sieve back into the cleaned pan. Return to the heat and boil until it has reduced to a sticky liquid, about 200ml in volume. Taste and adjust the seasoning if necessary. Leave to cool, but not until set.

Remove all of the meat from the rabbit and pig's trotter, including all the bits of gelatinous skin. Mix the pieces of meat with the liquid and transfer to a terrine mould, bowl, pie dish or other suitable container. Cover and leave to set in the fridge overnight.

To serve, cut the rabbit brawn into very fine slices using a very sharp knife and arrange over individual plates with a leafy salad.

# MUTTON SCRUMPETS WITH WILD GARLIC MAYONNAISE

300–400g boneless breast of mutton or lamb
sea salt and freshly ground black pepper
1 head of garlic, halved and roughly chopped
a few sprigs each of rosemary and thyme
2–3 tbsp plain flour
2 medium eggs, beaten
60–70g fresh white breadcrumbs
vegetable or corn oil, for deep-frying
2–3 tbsp mayonnaise (see page 295)
1 tbsp wild garlic sauce (see page 298), or
    chopped garlic chives
1 lemon, quartered, to serve

SERVES 4

Preheat the oven to 160°C/gas mark 3. Place the mutton in an ovenproof dish (with a tight-fitting lid). Season well and scatter over the chopped garlic and herbs. Cover and cook in the oven for 2 hours or until very tender, basting regularly and turning the oven down if necessary. Leave to cool overnight.

Scrape away any fat residue from the mutton and any fat that hasn't rendered down during cooking. Cut the breast into 1cm wide strips, 3–4cm long.

Have 3 bowls ready, one with the flour, one with the eggs and the third with the breadcrumbs. Season the flour. Heat a 8cm depth of oil in a deep-fat fryer or other suitable deep, heavy pan to 160–180°C.

Mix the mayonnaise with the wild garlic sauce or garlic chives.

Pass the mutton strips through the seasoned flour, shaking off the excess, then through the egg and finally coat in the breadcrumbs. Deep-fry the strips in batches for 2–3 minutes, moving them around in the oil until golden and crisp. Lift out with a slotted spoon and drain on kitchen paper.

Serve the mutton scrumpets with lemon wedges and the wild garlic mayonnaise on the side.

# COLD OX TONGUE WITH BABY BEETS

800g–1kg piece of salted ox tongue
1 onion, peeled and halved
2 carrots, peeled and trimmed
10 black peppercorns
1 bay leaf
1kg young beetroot, cleaned
sea salt and freshly ground black pepper
2 tsp cider vinegar
2 tbsp cold-pressed rapeseed oil
a handful of small salad leaves (red mustard leaf,
    young beetroot leaves, purslane or red orach)

SERVES 4

Put the ox tongue into a large saucepan with the onion, carrots, peppercorns and bay leaf. Bring to the boil, lower the heat and simmer for about 2–2½ hours. Leave to cool in the liquid. While still warm, peel the skin away, using your fingers. You can either keep the tongue as it is, or fit it snugly into a pudding basin or similar mould and put a small plate and weights on top to press it. Either way, refrigerate to set.

Cook the beetroot in their skins in a pan of salted water for about 50 minutes to 1 hour, depending on their size. Test with the point of a sharp knife; it should slide in fairly easily once they are cooked. Drain the beetroot and allow them to cool a little, then don a pair of rubber gloves and rub off the skins (if using larger beetroot cut into wedges). Place in a bowl.

Mix the cider vinegar and rapeseed oil together to make a dressing, season with salt and pepper to taste and pour over the beetroot.

To serve, carve the tongue into thin slices using a sharp knife. Arrange on a large plate or individual ones and pile the beetroot and salad leaves on top.

Try to buy fresh young beetroot for this dish – you may need to pre-order them from your greengrocer. Otherwise you could use normal beetroot and cut them into quarters. Cook the ox tongue one or two days in advance if you like, so it is cold and ready to serve. Similarly, you can prepare the beetroot ahead.

# JELLIED HAM HOCK WITH PICCALILLI

1kg ham hock or a 700g ham joint, soaked overnight in
   plenty of cold water
a few sprigs of thyme
1 bay leaf
2 onions, peeled and quartered
3 celery stalks, roughly chopped
10 black peppercorns
9–12g leaf gelatine (3–4 sheets), using the smaller
   quantity if using a hock
2 tbsp chopped flat-leaf parsley

FOR THE PICCALILLI
1 medium cucumber, halved and deseeded
½ large cauliflower, cut into small florets
1 onion, peeled and chopped
1 tbsp salt
150g caster sugar
65g English mustard
½ tsp ground turmeric
1 small chilli, deseeded and finely chopped
150ml malt vinegar
125ml white wine vinegar
1 tbsp cornflour

SERVES 6–8

First make the piccalilli. Cut the cucumber into 1cm pieces. Halve the cauliflower florets and place in a dish with the cucumber and onion. Sprinkle with the salt and leave for 1 hour. Rinse well, drain and put into a bowl. Put the sugar, mustard, turmeric, chilli and vinegars into a saucepan. Dissolve over a low heat, then simmer for 2–3 minutes. Mix the cornflour with 150ml water and whisk into the vinegar mixture. Simmer gently, stirring, for 5 minutes. Pour the hot liquid over the vegetables and leave to cool. Pour into sterilised jars and refrigerate for at least a week before use, or up to 6 months.

Put the ham in a large saucepan with the thyme, bay leaf, onions, celery and peppercorns. Add water to cover, bring to the boil and simmer until the ham is tender, about 2 hours depending on the cut and size (refer to pack guidelines if applicable). Remove the ham from the liquid and leave to cool.

Skim the cooking liquor, measure 350ml and bring to the boil in a pan. Meanwhile, soak the gelatine in cold water for a few minutes to soften, then squeeze out the excess water. Remove the liquor from the heat and add the gelatine, with the parsley, stirring to dissolve. Leave until cool, but not set.

Meanwhile, remove the ham from the bone and cut roughly into 1cm cubes, discarding any fat and gristle, and put it into a bowl. Mix in a little of the cooled jellied liquor and pack into a 1.2 litre terrine. Top up with the remaining liquor (you may not need all of it). Cover with cling film and leave to set in the fridge overnight.

To serve, briefly dip the terrine into a bowl of boiling water and invert on to a chopping board to turn out. With a carving knife, cut it into 2cm thick slices. Serve on individual plates, with the piccalilli.

This is a great way to use some of the meat from a home-cooked ham joint. Make the piccalilli at least a week ahead, and soak the ham overnight before cooking as it can sometimes be salty.

# HEAVEN AND EARTH

300–400g good-quality soft black pudding
about 100ml chicken stock, if needed (see page 293)
about 100g caul fat, rinsed
300g potatoes, peeled and quartered
sea salt and freshly ground black pepper
1 cooking apple
½ tbsp caster sugar
about 120g butter

SERVES 4

Unless your black pudding is already soft, place it in a bowl and mix in enough stock to give a soft but not wet consistency. Spread the caul fat out on a work surface and pat dry with kitchen paper. Shape the black pudding into 4 balls and cut a piece of caul large enough to wrap around each one. Wrap securely and overlap slightly. If the caul is very thin, add another layer.

Simmer the potatoes in a pan of salted water until just tender. Meanwhile, peel, quarter and core the apple, then cut into chunks and place in a saucepan with the sugar. Cook over a low heat, stirring every so often, until soft and almost falling apart.

Drain the cooked potatoes and return to a low heat for 30 seconds or so to dry out. Crush lightly with a fork or potato masher, season and stir in the apple and half of the butter; keep warm.

Preheat the grill to medium. Melt the remaining butter in a small pan. Place the black pudding parcels on a grill tray and brush with melted butter. Grill for 6–7 minutes until evenly browned, turning and basting with more butter during cooking.

To serve, spoon the apple and potato into the centre of each warmed plate and flatten slightly with the back of a spoon. Place the black pudding in the middle and serve at once.

❝This is based upon *himmel und erde*, a popular German dish. According to my mate, Steve Claydon, who is a huge fan, the soft, silky black pudding is the heaven (*himmel*) upon the earth (*erde*) of crushed up apples and potatoes. Until recently the closest I could find to the German soft black pudding was Spanish morcilla, which works pretty well. Then Peter Gott of Sillfield Farm in the Lake District kindly developed a soft version of his black pudding for me, which is perfect. Wrapping the pudding in pig's caul stops it bursting during cooking.❞

# SALADS

## POTATO SALAD WITH BACON AND SPRING ONIONS

300–350g Anya or other waxy new potatoes
  (unpeeled)
sea salt and freshly ground black pepper
1 medium onion, peeled and finely chopped
3 rashers of rindless streaky bacon, finely chopped
1 tsp cumin seeds
3 tbsp cider vinegar
250ml chicken stock (see page 293)
3–4 tbsp cold-pressed rapeseed oil
4 spring onions, trimmed and finely chopped

SERVES 4–6

Cook the potatoes in a pan of boiling salted water for 12–15 minutes until just tender. Drain and leave until cool enough to handle.

Meanwhile, put the onion, bacon, cumin seeds, cider vinegar and chicken stock into a saucepan and simmer gently until the liquid has reduced by about two-thirds, then take off the heat.

Peel the potatoes and cut into 3mm thick slices. Add to the onion and bacon mixture, along with the rapeseed oil. Toss gently to mix and season with salt and pepper to taste.

Cover and leave for up to an hour until ready to serve, giving an occasional stir to encourage the potatoes to absorb all the flavours. Just before serving, add the spring onions and toss gently.

I discovered this great warm potato salad years ago while working at The Dorchester. It goes with just about anything – from sausages to a piece of grilled salmon – or you can serve it as part of a buffet salad selection. You could use other waxy potatoes, such as Charlotte or Pink Fir Apple.

## BROAD BEAN, PEA AND GIROLLE SALAD

1 garlic clove, peeled and sliced
4 tbsp cold-pressed rapeseed oil
a few sprigs of tarragon, leaves removed and
  stalks reserved
sea salt and freshly ground black pepper
200–250g girolles, cleaned
200g podded peas
200g podded broad beans
a pinch of caster sugar
1 tbsp cider vinegar
a handful of pea shoots (optional)

SERVES 4

Put the garlic, oil and tarragon stalks into a wide saucepan with about 3 tablespoons of water. Season well and bring to the boil. Add the girolles, cover with a lid and cook over a low heat for 3–4 minutes, turning them every so often. Take off the heat, remove the lid and leave to cool a little.

Cook the peas and broad beans separately in boiling salted water for a few minutes until just tender, adding a little caster sugar to the cooking water for the peas. Drain and remove the tough skins from any larger beans; leave small ones as they are.

Remove the girolles from their liquid with a slotted spoon and set aside on a plate.

To make the dressing, carefully pour off the oily part of the girolle cooking liquid into a bowl, leaving the watery liquid behind in the pan. Whisk the cider vinegar into the oil. Chop the tarragon leaves and stir these in, too. Check the seasoning.

Toss the peas and broad beans in the dressing, then spoon onto serving plates. Scatter the girolles on top, along with a few pea shoots, if using. Spoon a little more dressing over the salad and serve.

You can vary the beans you use here if you wish, perhaps adding some runners or bobby beans in place of the broad beans.

"This is a really simple, fresh-tasting salad – one of those dishes that you take one look at and know it's summer."

# CELERY AND PICKLED WALNUT SALAD

1 head of very leafy celery (you may need 2 heads to obtain enough leaves), washed
12 pickled walnuts, or more if you like

FOR THE DRESSING
1 tsp walnut pickling vinegar
1 tbsp cider vinegar
3–4 tbsp cold-pressed rapeseed oil
1 tsp Tewkesbury mustard
sea salt and freshly ground black pepper

SERVES 4

Remove all the leaves from the celery and give them a good wash and dry. Tear larger leaves into smaller pieces. Finely slice the celery hearts and place them in a bowl with the leaves. (Use the rest of the celery stalks to flavour a soup or casserole.)

To make the dressing, whisk all of the ingredients together in a bowl to combine, seasoning with salt and pepper to taste.

Drizzle the dressing over the celery and toss lightly. Arrange on individual plates. Scatter the walnuts over the salad, breaking any large ones in half. Serve at once.

66 This makes for a refreshing starter or side salad. For a more substantial salad, crumble in some blue or goat's cheese. I usually rely on shop-bought pickled walnuts as it can be tricky to get the walnuts at the stage needed for pickling. 99

# FENNEL SALAD

2 young fennel bulbs, trimmed and green
  tops reserved
2–3 tbsp cider vinegar
sea salt and freshly ground white pepper
2–3 tbsp cold-pressed rapeseed oil

SERVES 4

Halve the fennel bulbs and slice them as thinly as possible, using a mandolin or very sharp knife. Tip into a bowl, add the cider vinegar and season to taste. Toss to mix and leave for about an hour, stirring every so often.

Chop the green fennel tops and add to the fennel with the rapeseed oil. Toss to combine, then taste and adjust the seasoning if necessary. Serve within a couple of hours.

Fennel is an underused vegetable in this country, though it has many possibilities – both raw and cooked. Try serving this salad with marinated or smoked fish. You could also combine it with thinly sliced cucumber (that has been halved lengthways and deseeded) for a light summery garnish to grilled fish.

“A simple beetroot salad makes a great light starter for a dinner party and it will look stunning if you are able to source different coloured beetroot varieties from a farmers' market or good greengrocer. Cook the different beets separately as their cooking times will vary slightly, also because the red beetroot is likely to stain the others.”

# BEETROOT SALAD WITH WALNUTS

500–600g mixed young beetroot (red, golden and
    white or candy-striped)
sea salt and freshly ground black pepper
30g good-quality shelled walnuts
1 tsp good-quality sea salt
1 tbsp cold-pressed rapeseed oil
a couple of handfuls of small salad and herb leaves,
    such as silver sorrel, red chard, orach, pea shoots,
    chives, etc.

FOR THE DRESSING
1 tbsp cider vinegar
1 tsp Dijon or Tewkesbury mustard
4 tbsp cold-pressed rapeseed oil

SERVES 4

Cook the beetroots separately in a pan of salted water for about an hour, depending on the variety and size, until they feel tender when pierced with a sharp knife. Drain and leave until cool enough to handle. Then peel away the skins with your fingers, wearing rubber gloves to stop the red beetroot staining your hands.

Preheat the oven to 180°C/gas 4. Toss the walnuts with the sea salt and rapeseed oil and spread out on a baking tray. Roast in the oven for 4–6 minutes, turning them once or twice, until lightly coloured.

To make the dressing, whisk the ingredients together in a small bowl and season with salt and pepper to taste.

Cutting the red ones last so that you don't stain the lighter coloured ones, cut the young beetroot into even-sized wedges or halves if they are small.

Arrange the beetroots and salad leaves on plates, season lightly and spoon over the dressing. Scatter over the walnuts and serve.

## SORREL, BEETROOT AND GOAT'S CHEESE SALAD

1 small piece of soft goat's cheese, about 150g, at
    room temperature
a good handful of silver sorrel leaves, or other small
    salad leaves
200g baby beetroots, cooked and peeled
a few chives, snipped into 7–8cm lengths

FOR THE DRESSING
2 tbsp white wine vinegar
1 tbsp clear runny honey
6–7 tbsp cold-pressed rapeseed oil or olive oil
sea salt and freshly ground black pepper

SERVES 4–6

Make the dressing by mixing all of the ingredients
together and add seasoning to taste.

Break the cheese into rough 1cm pieces and arrange
on plates with the sorrel leaves and the beetroot.
Sprinkle generously with the dressing and scatter
the chives over the top.

"Soft goat's cheeses lend themselves
perfectly to a refreshing starter or main
course salad. There is a great salad leaf
I discovered a couple of years ago called
silver sorrel, which has a small, almost
heart-shaped leaf and the citrus-like
flavour of the large-leaved common
sorrel. Teamed with some young
beetroots, this makes a great salad and
is a good excuse to get out the cold-
pressed rapeseed oil."

## BLUE MONDAY SALAD

25–30 cobnuts, shelled
½ tbsp cold-pressed rapeseed oil
2–3 tsp Cornish or flaky sea salt
4 small Little Gem lettuce
blue cheese dressing (see page 300)
50–60g Blue Monday, or other blue cheese

SERVES 4

Heat the grill to medium. Place the cobnuts on a
grill tray and mix with the rapeseed oil and salt.
Grill until lightly toasted, then leave to cool.

Toss the salad leaves in the dressing and arrange
on serving plates or bowls. Break the cheese into
pieces and scatter over the top of the salad, along
with the toasted cobnuts.

Blue Monday, created by the Evenlode
Partnership, has become my favourite
British blue cheese. You can serve this
salad as a starter or side dish, but bear
in mind the intensity of the dressing
for the rest of the meal. If you can't get
hold of any cobnuts, substitute with
walnuts or hazelnuts.

# TOMATO AND LOVAGE SALAD

300–400g mixed tomatoes
a few sprigs of lovage
2 tbsp finely chopped spring onions or chives
   (optional)
a little malt vinegar or cider vinegar, to drizzle
2–3 tbsp cold-pressed rapeseed oil
sea salt and freshly ground black pepper

SERVES 4

Cut the tomatoes into chunks, wedges or halves; leave small ones whole. Arrange on plates and tear the lovage leaves over them. Scatter over the spring onions or chives if using. Drizzle with a little vinegar and oil as desired, and sprinkle with salt and pepper to taste.

66 If you have a good selection of tasty tomatoes, you really don't need to do anything too clever to them. Just some torn lovage leaves, and perhaps a few spring onions, is enough to turn them into a simple but special salad. 99

Like basil, lovage has a way of working itself into dishes to give them a real lift, but it can be overpowering and needs to be used in moderation.

# SHAVED ASPARAGUS AND FENNEL WITH AGED CAERPHILLY

4–6 thick or 8–10 medium very fresh asparagus spears
1 young fennel bulb, trimmed, a few feathery tops
    reserved
a handful of small salad leaves, such as silver sorrel,
    landcress etc.
70–80g good-quality aged Caerphilly cheese, such as
    Gorwydd

FOR THE DRESSING
grated zest and juice of ½ lemon
4–5 tbsp cold-pressed rapeseed oil
sea salt and freshly ground black pepper

SERVES 4

“Slicing freshly picked asparagus into thin slivers and eating it raw may not seem the obvious way to serve this delicious vegetable, but combined with just a few other simple ingredients it works a treat. Choose thicker stems of asparagus as they are easier to shave.”

Cut off the woody ends of the asparagus and peel the lower end of the stalks. Using a mandolin or very sharp knife, cut the asparagus on the diagonal into very fine slices.

Halve the fennel and, again, using a mandolin or very sharp knife, slice the fennel as thinly as possible and place into a bowl with the sliced asparagus.

Shake the ingredients for the dressing together in a screw-topped jar and season with salt and pepper to taste.

Add the leaves and feathery fennel tops to the asparagus and fennel and season lightly. Toss with the dressing and arrange on plates. Shave the cheese with a small, sharp knife or a vegetable peeler and scatter over the salad.

# RED MULLET AND SAMPHIRE SALAD WITH TOMATO VINAIGRETTE

150g samphire, trimmed

a little olive oil, for frying

4 red mullet fillets, each about 115g, any residual bones removed and fillets halved

60g small salad leaves, such as purslane, baby spinach, corn salad

FOR THE TOMATO VINAIGRETTE

1 tbsp tarragon vinegar

1 small tomato, skinned and deseeded

4 tbsp olive oil

sea salt and freshly ground black pepper

SERVES 4

Heat a large pan of water to blanch the samphire. Make the dressing: in a processor, blend the vinegar, tomato and oil with 1 tablespoon of water until smooth. Strain and season with salt and pepper.

Heat a little olive oil in a non-stick frying pan over a medium heat. Season the red mullet fillets with salt and pepper and fry them, skin side down first, for 1½ minutes on each side.

Meanwhile, blanch the samphire in the boiling water for 30 seconds only, then drain in a colander.

Dress the salad leaves with the dressing, lightly season with salt and pepper, and arrange on plates with the samphire and red mullet.

"Red mullet has a rich, almost gamey flavour, hence one of the French terms for it, *bécasse de mer* (woodcock of the sea). It is a beautiful-looking fish and normally has a price tag to match. Ideally, it should be cooked and garnished simply."

# MONKFISH CHEEK AND
# CHANTERELLE SALAD

2 handfuls of watercress or other small winter
  salad leaves
12–15 monkfish cheeks, about 200–250g in total
60–70g butter
150g chanterelles, cleaned

FOR THE DRESSING
1 tbsp cider vinegar
juice of 1 lemon
1 tsp mustard, such as Tewkesbury
4–5 tbsp cold-pressed rapeseed oil
sea salt and freshly ground black pepper

SERVES 4

For the dressing, whisk all the ingredients together in a bowl and season with salt and pepper; set aside.

Wash the salad leaves, trim and pat dry, then arrange on individual serving plates.

Season the monkfish cheeks and cut them in half if they are large. Heat half of the butter in a heavy-based frying pan until foaming and cook the monkfish cheeks for 4–5 minutes, turning them until nicely coloured all over. Remove the cheeks to a plate and keep warm. Wipe out the pan.

Add the rest of the butter to the pan and heat until foaming, then add the chanterelles, season and cook for about 30–40 seconds, turning every so often.

Arrange the warm monkfish cheeks on the salad leaves and spoon over the dressing. Top with the chanterelles and serve immediately.

“ Monkfish cheeks are not commonly seen on fishmongers' slabs and you'll probably need to pre-order them. Using these types of cuts is certainly the way forward to helping the sustainability problem; mind you the fisherman whose task it is to cut them out might well disagree with me. ”

You can treat both monkfish and ray cheeks in the same way as any cut of fish, except that they have the added advantage of responding well to a bit of slow cooking – in a stew, curry or fish soup, for example. They also freeze really well, so it's worth ordering extra that you can store in the freezer in small, usable batches.

"We developed this salad at the Hix Oyster & Fish House in Lyme Regis, making good use of the diverse seafood and seashore vegetables available along the Dorset coast. It occasionally appears on the menu in London and is a reminder of the great seafood we have in our coastal waters. You can really use whatever seafood and seashore vegetables you can get your hands on. When rock samphire is around, we pickle it and use it to add a little acidity to the salad, but you could use capers in much the same way."

## SEASHORE SALAD

150–200g cockles or surf clams, cleaned
150–200g mussels, cleaned
50ml white wine
4 medium scallops, shelled and cleaned
sea salt and freshly ground black pepper
a couple of handfuls of sea vegetables, such as small
    leaves of sea beet, samphire, sea purslane, sea aster,
    wild fennel, trimmed of woody stalks and washed
2–3 tbsp freshly picked white crab meat
other seafood, such as cooked lobster, prawns etc.
    (optional)
4 oysters, shucked and left in the half-shell

FOR THE DRESSING
juice of ½ lemon
1 tbsp cider vinegar
4–5 tbsp cold-pressed rapeseed oil

SERVES 4

Put the cockles and mussels in a pan with the white wine. Cover with a tight-fitting lid and cook over a high heat for 3–4 minutes, shaking the pan every so often until they open. Tip into a colander, reserving the juices; discard any molluscs that remain closed.

Strain the liquor through a fine-meshed sieve into a small saucepan and bring to the boil. Halve the scallops, lay in a small dish and pour the hot liquid over them; leave to cool.

Bring a pan of water to the boil and blanch your chosen sea vegetable for 20 seconds, then refresh under the cold tap.

For the dressing, whisk the lemon juice, cider vinegar and rapeseed oil together with a little of the liquid from the scallops and season to taste.

To serve, remove half of the mussels and cockles from their shells. Arrange together with the sea vegetable(s) and the rest of the shellfish, except the oysters, on individual plates or one large platter. Spoon over the dressing and sit the oysters on top.

## BRADEN ROST SALAD WITH PICKLED CUCUMBER AND HORSERADISH

1 medium cucumber
1–2 tsp cold-pressed rapeseed oil
8 spring onions, trimmed and cut into 3–4cm lengths
300–400g piece Braden rost (hot smoked salmon)
2–3 handfuls of small salad leaves, such as baby spinach,
    pea shoots, ruby chard, rocket, red mustard leaf etc.
a few chives, snipped
2 tbsp freshly grated horseradish

FOR THE PICKLED CUCUMBER
1 medium cucumber
1 tbsp good-quality white wine vinegar
grated zest of 1 lemon
2 tbsp cold-pressed rapeseed oil
a good pinch of salt
2 tbsp chopped dill

FOR THE CIDER DRESSING
1 tbsp cider vinegar
1 tsp clear runny honey
1 tsp grain mustard
2 tbsp cold-pressed rapeseed oil
2 tbsp vegetable or corn oil
sea salt and freshly ground black pepper

SERVES 4

For the pickled cucumber, halve the cucumber lengthways and scoop out the seeds, then cut the flesh into 3mm slices and place in a bowl. Add the vinegar, zest, oil, salt and dill and toss to mix. Cover and leave to stand for 45 minutes before serving.

For the dressing, whisk all of the ingredients together in a bowl and season to taste. Set aside.

Cut the fresh cucumber on the diagonal into 5mm thick slices. Heat the oil in a frying pan and sauté the cucumber slices for 3–4 minutes, seasoning and turning them every so often, until lightly coloured. Remove with a slotted spoon and set aside.

Sauté the spring onions in the same pan for 2–3 minutes until lightly coloured. Take off the heat.

Remove the skin from the salmon and break into pieces. Toss the leaves in the dressing, season lightly and divide among plates. Arrange the salmon, pickled and sautéed cucumbers, spring onions and chives with the leaves and drizzle over any remaining dressing. Top with the horseradish.

# FISH HOUSE SALAD

150ml cold-pressed rapeseed oil
1 small onion, peeled and finely chopped
2 garlic cloves, peeled and sliced
1 red chilli, halved and deseeded
½ tsp cumin seeds
a few sprigs of thyme
2 tbsp cider vinegar, plus a little extra for the dressing
juice of ½ lemon
sea salt and freshly ground black pepper
4 medium or 8 small mackerel fillets
12–16 new potatoes (unpeeled)
80–100g green beans
100–120g podded broad beans
4 medium eggs
200–250g ripe tomatoes, mixed or 1 variety
2 Little Gem lettuces

SERVES 4–6

Heat 3 tbsp of the rapeseed oil in a saucepan and gently cook the onion and garlic with the chilli, cumin and thyme for 2–3 minutes, without colouring, until soft. Add all but 1 tbsp of the remaining rapeseed oil with the cider vinegar and lemon juice. Bring to a gentle simmer and season well with sea salt.

Meanwhile, lightly season the mackerel fillets with salt and pepper and heat 1 tbsp rapeseed oil in a non-stick frying pan. Fry the mackerel fillets, skin side down first, over a high heat, for 2–3 minutes on each side. Now immerse the mackerel fillets in the flavoured oil, remove from the heat and leave to cool.

Add the potatoes to a pan of salted water, bring to the boil and cook for 12–15 minutes until just tender. Drain and leave until cool enough to handle, then halve or quarter them.

Cook the green beans and broad beans separately in boiling salted water until just tender, then drain and refresh under cold water. Remove the skins from any larger broad beans.

Bring a pan of water to the boil and carefully drop in the eggs, using a slotted spoon. Simmer for 6–8 minutes, then drain and refresh under the cold tap. Shell the eggs and halve or quarter them.

Remove the mackerel from the oil with a slotted spoon and set aside. For the dressing, strain the flavoured oil through a fine-meshed sieve into a bowl. Whisk well and add a little more cider vinegar to taste.

To serve, cut the tomatoes into wedges or chunks. Toss the lettuce leaves with the green beans, broad beans, potatoes, tomatoes and some of the dressing. Season, then arrange in serving bowls. Break the mackerel into chunks and arrange on top of the leaves with the eggs. Spoon over some more dressing and serve.

"This is my British take on a *salade niçoise*, using fresh mackerel in place of the typical tinned tuna. Cooking the mackerel in oil in the way I have here gives a flavour that is comparable to tinned tuna, but better in my view and, of course, it's a much more sustainable option."

# LOBSTER AND JERSEY ROYAL SALAD WITH BACON

2 live lobsters, each about 500g

500g Jersey Royals, Cornish Earlies or other new potatoes, peeled

sea salt and freshly ground black pepper

4 thick slices of rindless smoked streaky bacon

1 tbsp vegetable oil

a handful of small salad leaves, such as silver sorrel, baby spinach, nasturtiums, flat-leaf parsley, bittercress, landcress etc.

FOR THE COURT BOUILLON

1 onion, peeled and quartered

2 carrots, peeled and roughly chopped

1 bay leaf

a few sprigs of thyme

1 tsp fennel seeds

10 black peppercorns

a few flat-leaf parsley stalks

FOR THE DRESSING

1 tbsp cider vinegar

4 tbsp cold-pressed rapeseed oil, or shellfish-infused oil (see page 297)

a few sprigs of tarragon

1 garlic clove

SERVES 4

An hour or so before cooking the lobsters, place them in the freezer to make them sleepy (this is deemed to be the most humane way of preparing live lobsters for cooking).

To make the court bouillon: put all the ingredients into a saucepan that will be large enough to also fit both lobsters. Cover with cold water, bring to the boil and simmer for 10 minutes. Drop the lobsters into the court bouillon, simmer for 5 minutes, then set aside to cool.

Meanwhile, cook the new potatoes in boiling salted water for 12–15 minutes until just cooked. Drain and leave to cool.

When the lobsters are cool enough to handle, split them in half with a heavy chopping knife and remove the meat from the shell, reserving any juices. Cut the meat into bite-sized chunks. Crack the claws and leg joints with the back of the knife and take out the meat.

Whisk all of the ingredients together for the dressing and season with salt and pepper. Set aside.

Cut the bacon roughly into 5mm cubes. Heat the oil in a frying pan and fry the bacon for 3–4 minutes until crisp all over, then drain on some kitchen paper.

Arrange the potatoes, bacon, lobster and some salad leaves on serving plates. Strain the dressing and drizzle over the salad, dressing it well. Top with a few more leaves and serve.

# OCTOPUS AND POTATO SALAD WITH SAMPHIRE

1 octopus, about 1–1.5 kg, cleaned

125g samphire, trimmed

200g waxy new potatoes, such as Charlotte, Roseval or Anya, cooked in their skins, peeled and halved

30g capers, rinsed

FOR THE COOKING LIQUOR

½ tsp fennel seeds

1 tsp white peppercorns

2 bay leaves

5 garlic cloves, peeled and roughly chopped

2 small onions, peeled and roughly chopped

2 celery stalks, roughly chopped

100ml white wine

1 lemon, halved

3 tbsp salt

FOR THE DRESSING

5 tbsp olive oil

juice of ½ lemon

1 tbsp good-quality white wine vinegar, such as Chardonnay or white balsamic

sea salt and freshly ground white pepper

SERVES 4–6

Put all of the ingredients for the cooking liquor in a large pan with enough water to be able to eventually cover the octopus when it is added later, bring to the boil and simmer gently for 15 minutes.

Add the octopus, bring back to the boil (you may need to put a pan lid slightly smaller than the one you are using on the octopus to keep it submerged in the water) and simmer gently for 50 minutes, or another 10 minutes for larger ones above 1.5kg. Leave to cool completely in the liquid until required.

Blanch the samphire in boiling unsalted water for 30 seconds, then drain in a colander and refresh in cold running water.

Make the dressing by mixing all the ingredients together and seasoning with salt and pepper.

Remove the octopus from the cooking liquor and drain it on kitchen paper. Cut the legs and body into 2–3cm chunks and put them in a bowl with the samphire and new potatoes. Season with salt and pepper and mix with half the dressing.

Arrange on plates, then scatter over the capers and spoon over the rest of the dressing.

"It's unfortunate that those pre-made seafood salads that you can buy in supermarkets and jars – and that are even served in some restaurants – include baby octopus that taste like rubber. The fresh stuff is pretty simple to cook and well worthwhile, but if you can't find fresh octopus, the frozen ones are fine."

You hear stories of Greek fishermen bashing octopuses over the rocks to tenderise them. I'm not sure if that really works, as really it is the cooking that determines the tenderness; undercooked, octopus is completely inedible. This method is simple enough, but you could also try cooking the octopus with no liquid at all in a covered pot with some seasoning for about the same amount of time.

# CRAB AND SAMPHIRE SALAD

40g podded peas
sea salt and freshly ground black pepper
a pinch of sugar
a handful of samphire, trimmed
60g podded broad beans
a handful (50–60g) of small salad leaves, such as pea
    shoots, landcress or harvested sea vegetables
200–250g freshly picked white crab meat

FOR THE DRESSING
1 tbsp cider vinegar
1 tsp Tewkesbury mustard
4 tbsp cold-pressed rapeseed oil

SERVES 4

Cook the peas in a pan of boiling salted water with the sugar for 3–4 minutes until tender, drain and leave to cool. Blanch the samphire briefly in unsalted boiling water, then drain and leave to cool. Cook the broad beans in some boiling salted water for 3–4 minutes until tender, drain and leave to cool. If the broad beans are large, remove the outer skins.

Make the dressing by mixing all of the ingredients together and seasoning lightly.

To serve, toss the vegetables and salad leaves in the dressing, season and arrange on plates, then scatter the crab meat over the salad.

# FARMHOUSE SALAD WITH SCOTCH DUCK'S EGG

80–100g piece of smoked streaky bacon or lardons

180–200g good-quality black pudding, skinned

2 thick slices of bread

4 duck's eggs

200g good-quality Cumberland sausagemeat

1 tbsp plain flour

1 egg, beaten

40–50g fresh white breadcrumbs

2–3 tbsp vegetable oil, plus extra for deep-frying

4 rabbit saddle fillets (optional)

a knob of butter

2 handfuls of small salad and herb leaves (about 80–90g)

100ml tarragon dressing (see page 301)

sea salt and freshly ground black pepper

**SERVES 4**

Cut the bacon, black pudding and bread roughly into 1cm chunks and set aside.

Lower the eggs into a pan of simmering water and cook for 3–5 minutes to soft-boil them, then remove and refresh in cold water. Once cool, carefully peel the eggs, keeping them intact. Divide the sausagemeat into 4 balls and flatten them into patties. Wrap each patty around an egg, moulding it to cover evenly with your hands.

Have three shallow containers ready, one containing the flour, one with the egg and the third with the breadcrumbs. One at a time, coat the duck's eggs with the flour first, shaking off any excess, then put through the beaten egg and finally into the breadcrumbs. Turn to coat all over and re-mould as necessary.

Heat a 8cm depth of oil in a deep-fat fryer or other suitable large, deep, heavy-based pan to 140–150ºC. Deep-fry the eggs for 3–4 minutes, turning occasionally to colour evenly. Remove and drain on kitchen paper.

Heat 1 tablespoon of oil in a frying pan. Add the bacon, black pudding and rabbit fillets if using. Cook, stirring, for 2–3 minutes until lightly coloured, then remove with a slotted spoon and keep warm. Heat the rest of the oil in the pan, then add the bread cubes with the butter and fry until crisp and golden; remove and drain.

To serve, dress the leaves with some of the dressing, season and arrange in wide bowls or on plates. Cut each rabbit fillet, if using, into 4 or 5 slices then scatter over the salad leaves with the fried bread, bacon and black pudding. Cut the Scotch eggs in half and arrange on the salad. Drizzle over the rest of the dressing and serve.

# WOOD PIGEON, SILVER SORREL AND COBNUT SALAD

2 oven-ready wood pigeons
sea salt and freshly ground black pepper
a couple of sprigs of thyme
a few knobs of butter
25–30 cobnuts, shelled
1 tsp sea salt
5 tbsp cold-pressed rapeseed oil
2 thick slices of smoked streaky bacon, cut into
    5mm cubes
1 tbsp cider vinegar
1 tsp Tewkesbury mustard
a couple of handfuls of silver sorrel or other small leaves

SERVES 4

Preheat the oven to 220°C/gas mark 7. Season the pigeons inside and out. Put a thyme sprig and a knob of butter inside each cavity. Rub the breasts with butter. Roast for 10-12 minutes, keeping the meat nice and pink.

Meanwhile, toss the cobnuts with the sea salt and 1 tbsp of the oil and spread out on a baking tray. Place in the oven for 3-4 minutes to colour lightly.

Transfer the roasted pigeons to a warm plate and set aside to rest. Tip the bacon pieces into the roasting pan and fry over a medium heat for 3-4 minutes until lightly coloured. Remove with a slotted spoon and put to one side. Add a tablespoonful of water to the pan and stir over a low heat for a minute to scrape up any residue from the bottom. Spoon into a small bowl and whisk in the vinegar, mustard, remaining oil and seasoning to make the dressing.

Take the legs off the pigeon and remove as much meat from them as you can, then shred it. Cut the breasts from the birds with a sharp knife and cut each one into 6 or 7 thin slices.

To serve, toss the leaves with the bacon, dressing and leg meat and divide among plates. Arrange the sliced breasts on top and scatter the cobnuts over. Serve at once.

> If you can't find cobnuts, which are
> really particular to Kent, then use
> walnuts or hazelnuts instead.

# GROUSE SALAD WITH PARSNIP CRISPS AND BRAMBLE DRESSING

2 oven-ready grouse
2 small parsnips, scrubbed clean
vegetable or corn oil, for deep-frying
sea salt and freshly ground black pepper
a couple of knobs of butter, softened
4 rashers of streaky bacon, cut into 1cm pieces
a couple of handfuls of small flavoursome salad
    leaves and herbs
bramble dressing (see page 300)

SERVES 4

Preheat the oven to 240°C/gas mark 9 and have the grouse ready at room temperature. Top and tail the parsnips, leaving the skin on unless it is very brown. Using a mandolin or vegetable peeler, slice them lengthways as thinly as possible, rinse well and then pat dry with a clean tea towel. Heat about an 8cm depth of oil in a deep-fat fryer or other suitable deep, heavy pan to 180°C.

Fry the parsnip slices in the hot oil in small batches, stirring to ensure that they don't stick together. The parsnip slices will take a while to colour (avoid over-browning them) and even then may still appear soft (they will crisp up on drying). Remove with a slotted spoon, drain on kitchen paper and sprinkle with salt. Leave them to dry somewhere warm but not hot.

Season the grouse with salt and pepper and rub the breasts with butter. Roast for about 15 minutes, keeping them nice and pink, then set aside to rest in a warm spot. Meanwhile, fry the bacon pieces in a dry pan for a few minutes until crisp.

To serve, carefully remove the grouse breasts from the carcass and cut each one into 6 or 7 slices. Arrange the leaves on serving plates with the grouse and bacon. Spoon over the bramble dressing, then scatter or pile the parsnip crisps on top.

> Using the grouse breasts like this for
> a salad means you'll be able to get
> another meal out of the rest of the
> meat on the bird in the form of a soup
> or a broth (see page 113).

# SPRING LAMB SALAD

2 pieces of spring lamb neck fillet, about 200g in total
sea salt and freshly ground black pepper
1 tbsp vegetable oil
2–3 slices of lamb's liver, 120–150g in total
a few slices of roasted stuffed breast of lamb (see
    page 212, optional)
a couple of handfuls of small salad and herb leaves,
    such as flat-leaf parsley, chervil, bittercress,
    mint etc.

FOR THE DRESSING
2 tbsp good-quality white wine vinegar
1 tsp grain mustard
a few mint leaves
6–7 tbsp olive oil

SERVES 4

Season the lamb fillet with salt and pepper. Heat
the oil in a frying pan and fry the pieces of fillet for
about 4–5 minutes on each side until pink. Remove
from the pan and set aside on a warm plate to rest.

For the dressing, whiz all the ingredients together
in a blender and season to taste.

Just before serving, fry the lamb's liver slices in the
pan over a high heat for about 30 seconds on each
side, then remove and cut into strips. Briefly warm
the slices of cooked breast if using.

To serve, toss the leaves in the dressing and arrange
on serving plates. Carefully slice the lamb fillet and
arrange on top, with the liver and roasted stuffed
breast if using.

66 For this salad, you can use any
combination of your favourite lamb cuts
and offal – cooked pink and sliced up.
Slow-cooked belly, pan-fried until crisp,
shredded and scattered over the salad,
is a great addition. 99

# HAM HOCK AND PEA SALAD

FOR COOKING THE HAM
1 ham hock (smoked or unsmoked), about 1kg,
    soaked overnight in cold water
1 onion, peeled and quartered
1 leek, halved lengthways and washed
10 black peppercorns
1 bay leaf
a few sprigs of thyme
3 juniper berries

FOR THE SALAD
sea salt and freshly ground black pepper
1–2 tsp granulated sugar
a few good knobs of butter
120–150g freshly podded peas
a little vegetable oil (optional)
2 handfuls of pea shoots
100ml tarragon dressing (see page 301)

SERVES 4

Drain the ham, rinse and place in a large pot with
the rest of the cooking ingredients. Add enough
cold water to cover generously and bring to the boil.
Skim off any scum from the surface and simmer,
covered, for 2–2½ hours or until the ham is tender.

Leave the ham hock to cool in the liquid (unless
you're in a hurry, in which case remove it to a board
to cool more quickly).

Bring some water to the boil in a pan. Add salt, the
sugar and butter, then tip in the peas. Simmer for
3–5 minutes or until tender. Drain well.

Remove enough of the ham from the hock for the
salad and break it into flakes with your fingers. (You
could also dice some of the rind and fry it in a little
hot oil to crisp up if you like.)

Toss the shoots, peas and the ham in the dressing
and arrange on plates or in shallow bowls to serve.

A ham hock or knuckle has a fantastic
flavour and goes a long way. Once
cooked, you have a great stock base
for a soup. Simmer peas and/or
broad beans in it and blend to make a
smooth soup, or prepare a summery
minestrone, flaking some of the off-
cuts of the hock back in.

# SALAD OF SPROUT TOPS, SALSIFY AND HAM HOCK

1 small ham hock, cooked (see page 80), some of the
    cooking liquor reserved
6–7 salsify
juice of 1 lemon
a couple of handfuls of sprout tops, thick stalks
    removed and washed
a little vegetable oil (optional)

FOR THE DRESSING
2 shallots, peeled and finely chopped
1 tbsp cider vinegar
1 tsp English mustard
4 tbsp cold-pressed rapeseed oil
sea salt and freshly ground black pepper

SERVES 4

Have the ham hock cooked and ready with the reserved liquor.

For the salsify, have two bowls of water ready, one with the lemon juice added and the other for washing. Top, tail and half the salsify, then peel with a vegetable peeler, dipping them in the bowl of water as you're going, to ensure all the black skin is removed. As you've peeled each one, drop into the bowl of acidulated lemon water.

For the dressing, put the shallots into a small pan with the cider vinegar and 1 tablespoon of water and simmer until reduced by half, then remove from the heat and whisk in the mustard and oil. Season with salt and pepper to taste; set aside.

Add the salsify to a pan of well-salted water, bring to the boil and cook for 4–5 minutes until tender. Drain and leave to cool a little. Meanwhile, add the sprout tops to a pan of boiling salted water and cook for 3–4 minutes until tender, then drain.

Flake the ham hock into small pieces and reheat with a little of the cooking liquor, or pan-fry in a little oil until crisp if you prefer. Slice the salsify on the diagonal.

To serve, arrange the warm sprout tops and salsify on individual serving plates. Scatter the ham on top and spoon the dressing over.

# OXTAIL SALAD

FOR THE BRAISED OXTAIL

1kg oxtail, cut into 2–3cm thick pieces and trimmed of excess fat

sea salt and freshly ground black pepper

50g plain flour, plus extra for dusting

60g butter

1 onion, peeled and finely chopped

2 garlic cloves, peeled and crushed

1 tsp thyme leaves

2 tsp tomato purée

100ml red wine

2 litres dark meat stock (see page 292)

FOR THE DRESSING

1 tbsp cider vinegar

1 tsp English mustard

3 tbsp cold-pressed rapeseed oil

FOR THE SALAD

1 carrot, peeled

1 turnip, peeled

a handful of small salad and herb leaves, such as purslane, watercress, chervil, chives, etc.

SERVES 4–6

❝Braised oxtail may not be the obvious choice for a salad but I've often made this when I've had some left over from a dinner. It can be served in summer or winter – you just need to change the salad vegetables accordingly.❞

First braise the oxtail. Preheat the oven to 220°C/gas mark 7. Season the pieces of oxtail and dust them lightly with flour. Place in a roasting tray and roast in the oven for 30 minutes, turning them halfway through to make sure they are nicely coloured on both sides.

Heat the butter in a large heavy-based saucepan and gently cook the onion with the garlic and thyme for 3–4 minutes until softened, stirring every so often. Add the flour and tomato purée and stir well. Gradually pour in the wine and stock, stirring well to avoid lumps forming, and bring to the boil.

Add the pieces of oxtail, then lower the heat, cover and simmer very gently for about 2 hours. Check the pieces of oxtail: the meat should be tender and easily removed from the bone; if not, replace the lid and cook for another 15 minutes or so.

Meanwhile, for the dressing, whisk the ingredients together in a bowl and season with salt and pepper to taste. Shred the carrot and turnip into very fine matchsticks.

Drain the oxtail in a colander over a bowl to reserve the sauce. When the oxtail is cool enough to handle, take the meat off the bone in bite-sized pieces and place in a saucepan with a little of the sauce.

Toss the salad leaves, carrot and turnip with the dressing and arrange in the centre of individual serving plates. Reheat the oxtail a little and spoon around the salad, with a small amount of sauce just coating the meat. Spoon any remaining dressing over the oxtail.

## SALT BEEF AND GREEN BEAN SALAD

700–800g salted beef brisket or salted ox cheeks,
    soaked overnight in cold water
2 onions, peeled and quartered
2 carrots, peeled and trimmed
10 black peppercorns
4 garlic cloves, peeled
a few sprigs of thyme
100g French green beans, trimmed
2 large shallots, peeled and finely chopped

FOR THE VINAIGRETTE
1½ tbsp good-quality tarragon vinegar
2 tsp Dijon mustard
1 garlic clove, peeled
3 tbsp olive oil
3 tbsp vegetable or corn oil
sea salt and freshly ground black pepper

SERVES 4

First make the vinaigrette. Put all the ingredients into a screw-topped jar and season with salt and pepper. Shake and leave to infuse overnight. Cover the brisket with cold water and leave overnight.

Rinse the salt beef and put it into a saucepan with the onions, carrots, peppercorns, garlic and thyme sprigs. Cover well with water, bring to the boil and skim off the scum from the surface, then simmer, covered, for about 2 hours, topping up the water if necessary. It's difficult to put an exact cooking time on cuts of meat like this, so check it after 2 hours and if it's not tender cook for another half an hour or so. Leave to cool in the liquid, but don't refrigerate.

Cook the green beans in boiling salted water for 3–4 minutes until tender, then drain well.

Remove the beef from the cooking liquid and carve into 5mm thick slices, breaking these up into bite-sized pieces. Mix the beef with the beans and shallots, season with salt and pepper to taste and dress well with the vinaigrette to serve.

Salted ox cheeks are tricky to get, but salted brisket makes a good substitute. It has layers of fat running through it, which keeps the meat meltingly tender. Silverside is too lean.

## BEEF FLANK, CRISPY SHALLOT AND WATERCRESS SALAD

2 butcher's steaks, each about 300g (see page 180)
5–6 shallots, peeled
vegetable oil, for deep-frying
plain flour, for dusting
sea salt and freshly ground black pepper
100ml milk
100–150g watercress, trimmed and thick stalks
    removed

FOR THE DRESSING
1 tbsp good-quality cider vinegar
3 tbsp cold-pressed rapeseed oil
1 tsp English or Tewkesbury mustard

SERVES 4

Trim the steaks of any excess fat and set them aside at room temperature.

Slice the shallots into thin rings. Heat about an 8cm depth of oil in an electric deep-fat fryer or other suitable heavy-based pan to 160–180°C. Season the flour for dusting generously with salt and pepper.

Toss the shallot rings in the seasoned flour to coat, shaking off any excess, then pass through the milk and then through the flour again, shaking off any excess. Deep-fry the shallot rings a handful at a time for 3–4 minutes until crisp, then remove with a slotted spoon and drain on kitchen paper. Repeat with the rest (you don't need to worry about keeping the onions hot).

Heat a ridged griddle pan or a heavy-based frying pan, or better still a barbecue. Season the steaks well and cook to your liking. Allow about 3–4 minutes on each side for rare to medium-rare, which I'd recommend, especially for a salad.

Meanwhile, make the dressing. Whisk the ingredients together in a bowl and season with salt and pepper to taste. Dress the watercress and arrange on serving plates. Slice the steaks and place on top of the watercress, then scatter the crispy shallots over and serve.

SOUPS

## CELERY AND STILTON SOUP

1 small leafy head of celery
a good knob of butter
1 small onion, peeled and chopped
1.5 litres vegetable stock (see page 292)
sea salt and freshly ground black pepper
2 tbsp double cream
60g Stilton, rind removed, cut into chunks
1 tsp celery salt

SERVES 4–6

Separate the leaves from the celery stalks, wash and pat dry, then set the leaves aside for later. Roughly chop the stalks.

Heat the butter in a medium saucepan. Add the onion and celery stalks, cover and cook gently for 3-4 minutes without colouring, stirring occasionally. Add the stock, season lightly and bring to a simmer. Cover and simmer for 30 minutes. Now add all but a handful of the celery leaves and simmer for another 5-6 minutes. Remove from the heat.

Whiz the soup to a purée in a blender, in batches if necessary. Pass through a sieve into a clean pan to remove any stringy bits. Reheat if necessary and stir in the cream. Pour into warm soup plates and crumble in the Stilton. Roughly tear the reserved celery leaves and scatter over the soup. Sprinkle with a little celery salt and serve.

"Celery and Stilton are familiar cheeseboard partners, but they also marry brilliantly in a soup. Serve this with some good, crusty bread."

## WATERCRESS SOUP WITH GOAT'S CHEESE

250g watercress, washed
1 tbsp vegetable or corn oil
1 leek, trimmed, roughly chopped and rinsed
1 small floury potato, about 80–100g, peeled and diced
1.2 litres vegetable stock (see page 292)
sea salt and freshly ground black pepper
100g soft goat's cheese

SERVES 4–6

Cut the main stalks from the watercress and reserve. Heat the oil in a pan, add the leek and potato, cover and cook gently for about 10 minutes until soft, without allowing them to colour. Add the vegetable stock, season and bring to the boil. Simmer for 10 minutes, then add the watercress stalks and simmer for another 5 minutes.

Remove from the heat and add the watercress sprigs. Whiz the soup in a blender or using a hand-held blender until smooth, then pass through a fine-meshed sieve into a clean pan. If serving hot, reheat the soup briefly and season again with salt and pepper, if necessary. If serving cold, cool, then chill and check the seasoning before serving.

Pour the watercress soup into bowls and top each portion with a spoonful of soft goat's cheese. Serve at once.

Like most soups and sauces that are made with leafy green herbs, brief cooking and quick chilling are essential to preserve the delicate flavour of the watercress. Try to buy soft creamy goat's cheese, which means that it is fresh not matured. You can serve this soup hot or cold.

❝Watercress farms are dotted
throughout Hampshire and Dorset, but
unfortunately, most of their wonderful
produce ends up garnishing roasts
and grills, often to be left on the plate.
This fresh-tasting soup is a great way
to appreciate the true flavour of this
underused peppery salad leaf.❞

## CHILLED PEA AND LOVAGE SOUP

1 tbsp vegetable, corn or cold-pressed rapeseed oil
1 leek (both green and white parts), trimmed,
   roughly chopped and washed
1.2 litres vegetable stock (see page 292)
sea salt and freshly ground black pepper
450g freshly podded peas (or frozen ones will do)
10–12 lovage leaves

SERVES 4

Heat the oil in a pan, add the leek and cook gently
for 3-4 minutes, stirring occasionally until soft. Add
the stock and some seasoning and simmer gently
for 10-12 minutes.

Tip in the peas and simmer for another 5 minutes
or until tender (frozen peas will only need a couple
of minutes once they come back to a simmer). Add
the lovage and immediately take off the heat.

Whiz the mixture in a blender until smooth, then
taste. Adjust the seasoning and blend in some more
lovage if you think the soup needs it. Pass through
a sieve if you wish (some blenders do a better job
than others). Cool the soup down, then refrigerate
for a few hours until well chilled or put it into the
freezer if you're in a rush.

" Pea and mint is of course a classic
combination and may be the obvious
choice, but lovage also complements
peas really well. Like mint, it is very
fragrant and has a special flavour but it
is an underused herb, probably because
of its potency. Certainly, lovage must be
added with caution or it will overpower
other flavours. I always have some in
the garden because it's great walking
out the back door and grabbing a few
leaves of something that's so hard to
find in the shops. "

## CHILLED GOLDEN BEETROOT SOUP WITH HORSERADISH

400g medium yellow beetroots
sea salt and freshly ground black pepper
1 tbsp cold-pressed rapeseed or olive oil
1 small onion, peeled and roughly chopped
1 litre vegetable stock (see page 292)
cream, crème fraîche or soft goat's cheese, to serve
1 tbsp freshly grated horseradish

SERVES 4

Cook the beetroots in a pan of salted water for
about 1 hour until they feel tender when pierced
with a knife. Drain and leave until cool enough to
handle, then peel and roughly chop.

Heat the oil in a large saucepan, add the onion,
cover and cook gently for 3-4 minutes to soften.
Add the vegetable stock, bring to the boil, season
and simmer for 30 minutes.

Add the beetroot, then remove from the heat.
Purée in a blender until smooth, then pass the
soup through a fine-meshed sieve into a large bowl.
Re-season if necessary. Cool the soup down, then
refrigerate for a few hours until well chilled or put
it into the freezer if you're in a rush.

Serve in soup plates topped with a dollop of cream,
crème fraîche or soft goat's cheese and a sprinkling
of grated horseradish.

This is a great soup to trick guests and
keep them guessing as to what you
are serving. Beetroot would be the last
thing they would think of, but golden
beet – one of several old varieties on
the market – makes a stunning soup.
You can finish it with all sorts of things –
horseradish will give the soup a kick, or
you might prefer a little shredded ham
or salted ox tongue.

# ICED PLUM TOMATO SOUP WITH HORSERADISH

250g ripe red tomatoes, halved and deseeded
250g cherry tomatoes
150ml tomato juice
1 garlic clove, peeled and blanched in
    boiling water for 2 minutes
sea salt and freshly ground black pepper

FOR THE GARNISH
60–70g mixed tomatoes such as red and
    yellow, cherry, plum, etc.
20–30g freshly grated horseradish
2 tbsp olive oil

SERVES 4

Put the ripe red tomatoes in a blender with the cherry tomatoes, tomato juice and garlic. Whiz to a purée, then pass through a fine sieve into a bowl. Season with salt and pepper to taste, then chill in the fridge for an hour or two, or the freezer for 20-30 minutes if you're in a hurry.

To serve, divide the soup among chilled soup plates. Cut the mixed tomatoes into even-sized chunks and add to the soup. Scatter the grated horseradish on top and drizzle with the olive oil.

I suppose this delicious chilled soup is verging on being a Bloody Mary – a brunchy hangover soup maybe, or just a clever lunch dish or dinner party starter. I've included some tomato juice here, just to intensify the flavour a little, but if you've got really ripe, great flavoured tomatoes you needn't bother.

# SUMMER VEGETABLE BROTH

1.5 litres vegetable stock (see page 292)
1 small leek, trimmed, cut into 1cm dice and washed
1 celery stalk, peeled if necessary and cut into 5mm dice
sea salt and freshly ground black pepper
150g podded broad beans
100g podded peas
60g green or runner beans, cut into 5mm lengths
1 tbsp chopped flat-leaf parsley
1 tbsp chopped chives

SERVES 4

Pour the stock into a large saucepan, add the leek and celery and bring to a simmer. Season lightly with salt and pepper and let simmer for 15 minutes.

Meanwhile, blanch the broad beans in boiling salted water for 3-4 minutes, then drain and refresh under the cold tap. Remove the tough skins from any larger broad beans; leave small ones as they are.

Add the peas and green or runner beans to the simmering stock and cook for a further 10 minutes. Add the broad beans, chopped parsley and chives, and simmer for another 5 minutes. Re-season if necessary before serving.

" This is a nice light broth that uses summer peas and beans. You can vary the vegetables according to what is available. Asparagus is a great addition when it's in season, and adding some diced new potatoes will make the soup a bit more substantial. "

# CABBAGE AND BACON SOUP

150–200g piece of smoked streaky bacon
a good knob of butter
1 large onion, peeled and finely chopped
2 garlic cloves, peeled and crushed
2 litres chicken stock (see page 293)
8–10 leaves of Savoy, pointed hispi or green cabbage
10–12 small waxy potatoes, such as Anya, Ratte or
    Charlotte, peeled
sea salt and freshly ground black pepper
2 tbsp coarsely chopped flat-leafed parsley

SERVES 4–6

Cut the bacon roughly into 1cm cubes. Heat the butter in a large saucepan and add the onion, garlic and bacon. Cover the pan and cook gently for 4–5 minutes, stirring every so often. Add the stock, bring to the boil and simmer gently for 40 minutes.

Meanwhile, cut the cabbage leaves roughly into 1cm pieces and thinly slice the potatoes. Add the cabbage and potatoes to the pan with a little salt and some pepper and simmer for 10–12 minutes.

Add the parsley and check the seasoning. Simmer for another couple of minutes.

Ladle the soup into warm bowls and serve with some good bread.

## SPICED PARSNIP
## AND APPLE SOUP

2–3 large Russet or Cox's apples, about
   400–500g in total
500g parsnips
60g butter
1 tsp chopped fresh root ginger
1 tsp ground cumin
½ tsp ground cinnamon
1 tsp fenugreek seeds
½ tsp ground turmeric
100ml cider
about 1.5 litres vegetable stock (see page 292)
sea salt and freshly ground black pepper
90ml double cream
2 tsp toasted cumin seeds

SERVES 4–6

Peel, core and roughly dice the apples and parsnips. Melt the butter in a large saucepan, tip in the diced parsnips and apples, then add the fresh ginger and spices. Cover and cook gently for about 5 minutes, giving it an occasional stir; don't let it colour.

Remove the lid, add the cider and vegetable stock and bring to the boil. Season with salt and pepper and simmer gently for about 15 minutes until the parsnip is soft.

Purée the soup in a blender until smooth, then strain through a fine sieve back into the cleaned pan. Bring back to a low simmer, then stir in the cream. If the soup is too thick, adjust the consistency with a little water or additional stock.

Divide between warm soup bowls, sprinkle with a pinch of cumin seeds and serve.

## ROAST AUTUMN SQUASH
## AND WALNUT SOUP

1kg butternut or onion squash
a large knob of butter
1 small leek, trimmed, chopped and washed
1 small onion, peeled and roughly chopped
1.2 litres vegetable stock (see page 292)
sea salt and freshly ground black pepper
1 tbsp pumpkin seeds, lightly toasted
12–15 fresh walnuts, shelled and roughly broken

SERVES 4

Peel the squash, halve and remove the seeds and fibrous bits, then chop the flesh into small cubes. Heat the butter in a large saucepan and gently cook the leek and onion for 4–5 minutes until softened.

Add the squash and stock, bring to the boil and season with salt and pepper. Leave to simmer for 20 minutes. Scoop out a spoonful of the cubed squash, using a slotted spoon, and reserve for serving.

Whiz the soup in a blender until smooth, then – if necessary – strain through a fine sieve back into the pan. Reheat gently, stirring in a little more vegetable stock or water if the soup is too thick. Taste and adjust the seasoning.

Pour the soup into warm soup plates and add the reserved squash cubes. Top with a light sprinkling of toasted pumpkin seeds and walnut pieces and serve straight away.

**"** Parsnips make a hearty, sweet soup – ideal when the weather begins to get a bit chilly. Teamed with apples like Russets or Cox's and mild background spices, they are amazingly good. This is a mildly curried soup; increase the quantities of spices if you want it to be more fiery. **"**

"Closer-textured orange-fleshed squash – like
butternut and onion – are particularly good for using
in soups. These varieties tend to have a better ratio of
usable flesh to skin than some of the larger squashes
and pumpkins that you find. Fresh walnuts make a
natural crunchy accompaniment."

# HORSERADISH SOUP

50g butter
1 onion, peeled and roughly chopped
1 large leek, trimmed, roughly chopped and washed
1 tbsp plain flour
1.5 litres vegetable stock (see page 292)
sea salt and freshly ground black pepper
100g freshly grated horseradish, or more to taste
1–2 tbsp double cream

SERVES 4

Melt the butter in a large saucepan. Add the onion and leek, cover and cook gently without colouring for 3-4 minutes, stirring every so often, to soften. Stir in the flour and cook over a low heat for 30 seconds, then gradually stir in the stock. Bring to the boil, season and simmer for 30 minutes.

Add about two-thirds of the horseradish to the soup and simmer for 5 minutes, then take off the heat. Purée in a blender until smooth, then pass through a fine-meshed sieve into a clean saucepan.

Taste for seasoning and the horseradish, adding more to taste. You don't need to blend the soup again - the extra horseradish gives a nice texture. Add the cream, bring back to a simmer and serve.

**"**I first had this soup in Poland. It was so good that I vowed to make my own version and put it on the menu. We have loads of horseradish growing in the UK but don't seem to make much use of it, apart from the ubiquitous horseradish sauce for roast beef and the odd grating for a Bloody Mary.**"**

# WILD GARLIC AND NETTLE SOUP

a couple of good knobs of butter
2 leeks, trimmed, chopped and washed
1 tbsp plain flour
1.5 litres vegetable stock (see page 292)
sea salt and freshly ground black pepper
a handful of young nettle tops
a handful of wild garlic leaves, chopped
3–4 tbsp double cream

SERVES 4

Melt the butter in a heavy-based pan and gently cook the leeks for 2-3 minutes to soften, stirring every so often. Stir in the flour, then gradually stir in the vegetable stock and season with salt and pepper. Bring to the boil, lower the heat and simmer for about 20 minutes.

Add about two-thirds of the nettles and wild garlic leaves and simmer for a few minutes. Whiz the soup in a blender until smooth, in batches if necessary, then return to the pan.

Stir in the cream and the rest of the nettles and wild garlic. Simmer for a few more minutes, then taste and adjust the seasoning if necessary. Serve piping hot, with some good bread.

When you have wonderful wild ingredients at hand, it makes sense to use them. Both young nettles and wild garlic are abundant in spring and are easy to gather – just remember to take a rubber glove with you for gathering the nettles. And don't worry, cooking takes the prickle out of young nettles so they won't sting your throat on the way down.

# SPRING VEGETABLE MINESTRONE WITH LANGOUSTINES

16 small live langoustines
sea salt and freshly ground black pepper
1.5 litres vegetable or fish stock (see pages 292–293)
1 bay leaf
a few sprigs of thyme
150g podded broad beans
1 small leek, trimmed, cut into rough 1cm dice and
   well rinsed
100g podded peas
60g green beans, cut into 5mm pieces
1 tbsp chopped flat-leaf parsley
2 tbsp cooked risotto rice or soup pasta (optional)

SERVES 4

❝Spring is the best time for those tender little peas and beans, and langoustine tails complement them beautifully. They also add the perfect colour contrast.❞

Bring a pan of water large enough to fit the langoustines to the boil. Stir in a good tablespoon of salt, then plunge in the langoustines, bring back to the boil and simmer for 3 minutes. Drain in a colander and leave to cool for 6–7 minutes.

Remove the heads and shells and put the tails in the fridge. Wash the shells in cold water and put them into a saucepan with the fish or vegetable stock and herbs. Bring to the boil and simmer gently for 30 minutes, skimming occasionally.

Meanwhile, blanch the broad beans in boiling salted water for 3 minutes, drain and remove their skins.

Strain the soup through a fine-meshed sieve into a clean saucepan. Add the leek, peas and green beans to the soup, and simmer for 10 minutes. Add the broad beans and parsley, and simmer for another 5 minutes. Add the langoustine tails and rice or pasta if using them. (You can cook these in the soup, but they will make it go slightly cloudy.) Season again with salt and pepper, if necessary.

The actual vegetables and pulses used in a minestrone can be varied almost infinitely. Tomatoes, young carrots and celery, and courgettes can be added in spring; add other seasonal veg throughout the year, particularly Savoy cabbage in winter. Instead of the broad beans you could also use borlotti and/ or cannellini beans.

# CRAYFISH SOUP WITH CIDER BRANDY

the shells from 1kg freshly cooked crayfish, any excess
   tail meat reserved
1 tbsp vegetable oil
1 small onion, peeled and roughly chopped
1 small leek, trimmed, roughly chopped and washed
2 celery stalks, roughly chopped
3 garlic cloves, peeled and roughly chopped
½ tsp fennel seeds
a pinch of saffron strands
a few sprigs of thyme
a couple of sprigs of tarragon
1 bay leaf
40g butter
3 tbsp plain flour
2 tbsp tomato purée
100ml white wine
1.5 litres fish stock (see page 293)
sea salt and freshly ground white pepper
100ml double cream
1–2 tbsp Somerset cider brandy

SERVES 6–8

Chop up the crayfish shells. Heat the oil in a large heavy-based saucepan and add the crayfish shells with the vegetables. Fry over a high heat, stirring every so often, for about 5 minutes until they begin to colour. Add the garlic, fennel seeds, saffron, thyme, tarragon and bay leaf, and continue cooking for another 5 minutes or so.

Add the butter and once it has melted, stir in the flour. Cook over a medium heat for about 5 minutes, stirring frequently, until the mixture turns a dark sandy colour. Add the tomato purée, stir well and cook over a low heat for a minute or so. Add the wine, then slowly add the fish stock, stirring to avoid lumps. Bring to the boil, season with salt and pepper, and simmer for 1 hour.

Liquidise the soup, shells and all, in a strong blender or food processor until smooth, then strain through a fine-meshed sieve into a clean pan. You'll need to do this in batches.

Bring to a simmer, then add the cream and any crayfish tail meat. Season again if necessary and stir in the cider brandy. Serve in warmed soup plates.

66The potential waste with crayfish, crabs, lobsters, and other crustaceans is pretty high if you don't put their shells to good use. All of a sudden, expensive shellfish like these become good value once you have used the shells to make a few bowls of rich velvety soup. I've added a few splashes of Julian Temperley's Somerset cider brandy at the end here to give the soup a West Country kick.99

# JELLIED TOMATO SOUP WITH CRAYFISH AND WILD FENNEL

2 garlic cloves, peeled
1.5kg ripe tomatoes, halved
a few sprigs of basil
300ml good-quality tomato juice
sea salt and freshly ground black pepper
9g of leaf gelatine (3 sheets)
1 tbsp fennel seeds
1kg live freshwater crayfish
a few sprigs of wild fennel or dill

SERVES 4–6

Add the garlic cloves to a pan of boiling water and blanch for 2 minutes, then drain and place in a food processor. Add the tomatoes, basil, 250ml of the tomato juice and season with salt and pepper. Briefly blend in a food processor to a coarse texture.

Line a colander with a double layer of muslin or a clean tea towel and set over a large bowl. Pour the tomato pulp into the colander, cover loosely and place in the fridge. Leave overnight to allow the juice to drip through slowly.

The next day you should have about 600–700ml of clear juice in the bowl. Gently squeeze the pulp to extract as much juice as possible.

Soak 3 sheets of gelatine (or 4 if you have more than 750ml tomato juice) in cold water to soften.

Meanwhile, take a small ladleful of the clear tomato juice and heat it in a pan.

Squeeze the excess water from the gelatine leaves, then add them to the hot tomato juice and stir until dissolved; do not allow to boil. Add this to the rest of the strained juice with the remaining 50ml tomato juice and stir well. Cover and refrigerate for 1–2 hours until set.

In the meantime, bring a large saucepan of water to the boil with the fennel seeds and plenty of salt added. Plunge in the crayfish, bring back to the boil and simmer for 3 minutes, then drain in a colander and leave to cool a little. Carefully peel the crayfish tails; if the claws are large, crack them open to extract the meat.

To serve, break the jelly up a little, then spoon into serving bowls and top with the crayfish. Scatter over the fennel or dill and serve.

Once you've made this, try preparing the soup opposite with the crayfish shells. Also, the pulp left from making the jelly can be transformed into a tomato salsa for dipping or to use as a sauce for pasta: just cook it in a pan over a low heat, season and spice it up with a chilli and coriander, if you wish.

"You may think this looks and sounds a bit fancy for me, but it is actually very straightforward. It's amazing how much flavour you can extract from a few really ripe tomatoes in the form of a clear jelly. You may need to order freshwater crayfish from your fishmonger, or you could use lobster or crab."

# MOUCLADE

1kg mussels, beards removed and well cleaned,
    discarding any which remain resolutely open
100ml dry white wine
1 tbsp chopped flat-leaf parsley

FOR THE BROTH
30g butter
2 shallots, peeled and finely chopped
1 garlic clove, peeled and crushed
small piece of fresh ginger, peeled and finely chopped
½ tsp ground turmeric
½ tsp ground cumin
½ tsp curry powder
½ tsp fennel seeds
a few curry leaves
a pinch of saffron strands
1 tbsp plain flour
1.1 litres fish stock (see page 293)
300ml double cream
sea salt and freshly ground black pepper

SERVES 4

First, make the broth: melt the butter in a heavy-based pan and gently cook the shallots, garlic and ginger without allowing them to colour. Add all the spices and cook for another minute to release the flavours. Add the flour and stir well over a low heat for 30 seconds, then gradually add the fish stock, bring to the boil and simmer for about 20 minutes. Pour in the cream and simmer gently for another 10 minutes. Blend the broth in a liquidiser until smooth and strain through a fine-meshed sieve. Adjust the seasoning.

While the broth is cooking, put the mussels into a large saucepan with the white wine and cover with a tight-fitting lid. Cook over a high heat for 3–4 minutes, removing the lid and giving them an occasional stir, until they have all opened.

Tip them into a colander over a bowl to catch the juices and leave to cool for 10 minutes. Strain through a fine-meshed sieve into the soup.

Remove all but 32 of the mussels from the shells. Add the shelled and shell-on mussels to the soup with the parsley and bring back to the boil to serve.

# COCKLE, PARSLEY AND CIDER BROTH

1kg live cockles
150ml cider
30g butter
1 onion, peeled and finely chopped
4 garlic cloves, peeled and crushed
25g plain flour
1 litre fish stock (see page 293)
2 tbsp finely chopped flat-leaf parsley
3–4 tbsp double cream
sea salt and freshly ground black pepper

SERVES 4

To clean the cockles, leave them under slow running water for about 15 minutes, agitating them with your hands every so often to release any trapped sand. Give the cockles a final rinse and drain.

Put the cleaned cockles in a large saucepan with the cider. Cover with a tight-fitting lid and cook over a high heat for about 2–3 minutes, shaking the pan every so often, until the cockles open.

Drain the cockles in a colander over a bowl, to catch the cooking liquor, then strain the liquor through a fine-meshed sieve into another bowl and set aside.

Melt the butter in a clean saucepan and gently cook the onion and garlic for 3–4 minutes without colouring. Add the flour and stir over a low heat for 30 seconds, then gradually whisk in the strained cooking liquor and fish stock. Bring to the boil, lower the heat and simmer gently for 30 minutes. By now the liquid should have reduced by about one-third and have a good flavour.

Remove about two-thirds of the cockles from their shells. Add the parsley and cream to the soup and simmer for a couple of minutes. Taste and adjust the seasoning as necessary, then divide the shelled and shell-on cockles between warmed soup plates and pour the hot soup over them to serve.

In my opinion, cockles have a better flavour than clams, and are a fraction of the price. That said, you can use clams or mussels if you like. Cockles have a tendency to be a bit gritty, so make sure you wash them really thoroughly.

# CRAB SOUP

500–700g crab shells

1 tbsp vegetable oil

1 small onion, peeled and roughly chopped

1 small leek, trimmed, roughly chopped
 and washed

1 small fennel bulb, trimmed and roughly chopped

4 garlic cloves, peeled and chopped

1 tsp fennel seeds

a few sprigs of thyme

1 bay leaf

a few good knobs of butter

2 tbsp tomato purée

3 tbsp plain flour

100ml white wine

2 litres fish stock (see page 293)

sea salt and freshly ground white pepper

3–4 tbsp double cream

about 100g white crab meat (optional)

SERVES 4–6

Put the shells into a strong carrier bag and smash them up with a steak hammer or rolling pin into small pieces (the bag will stop the shells flying around all over your kitchen worktop).

Heat the oil in a large heavy-based saucepan and fry the crab shells over a high heat for about 5 minutes, stirring every so often until they begin to colour. Add the onion, leek, fennel, garlic, fennel seeds, thyme and bay leaf, and continue cooking for another 5 minutes or so until the vegetables begin to colour.

Stir in the butter, followed by the tomato purée and flour. Cook, stirring, over a low heat for a minute or so. Add the wine, then slowly add the fish stock, stirring to avoid any lumps. Bring to the boil, season with salt and pepper, and simmer gently for about 1 hour.

Strain the soup, shells and all, through a colander set over a bowl, stirring the shells so that any very small pieces of meat go into the liquid. Pick out about a third of the softer white body shells in the sieve (not the hard claws or main shell). Add these to the strained liquor and discard the rest of the sieve contents. Tip the liquor and reserved shells into a strong blender or food processor and whiz until smooth, then strain through a fine sieve into a clean pan.

Taste the soup and adjust the seasoning as necessary, then bring to the boil. Stir in the cream, check the seasoning again and serve. If you like, stir a spoonful of flaked white crab meat into each portion before serving.

Crab isn't cheap, so it makes sense to get full value from it. Once you've enjoyed your crab feast, or made a sandwich or salad, crush the shells and freeze them for later use, or make this soup straight away, and freeze it. You can also convert this soup into a delicious crab sauce to serve with fish dishes, or even chicken. Once you've puréed it, add about 300ml double cream and simmer until it has thickened to the required consistency, then strain through a fine sieve.

# CULLEN SKINK

1 leek, trimmed and washed

a good knob of butter

1.2 litres fish stock (see page 293)

1 floury potato, about 200g, peeled and roughly
    chopped

1 bay leaf

300g undyed smoked haddock fillets

sea salt and freshly ground white pepper

4 tbsp double cream

1 tbsp chopped flat-leaf parsley

SERVES 4–6

&#x201C;Cullen is the village on the coast of the
Moray Firth where this classic Scottish
soup originated, and 'skink' is an
ancient word for a broth or soup. This
is substantial enough to be served as a
main course or brunch dish. Avoid the
yellow-dyed smoked haddock and buy
the lighter coloured natural smoked
fillets or Arbroath smokies, which are
on the bone.&#x201D;

Roughly chop the leek and rinse thoroughly in cold water, then drain
and pat dry. Melt the butter in a pan, stir in the leek, cover and cook
gently for a few minutes until soft.

Add the fish stock, potato, bay leaf and smoked haddock. Bring to
a simmer, season and cook gently for 15 minutes. With a slotted
spoon, carefully remove the smoked haddock from the pan to a plate
and put to one side. Simmer the soup for a further 15 minutes.

Remove the bay leaf and whiz the soup in a blender or using a hand-
held blender until smooth. Pass through a fine-meshed sieve into a
clean pan.

Skin and flake the smoked haddock, checking for any bones. Stir the
cream and parsley into the soup and bring back to a simmer. Add the
flaked haddock and adjust the seasoning, if necessary. Heat through
gently, then serve.

# FISH SOUP

2 tbsp olive oil

500g fish (heads, tails and all), roughly chopped

1 small onion, peeled and roughly chopped

½ leek, trimmed, well rinsed and roughly chopped

½ fennel bulb, roughly chopped

½ red pepper, deseeded and roughly chopped

1 small potato (about 125g), peeled and roughly chopped

3 garlic cloves, peeled and chopped

a good pinch of saffron strands

5 black peppercorns

2 juniper berries

1 bay leaf

a few sprigs of thyme

3 tbsp tomato purée

150g chopped tomatoes

150ml red wine

1.5 litres fish stock (see page 293)

sea salt and freshly ground black or white pepper

1 baguette, sliced at an angle and toasted, to serve (optional)

FOR THE ROUILLE (OPTIONAL)

a good pinch of saffron strands

3 garlic cloves, peeled and crushed

1 thick slice of white bread, crusts removed and torn into pieces

1 egg yolk

3 tbsp extra-virgin olive oil

3 tbsp vegetable oil

a pinch of cayenne pepper

1 tsp lemon juice

SERVES 4–6

Heat the olive oil in a large heavy-based pot and gently fry the fish, vegetables, garlic, spices and herbs for about 10 minutes. Add the tomato purée, chopped tomatoes, red wine and fish stock. Bring to the boil, season with salt and pepper, and simmer for 50 minutes.

Blend about one-third of the soup (bones and all) in a liquidiser. Return it to the pot and simmer gently for another 20 minutes.

Strain the soup by pushing it through a medium-meshed sieve or conical strainer with the back of a ladle, and adjust the seasoning, if necessary, with salt and pepper.

If you like, make a rouille to serve with the soup: ladle about 100ml of the soup into a pan and simmer the saffron and garlic in it for a couple of minutes. Stir in the bread, remove from the heat and let cool a little. Pour into a blender and process well with the egg yolk. Slowly trickle in the mixed oils, stopping the machine occasionally and scraping down the sides. When nicely blended and thick, season to taste with a little salt and cayenne and the lemon juice.

You can float a slice of baguette spread with rouille in the centre of each bowl, or simply ladle out the soup and then let everyone add the toasts and rouille themselves.

66 This is a perfect way to use up fish that's a bit too bony or doesn't have enough flesh to hold its own on a plate. Otherwise, if you are lucky enough to have a good fishmonger, he will probably sell his own 'fish soup mix', which will contain things like rascasse, conger eel, rockfish, gurnard – all the bony fish that are full of flavour. As the soup is blended and strained, the bones don't matter. You can use a wide range of fish, however, as long as you have several varieties and try to include at least one whole fish (I find snapper, gurnard or red mullet is best), but avoid oily fish. 99

The soup freezes well, so you could make a double batch when lucky enough to have the right mix. If you don't feel up to making the rouille, just sprinkle some grated cheese, preferably Gruyère, on the toasts to serve with the soup.

# FISH STEW

3–4 tbsp olive oil

sea salt and freshly ground black pepper

200g monkfish, cut into 1–2cm slices on the bone

250g sea bream, red or black, scaled and cut like the monkfish

100g cleaned squid, cut into 3–4cm chunks

250g mussels, debearded and scrubbed, discarding any that refuse to close

3 garlic cloves, peeled and crushed

2 tbsp chopped flat-leaf parsley

1 tbsp ground almonds

1 recipe quantity of fish soup (see opposite) or ½ quantity of Cornish red mullet soup (see page 107)

SERVES 4

Preheat the oven to 200°C/gas mark 6. Heat the oil in a frying pan, season the fish and lightly fry for a minute or so on each side. Transfer to an ovenproof dish.

Add the squid and mussels, then mix the garlic, parsley and almonds into the fish soup with about 100ml water. Add that to the pot, cover and cook in the oven for 15-20 minutes, stirring occasionally.

❝You can make this from scratch, but I find the use of a good fish soup for the base (instead of merely fish stock) improves it immensely. Serve this as they do in France – with thick slices of bread, grilled and brushed with olive oil and garlic.❞

"Cornish red mullet has a particularly fine flavour and, simply fried, the fillets make a delicious main course, leaving you the bones for a soup made in the tradition of Mediterranean fish soups as here."

# CORNISH RED MULLET SOUP

2 tbsp vegetable oil
1kg whole red mullet, fresh or frozen,
    roughly chopped
1 onion, peeled and roughly chopped
1 leek, trimmed, roughly chopped and washed
1 small fennel bulb, trimmed and roughly chopped
1 red pepper, deseeded and roughly chopped
1 potato (about 150–200g), roughly chopped
6 garlic cloves, peeled and chopped
a good pinch of saffron strands
1 tsp black peppercorns
3 juniper berries
1 bay leaf
a few sprigs of thyme
1 tbsp tomato purée
230g chopped tomatoes
100ml red wine
4 litres fish stock (see page 293)
sea salt and freshly ground black pepper

SERVES 8–10

Heat the oil in a large heavy pan and gently fry the mullet, vegetables, garlic, spices and herbs for about 10 minutes.

Add the tomato purée, chopped tomatoes, red wine and fish stock. Bring to the boil, season with salt and pepper and simmer gently for 50 minutes.

Blend about one-third of the soup in a liquidiser, bones and all, and return it to the pot. Simmer gently for another 20 minutes.

Strain the soup through a sieve or conical strainer and adjust the seasoning if necessary.

Fresh mullet is always preferable, but this recipe is just as successful with the frozen fish that can be bought at a reasonable price. This recipe is enough for about 8–10, because it freezes well, and it seems a rather pointless exercise just making a small batch for four people.

# CREAMED CHICKEN BROTH WITH ST GEORGE'S MUSHROOMS

1 raw free-range chicken carcass, chopped

2 free-range chicken legs (or just the thighs or drumsticks)

1 onion, peeled and roughly chopped

1 leek, trimmed, roughly chopped and washed

10 black peppercorns

1 bay leaf

a few sprigs of thyme

a few sprigs of tarragon, stalks separated, leaves roughly shredded

1.5 litres chicken stock (see page 293)

60g butter, plus an extra couple of knobs

50g plain flour

sea salt and freshly ground white pepper

100–120g St George's mushrooms, cleaned and sliced if large or halved or quartered

60ml double cream

SERVES 4–6

Put the chicken carcass and legs into a pan with the onion, leek, peppercorns, bay leaf, thyme, tarragon stalks and chicken stock. Bring to the boil, lower the heat and simmer gently for 35–40 minutes. Remove the chicken legs and set aside to cool. Strain the stock through a fine sieve.

Melt the butter in a clean saucepan and stir in the flour. Cook, stirring, over a medium heat for a minute, then gradually add the strained stock, a ladleful at a time, stirring well to avoid lumps from forming. Bring to the boil, season with salt and pepper and simmer gently for 30 minutes. Remove from the heat. Blitz the soup using a free-standing or hand-held stick blender to give it a nice silky finish. Return to the cleaned pan.

Melt a couple of knobs of butter in a frying pan and gently cook the mushrooms for 2–3 minutes without colouring them. Remove the meat from the chicken legs and shred into even-sized pieces with your fingers. Add to the soup with the mushrooms, cream and tarragon leaves. Taste and adjust the seasoning. Simmer gently for a minute or so before serving.

"There is something rather comforting about chicken and mushroom soup at any time of the year. If you've bought a whole bird and taken off the raw breasts for a dish, then this is the perfect way to use up the legs and carcass. All too often, not enough thought goes in to getting the best from a whole bird – they just tend to get roasted and that's it."

# COCK-A-LEEKIE

200g piece of stewing beef, such as shin or flank
2 litres chicken stock (see page 293)
200g large leeks, halved lengthways and washed well
sea salt and freshly ground black pepper
4 chicken legs, skinned
16 large good-quality pitted prunes, soaked in warm
　　water overnight
150g small finger leeks, halved if long and rinsed

SERVES 4

66 This ancient dish is usually
attributed to the Scots but is
also sometimes claimed by the
Welsh. Traditionally, this sort of
soupy stew would be made with
some shin of beef and a boiling
fowl or capon for the base stock,
then the meat would be used in
other dishes as well as serving
in the soup itself. If you want to
use a boiling fowl or capon then
fine, although the breast meat as
a meal can be a bit dry. Chicken
legs work well in this recipe as
they have the most flavour and
make a good broth. 99

Put the beef into a saucepan with the chicken stock. Add the large leeks, trimming them to fit the pan if necessary. Bring to the boil and skim off any scum that forms on the surface. Season with salt and pepper, then simmer gently for 1½ hours.

Meanwhile, cut the chicken legs in half at the joint, and chop the knuckles off the drumsticks. Add the chicken legs to the pan and simmer for another 30 minutes.

Drain though a colander into a bowl and reserve the chicken and beef, discarding the leeks. Skim the stock and strain through a fine sieve into a clean pan. Add the prunes and finger leeks. Cut the beef into 4 pieces and return to the pan with the chicken. Simmer for another 15 minutes, until the leeks are tender. Adjust the seasoning, if necessary.

Serve the cock-a-leekie as it is or, for a more refined soup, remove the chicken from the bone, shred the meat and return to the soup.

# GAMEY BROWN WINDSOR SOUP

vegetable oil, for frying
150–200g game meat and/or a couple of game
   carcasses from a roast
1 onion, peeled and roughly chopped
1 small carrot, peeled and roughly chopped
1 small leek, trimmed, roughly chopped and washed
a good knob of butter
2 tbsp plain flour
1 tsp tomato purée
1 garlic clove, peeled and crushed
a few sprigs of thyme
1 small bay leaf
3 litres dark meat stock (see page 292)
sea salt and freshly ground black pepper
2 tbsp cream sherry

SERVES 4–6

Heat the oil in a large heavy-based saucepan and
fry the meat and vegetables over a high heat until
nicely browned, stirring occasionally. Add the
butter, then stir in the flour and cook, stirring, for
a couple of minutes. Add the tomato purée, garlic,
thyme and bay leaf, then gradually add the stock,
stirring well to avoid lumps. Bring to the boil and
season with salt and pepper. Lower the heat and
simmer for 2 hours until the meat is tender.

Pick out a few pieces of meat and set aside. Whiz
the rest to a purée, using a hand-held stick blender.
Pass through a conical strainer or colander (not a
fine sieve) into a pan. The soup should be rich in
flavour and a nice brown colour; if not, simmer it
a little longer to concentrate the flavour. Add the
tender cubes of meat and check the seasoning.
Reheat and pour in the sherry just before serving.

66 This traditional soup, usually made
with beef, is out of favour these days,
though it doesn't deserve its bad
reputation. It's a nourishing, thick
wintry affair, especially when boosted
with sherry. 99

# PHEASANT, CHESTNUT AND CHANTERELLE SOUP

1 oven-ready pheasant
1 onion, peeled and roughly chopped
1 small leek, roughly chopped and washed
a few sprigs of thyme
2 litres chicken stock (see page 293)
100ml white wine
sea salt and freshly ground black pepper
40g butter
30g plain flour
16–18 fresh chestnuts in the shell
2–3 tbsp double cream
150g chanterelles, cleaned
2 tbsp chopped flat-leaf parsley

SERVES 6–8

Cut the legs from the pheasant using a sharp knife,
then carefully remove the breasts. Place the legs,
breasts and carcass in a pot with the onion, leek,
thyme, stock and wine. Season, bring to the boil,
then lower the heat and simmer for 10 minutes.

Take out the breasts and set aside. Continue to
simmer the soup for a further 20 minutes. Melt the
butter in a small saucepan and stir in the flour over
a low heat. Whisk the flour and butter mixture into
the simmering soup a little at a time to thicken it,
then continue to simmer for another 20 minutes.

Meanwhile, preheat the oven to 200ºC/gas mark
6. Score the chestnuts and place on a baking tray.
Cover with foil and bake for 12–15 minutes. Place on
a plate and leave until cool enough to handle. Peel
away the skins and cut each into 2–3 pieces.

Strain the soup through a fine sieve into a clean
saucepan and add the cream. Remove the pheasant
meat from the legs and cut the breast into bite-
sized pieces. Add to the soup with the chestnuts,
chanterelles and chopped parsley. Simmer gently
for 5 minutes. Check the seasoning and serve.

Pheasant has a tendency to dry out
during cooking, but this soup gets
around that problem. You can prepare
the soup base, roast the chestnuts
and get everything together the day
before, ready to reheat and assemble
everything just before serving.

"Rabbits are cheap and plentiful and so are oyster mushrooms, in fact both ingredients are free if you happen to be a hunter-gatherer. If not, then a rabbit will cost you a few quid and you can save the saddle fillets for a salad or other dish."

# WILD RABBIT AND OYSTER MUSHROOM SOUP

1 wild rabbit
1 small leek, trimmed, roughly chopped and washed
1 small onion, peeled and roughly chopped
2 garlic cloves, peeled
a couple of sprigs of thyme
1 bay leaf
10 black peppercorns
2 litres chicken stock (see page 293)
sea salt and freshly ground black pepper
60g butter
50g plain flour
120g oyster mushrooms, cleaned
2–3 tbsp double cream
1 tbsp chopped flat-leaf parsley

SERVES 4–6

Remove the fillets from the saddle of the rabbit (save them for another dish). Cut off the legs and halve at the joint, chopping through the bones.

Place the rabbit, leek, onion, garlic, herbs and peppercorns in a large saucepan. Pour in the chicken stock, season with salt and pepper and bring to the boil, then skim off any scum from the surface. Simmer for an hour, skimming every so often. If the leg meat is tender, remove and put to one side, otherwise leave in the pan.

Melt the butter in a small saucepan, stir in the flour and stir over a low heat for 20 seconds. Whisk this flour and butter paste into the simmering stock in small pieces. Continue to simmer gently, stirring occasionally for 20 minutes.

Strain the soup through a fine-meshed sieve into a clean pan. Cut the oyster mushrooms into even-sized chunks, add them to the soup and simmer for 10 minutes.

Meanwhile, strip the rabbit meat from the bones in bite-sized pieces and add to the soup with the cream and chopped parsley. Re-season if necessary before serving in warmed soup plates or bowls.

# GROUSE AND AUTUMN VEGETABLE BROTH

the carcasses from 2 or more grouse (raw or roasted)
1 tbsp vegetable oil
2 medium carrots, peeled
1 small onion, peeled and roughly chopped
2 garlic cloves, peeled and crushed
a couple of sprigs of thyme
4 juniper berries
a generous knob of butter
1 tbsp plain flour
1 tsp tomato purée
2 litres chicken stock (see page 293)
sea salt and freshly ground black pepper
1 small leek, trimmed
2 celery stalks, peeled to remove strings if necessary
a couple of green cabbage leaves

SERVES 4–6

Chop each of the grouse carcasses into 4 or 5 pieces. Heat the oil in a large, heavy-based saucepan over a medium heat. Roughly chop one of the carrots. Add the grouse carcasses with the onion, chopped carrot, garlic, thyme and juniper berries and fry for 3–4 minutes, stirring every so often, until lightly coloured.

Add the butter and once it has melted, stir in the flour. Cook, stirring for a few minutes, then add the tomato purée and chicken stock. Bring to the boil, season with salt and pepper and simmer gently for an hour.

In the meantime, cut the leek, celery, cabbage and second carrot roughly into 5mm pieces, washing the leek thoroughly after chopping.

Strain the broth through a fine-meshed sieve into a clean saucepan, reserving the pieces of carcass. Add the leek, celery and carrot and simmer for about 15 minutes or until they are tender. Add the cabbage and simmer for a further 5–6 minutes.

Meanwhile, remove as many bits of meat from the grouse carcasses as possible and add to the soup. Simmer for a final minute or two, re-season if necessary and serve in warmed soup plates.

# LONDON PARTICULAR

30g butter
1 onion, peeled and roughly chopped
a few sprigs of thyme
250g green split peas, or whole ones, soaked overnight
   in cold water
1.5 litres dark meat stock (see page 292)
a few pieces of leftover ham meat (see page 80)
sea salt and freshly ground black pepper

SERVES 4–6

Melt the butter in a heavy-based pan and gently
cook the onion for a few minutes until soft, without
allowing it to colour. Add the thyme, drained peas
and ham stock, checking it's not too salty; if it is,
replace some of it with water. Bring to the boil,
skim and add some pepper, then simmer for 1 hour.
The peas should be soft and beginning to fall apart;
if not, simmer for a little longer (you may have to
top up with more stock or water as necessary).
Cooking times can vary, depending on the peas.

Once they're cooked, blend the soup in a liquidiser
or with a stick blender as coarsely or as smoothly
as you wish; and add a little water if it is too thick,
or simmer for a little longer if too thin. Taste
and season again, if necessary. Shred some of
the cooked ham trimmings, add to the soup and
simmer a minute or so longer before serving.

" This thick and warming soup was given its name
by Charles Dickens and referenced in *Bleak House*
as 'London Particular', referring to the brown 'fog'
from the factories that often used to form a blanket
around London, a 'pea souper'. This could have
been the type of soup that Soyer fed the poor in his
Spitalfields soup kitchen, although he may have
left out the ham. "

# MUTTON BROTH

200g neck of mutton fillet
1 tsp chopped thyme leaves
1 onion, peeled and finely chopped
2 litres dark meat or chicken stock (see pages 292–293)
sea salt and freshly ground black pepper
1 medium carrot , peeled
1 medium parsnip, peeled
100–120g swede, peeled
1 small turnip, peeled
30g pearl barley, soaked in cold water for 1 hour
1 tbsp chopped flat-leaf parsley

SERVES 4

Cut the mutton roughly into 1cm cubes and put
into a large heavy-based pan with the thyme leaves
and onion. Pour on the stock to cover and season
with salt and pepper. Bring to the boil, then lower
the heat, cover and simmer very gently for about an
hour until the mutton is tender.

Cut all of the root vegetables into rough 5mm
cubes. Drain and rinse the pearl barley and add to
the broth with the vegetables. Simmer for another
30 minutes.

Add the chopped parsley and simmer for a further
10 minutes. Taste and adjust the seasoning, then
ladle into warm soup plates and serve.

Long, slow cooking not only suits
mutton, it also gives you a well-
flavoured stock to make the broth.
You can vary the vegetables and pulses
here, according to what you have in
your fridge and larder – add yellow or
green split peas, maple peas, celeriac
or any other root vegetable. Even a few
cabbage leaves at the end would add a
touch of colour and texture.

# FISH AND SEAFOOD

## OYSTER STEW

50g butter
1 medium onion, peeled and finely chopped
100g piece of rindless streaky bacon, cut into rough 1cm pieces
1 tbsp plain flour
50ml dry white wine
1 litre fish stock (see page 293)
2 celery stalks, cut into rough 1cm pieces
sea salt and freshly ground white pepper
1 leek, cut into rough 1cm pieces and washed
300g waxy potatoes, peeled and cut into rough 1cm cubes
100ml double cream
2 tbsp chopped flat-leaf parsley
12 large oysters, shucked and juices reserved

SERVES 4

Melt the butter in a large saucepan and gently cook the onion and bacon for 3–4 minutes without colouring until soft, stirring every so often. Stir in the flour and cook over a low heat for 30 seconds, then stir in the wine.

Gradually stir in the fish stock to avoid lumps forming, then bring to the boil. Add the celery and season with salt and pepper. Lower the heat and simmer for 20 minutes.

Add the leek and potatoes and simmer for a further 8–10 minutes or until the potatoes are tender. Ladle one-fifth of the soup into a blender and purée until smooth, then stir back into the soup.

Add the cream, chopped parsley and oysters together with any juices, re-season if necessary and simmer for another 2–3 minutes before serving.

“I'm not that keen on cooking oysters, but when you are confronted with large specimens that are slightly overwhelming, they are well suited to a dish like this.”

## MUSSEL BROSE

1 onion, peeled and finely chopped
a good knob of butter
250ml fish stock (see page 293)
150ml milk
sea salt and freshly ground black pepper
1kg mussels, well scrubbed and any beards removed, discarding any mussels that stay open when tapped
3 tbsp fine oatmeal, lightly toasted
2 tbsp chopped flat-leaf parsley

SERVES 4

In a large pot, gently cook the onion in the butter for 2–3 minutes until soft. Add the fish stock and milk and lightly season. Then add the mussels, cover with a lid and cook over a high heat, stirring or shaking the mussels, until they begin to open.

Drain the mussels in a colander over a bowl to catch the liquid. Pour the liquid back into the pan and stir in the oatmeal. Cook over a medium heat for a couple of minutes until the liquid thickens slightly and then add the parsley.

Put the mussels into warmed serving bowls and pour over the hot liquid.

“The term ‘brose’ can mean a number of very different dishes, from hearty soups to a sweet atholl brose, all of which are thickened with, or contain, oatmeal. I suppose a dish as simple as a mussel brose is rather similar to the classic *moules marinière*.”

You can add many other flavourings instead of the parsley, such as dill or chopped spring onions and a splash of wine, to suit your taste. When wild garlic leaves are in season in springtime, tear a handful of them into the soup to give it a special flavour.

# PRAWN BURGERS

550g (shelled weight) raw seawater prawns, shelled
   and deveined
150g firm white fish, boned and skinned
3–4 spring onions, finely chopped
1 tsp Worcestershire sauce
3 tbsp mayonnaise (see page 295)
a pinch of cayenne pepper
sea salt and freshly ground black pepper
fresh white breadcrumbs, to coat
vegetable oil, for deep-frying
4 burger buns, to serve

FOR THE SPICED TARTARE SAUCE
3 tbsp mayonnaise (see page 295)
20g capers, chopped
20g gherkins, chopped
4–5 drops of Tabasco sauce

SERVES 4

Put the prawns and white fish in a food processor
and blend to a coarse purée. Put this and all of the
remaining ingredients except the breadcrumbs, oil
and buns into a bowl, mix well and season with salt
and pepper. Make a tiny burger shape with a little
of the mix, dredge with some breadcrumbs and fry
in a little oil to test the seasoning of the mix. Add
more seasoning if necessary.

Divide the rest of the mix into 4 flat patties a little
larger than the buns and chill for 30–40 minutes.

Meanwhile, make the spiced tartare sauce by
mixing all of the ingredients together.

Preheat an 8cm-depth of oil to 170°C. Cover the
burgers in the breadcrumbs, pressing them into the
outside of the burgers to stick, and deep-fry for 4–5
minutes until golden.

Meanwhile, lightly toast the burger buns, spread
them with a spoonful of the spiced tartare sauce
and serve the burgers in them.

" I first saw this recipe in the American food magazine
*Saveur* and I have tweaked it and used it several times
since. It's important to use seawater prawns, as
opposed to freshwater, as the taste is far superior. "

# SCALLOPS WITH BLACK PUDDING AND JERUSALEM ARTICHOKE PUREE

300g Jerusalem artichokes, peeled and halved
sea salt and freshly ground black pepper
80g butter
150g good-quality black pudding
1 tbsp cold-pressed rapeseed or vegetable oil
12 medium scallops, cleaned and trimmed
a handful of flat-leaf parsley

SERVES 4

Cook the artichokes in a pan of lightly salted water
for 8–10 minutes or until tender. Drain well and
whiz in a blender or food processor to a purée.

Return to a clean pan and place over a low heat.
Warm the purée for a few minutes, stirring so
it doesn't stick, until it has reduced slightly to a
spoonable consistency; it shouldn't be wet and
sloppy. Season with salt and pepper to taste and stir
in about 30g of the butter; keep warm.

Cut the black pudding into small nuggets and set
aside ready to cook. Rub a non-stick heavy-based
frying pan with the tiniest amount of oil (too much
will make the scallops boil rather than fry). Heat
until almost smoking, then add the scallops and
cook over a medium-high heat for 1 minute on each
side. Immediately remove from the pan to avoid
overcooking and place on a plate; keep warm.

Lower the heat and add the black pudding, parsley
and the rest of the butter to the empty scallop pan.
Cook gently for 2–3 minutes to warm through,
stirring every so often.

To serve, spoon the Jerusalem artichoke purée onto
warm serving plates, place the scallops on top, then
spoon the butter and black pudding over.

If you're not confident about opening scallops yourself, ask your fishmonger to do it for you. Don't be tempted to buy those ready-prepared ones, unless you know that they have been freshly shucked; more often than not, they will have been soaked in water, frozen or washed to death and have practically no flavour left.

# GRILLED SQUID WITH CHICKPEAS AND PANCETTA

4 medium-sized squid, each about 200g
vegetable oil, for brushing
8 thin slices of pancetta or smoked streaky bacon
100g rocket, preferably wild

FOR THE CHICKPEA SALSA

125ml extra-virgin olive oil, plus more to dress
2 large shallots, peeled and finely chopped
1 small mild red chilli, deseeded and finely chopped
1 red pepper, deseeded and finely chopped
finely grated zest of ½ lime
160g (drained weight) good-quality tinned
    chickpeas, rinsed and drained
2 tsp sweet chilli sauce
1 tbsp finely chopped mint leaves
1 tbsp finely chopped flat-leaf parsley
sea salt and freshly ground black pepper

SERVES 4

To make the chickpea salsa, heat the olive oil in a saucepan and gently cook the shallots, chilli, pepper and lime zest for a few minutes until soft, but not allowing them to colour. Add the chickpeas, stir well and remove from the heat. Stir in the chilli sauce and fresh herbs, season with salt and pepper and set aside. If the salsa seems a bit dry, dress it with a little more oil.

Preheat a barbecue, griddle or cast-iron frying pan. Make a cut down the centre of each squid and open it out flat. With a sharp knife, score the body in criss-cross fashion with lines about 2cm apart. Season the squid bodies and tentacles with salt and pepper and brush with some vegetable oil.

Barbecue, griddle or fry the pancetta or bacon until crisp. Then use the same method to cook the squid for 2 minutes on each side.

Serve the squid with a pile of the rocket, a spoonful of the warm salsa and the pancetta or bacon on top.

**❝** Squid make perfect barbecue material, and are good for a summery lunch or dinner party. The squid needs to be cleaned, leaving the body tubes whole, with the tentacles cut just above the eyes so they stay attached to each other. **❞**

Instead of making the chickpea salsa, you could serve the grilled squid accompanied by some salsa verde, chilli salsa or spiced tartare sauce.

# ROASTED CRAYFISH FLAMED WITH CIDER BRANDY

2kg live freshwater crayfish
sea salt and freshly ground black pepper
100g butter
150ml Somerset cider brandy

SERVES 4

Preheat the oven to 220°C/gas mark 7 and heat a roasting tray, large enough to take all of the crayfish, in the oven. Add the crayfish, season with salt and pepper and roast for 10 minutes.

Take the tray out of the oven and place it on the hob over a medium heat. Add the butter and stir to coat the crayfish, then stand back a little and carefully add the cider brandy. It will ignite (well hopefully, otherwise you could use a long match). If you have a tabletop gas stove you can do this at the table.

As soon as the flames have died down, serve the crayfish, providing everyone with finger bowls and extra napkins.

## LOBSTER WITH SWEETBREADS AND TARRAGON

2 lobsters, each about 500g, cooked
500ml dark meat stock (see page 292)
3 shallots, peeled and roughly chopped
1 bay leaf
1 garlic clove, peeled
400g veal sweetbreads
lobster sauce (see page 154)
sea salt and freshly ground black pepper
plain flour, for dusting
a good knob of butter
½ tbsp chopped tarragon

SERVES 4

Remove the claws from the lobsters, then crack the shells, reserving them, and put the meat to one side. Remove the tail by twisting it away from the head, then, with a heavy, sharp knife, cut the tail in half lengthways.

In a large pan, bring the stock to the boil with the shallots, bay leaf and garlic. Add the sweetbreads, bring back to the boil, lower the heat and simmer for 10 minutes. Remove the sweetbreads with a slotted spoon and leave to cool on a plate. Reserve the cooking liquid for the sauce.

Using the shells and head from the lobster, make the lobster sauce as described on page 154, replacing some of the fish stock with the reserved sweetbread cooking liquor.

Trim any fat from the sweetbreads and cut them into 2cm-thick slices. Season with salt and pepper, lightly dust with flour and fry in some butter over a medium heat for 2 minutes on each side until golden, then drain on some kitchen paper.

Bring the sauce to the boil, add the lobster, sweetbreads and tarragon and simmer for 3–4 minutes. Serve with boiled or wild rice, green vegetables or boiled potatoes.

## ROASTED MIXED SHELLFISH

1 live lobster, about 700g
2–3 tbsp cold-pressed rapeseed oil
sea salt and freshly ground black pepper
4 medium or 12 queen scallops, cleaned, in the
    half-shell
500g cockles, clams or mussels (or a mix), cleaned
6 razor clams
120g butter
6 garlic cloves, peeled and crushed
a couple of handfuls of seashore vegetables, such as
    sea beet, samphire or sea purslane
2 tbsp chopped flat-leaf parsley

SERVES 2–4

Place the lobster in the freezer an hour or so before cooking to make them sleepy (deemed to be the most humane way of preparing live lobsters for cooking). Preheat the oven to 220°C/gas mark 7.

Heat a large roasting tray in the oven for about 10 minutes, adding the rapeseed oil for the last couple of minutes. Split the lobster in half through the head and down the back, using a heavy, sharp knife, and crack open the claws. Season the lobster and lay flesh-side down in the roasting tray. Roast in the oven for about 10 minutes.

Season the scallops and cockles (or clams or mussels). Add to the roasting tray and return to the oven for a further 5 minutes.

Finally add the razor clams, butter and garlic and roast in the oven for a further few minutes until they are just opened.

Meanwhile, plunge the seashore vegetables into a pan of boiling lightly salted water and blanch for 1 minute, then drain thoroughly.

Remove the roasting tray from the oven and toss in the seashore vegetable(s) and parsley. Transfer to a warmed serving dish and serve at once.

A dish of mixed shellfish is a great and indulgent dish. You can use any kind of shellfish but try to limit the selection to about 4 varieties, or you will have too many different cooking times to contend with.

## FILLET OF PIKE WITH SAUCE NANTUA

4 skinned pike fillets, each about 160–180g
sea salt and freshly ground white pepper
16–20 live crayfish
olive oil, for frying or roasting
a small knob of butter (optional)
sauce nantua (see page 296)
½ tbsp chopped tarragon

SERVES 4

Season the pike fillets with salt and pepper and steam for about 10 minutes. If you haven't got a steamer, preheat the oven to 190°C/gas mark 5, lay the fillets in a roasting tray with about 2cm of hot water, cover with foil and cook in the oven for 15 minutes. This steaming causes the flesh to shrink a little, leaving the bones protruding so they can be pulled out with a pair of pliers or tweezers. There are lots, so be patient - it's worth it.

Cook the crayfish in simmering salted water for 5 minutes, then plunge them into cold water. Remove the meat from the shells and the claws if they are big enough. Break the shells up a little with a heavy knife and use to make the sauce nantua.

Cook the pike fillets again. Either fry them in olive oil for 2–3 minutes on each side, then add a small knob of butter and continue to fry them until lightly browned; or preheat the oven to 200°C/gas mark 6, heat a couple of tablespoons of olive oil in a roasting pan and roast them for 10-12 minutes or until lightly coloured.

Meanwhile, if necessary, simmer the sauce until it is coating consistency, stir in the tarragon and drop in the peeled crayfish for a minute to re-heat them. To serve, spoon the sauce over the fish fillets.

This is a classic French dish in which both main ingredients – pike and crayfish – come from fresh water. Pike has an unusual bone structure, having not only a set of bones down its middle but two other sets, one on either side, and is a real pain to bone when raw. I've lightly steamed the pike so that the flesh can be easily removed from the bones – a top tip given to me by Mauro Bregoli, who for many years owned the brilliant Manor House in Romsey, Hampshire.

## HADDOCK SPECIALS

2 large baking potatoes
sea salt and freshly ground white pepper
150g haddock fillets, skinned and any residual bones removed
vegetable or corn oil, for deep-frying
plain flour, for dusting
crushed peas (see page 140) and/or tartare sauce (see page 295), to serve

FOR THE YEAST BATTER
4g easy-blend yeast
250ml milk, plus a little extra
1 small egg yolk, beaten
75g plain flour
75g cornflour
a pinch of cayenne pepper
¼ tsp baking powder

SERVES 4

Cook the baking potatoes in their skins in boiling salted water for 25 minutes and leave to cool.

Remove the skins from the potatoes and slice them into sixteen 1cm discs. Cut the haddock into pieces big enough to fit on top of 8 of the potato slices, season and sandwich them with another slice of potato, pressing firmly.

To make the batter, dissolve the yeast in a little milk and leave in a warm place for 10 minutes. In a larger bowl, mix the milk, egg, flour, cornflour, cayenne and baking powder and add the yeast mixture. Cover and leave at room temperature for 1½–2 hours, until it begins to ferment.

Meanwhile, heat an 8cm-depth of oil in a deep-fat fryer or heavy-bottomed pan (half full) to 160°C. Season the potato sandwiches and lightly flour them, then dip them in batter, allowing the excess to drip off, and fry them for about 4–5 minutes until golden. Remove them with a slotted spoon and transfer them to some kitchen paper to drain.

Serve with crushed peas and/or tartare sauce.

**"**These totally delicious treats take me right back to my childhood. The succulent flakes of white fish make them just sublime.**"**

# FISH FINGERS

500g firm white fish fillet, such as coley, pollack,
    cod or haddock, skinned
sea salt and freshly ground black pepper
plain flour, for dusting
1 large egg, beaten
100g fresh white breadcrumbs
vegetable or corn oil, for frying

TO SERVE
crushed peas (see page 140), to serve
tartare sauce (see page 295), to serve

SERVES 4

Cut the fish fillet into 8cm × 2cm fingers and season with salt and pepper. Put the flour in one shallow dish, the beaten egg in another and the breadcrumbs in a third dish. One at a time, dip each piece of fish first into the flour, then in the beaten egg and finally into the breadcrumbs to coat all over.

Heat a thin film of oil in a heavy-based frying pan and cook the fish fingers for about 2 minutes on each side until nicely browned.

Drain on kitchen paper and serve straight away, with crushed peas and tartare sauce.

❝These might be a bit more labour-intensive than reaching into the freezer for a packet of fish fingers, but they are far superior and well worth the extra effort. Kids love them, of course, but grown-ups do too, especially if you serve them with tartare sauce and crushed peas, or a salad and chips. I often serve them with posh mushy peas – made by simply blending frozen peas to a coarse purée.❞

# STARGAZY PIE

1 onion, peeled and finely chopped

3 rashers of rindless streaky bacon, chopped into rough 5mm dice

a good knob of butter

½ tbsp flour, plus more for dusting

3 tbsp dry white wine

250ml fish stock (see page 293)

300ml double cream

2 tbsp chopped flat-leaf parsley

2 hard-boiled eggs, shelled and chopped

sea salt and freshly ground black pepper

6 pilchards, herrings or small mackerel, filleted, any residual bones removed and heads reserved

200g ready-made all-butter puff pastry, rolled out to a thickness of about 3mm

1 egg, beaten

SERVES 4

In a small saucepan, gently cook the onion and bacon in the butter until soft. Add the flour and stir well, then slowly add the wine and fish stock, stirring well to prevent any lumps from forming. Bring to the boil and simmer for 10 minutes.

Add the cream, bring back to the boil and simmer until thickened and reduced by half. Remove from the heat; add the parsley and chopped egg, season and leave to cool.

Preheat the oven to 200°C/gas mark 6. Cut the fillets of fish in half and lay them in a shallow pie or flan dish, then lightly season. Pour the sauce over them, then lay the pastry over the dish and trim it to size. Make 6 small slits in the pastry and push the reserved fish heads through them, then brush the top with the beaten egg.

Bake for 40-45 minutes. Serve with greens in autumn and winter, or a selection of spring vegetables.

" You don't often see this on restaurant menus, and you are possibly not likely to... Imagine putting a pie in front of a guest with fish heads staring back up at him. The logic of the highly eccentric arrangement of the fish in this dish lies in preserving as much of the essential oils in the pilchards as possible; to this end, the heads are kept and the fish arranged so that their oils run back into the pie filling as it cooks. "

In Mousehole (pronounced 'mowzol'), near Penzance, a famous local tradition is that of Tom Bawcock's Eve, celebrated the night before Christmas Eve. The story goes that, one winter in the distant past, the sea was too stormy for any of the fishing boats to go out, and the people of the village faced starvation, let alone a bleak Christmas. Brave Tom ventured out and caught sufficient fish to feed the village, some of which was made into the first Stargazy Pie.

# FISH TAGINE

1kg monkfish or huss on the bone, skinned and
    cut into 3cm slices
sea salt and freshly ground white pepper
plain flour, for dusting
vegetable oil, for frying
1 tbsp olive oil
2 large onions, peeled and roughly chopped
4 garlic cloves, peeled and crushed
1 red chilli, deseeded and finely chopped
1 tbsp finely chopped root ginger
1 tsp ground cumin
½ tsp paprika
½ tsp crushed fennel seeds
a good pinch of saffron strands
4 tomatoes, skinned, deseeded and roughly diced
1 tsp tomato purée
1 litre fish stock (see page 293)
1 large fennel bulb, cored and quartered
1 preserved lemon, halved
1 tbsp chopped coriander leaves

SERVES 4

Season the fish pieces with salt and pepper and
lightly flour them. Heat some vegetable oil in a non-
stick or heavy frying pan and sauté them for 2–3
minutes on each side until lightly coloured. Remove
from the pan and set aside.

Meanwhile, heat the olive oil in a heavy-based
frying pan. Stir in the onions, garlic, chilli, ginger
and spices. Cover and cook gently for 7–8 minutes
until soft. Add the tomatoes, tomato purée and
stock, season with salt and pepper, and simmer for
30 minutes. Then add the fennel and simmer gently
for 30–35 minutes more, until the fennel is tender.

Add the fish, preserved lemon and coriander to the
sauce and simmer for a further 10 minutes. Adjust
the seasoning if necessary.

Moroccan food is often misinterpreted,
as 'spicy' doesn't always mean 'hot',
and subtle spices like fennel and
saffron give a delicate fragrance to
tagines, especially tagines of fish.

# FISH COLLAR CURRY

1.5kg fish collars
sea salt and freshly ground black pepper
60g ghee or vegetable oil
3 medium onions, peeled and roughly chopped
5 large garlic cloves, peeled and crushed
1 tbsp chopped or grated fresh root ginger
3 small, medium-strength chillies,
    deseeded and finely chopped
1 tsp cumin seeds
½ tsp fenugreek seeds
1 tsp fennel seeds
1 tsp mustard seeds
1 tsp cumin powder
½ tsp paprika
1 tsp ground turmeric
a pinch of saffron strands
5–6 curry leaves
2 tsp tomato purée
juice of 1 lemon
1.3 litres fish stock (see page 293)
3 tbsp chopped coriander leaves

SERVES 4–6

Season the fish with salt and pepper. Heat half of
the ghee in a large, heavy-based pan and fry the
pieces of fish over a high heat until lightly coloured.
Remove with a slotted spoon and put to one side.

Add the rest of the ghee to the pan and fry the
onions, garlic, ginger and chillies for a few minutes
until they begin to soften. Add all of the spices,
cover with a lid and cook for a couple of minutes to
allow the spices to release their flavours, lifting the
lid and stirring every so often.

Add the tomato purée, lemon juice and fish stock.
Bring to the boil, lower the heat, season and
simmer for 45 minutes. Take a cupful of sauce from
the pan and whiz in a blender until smooth, then
pour back into the sauce.

Add the pieces of fish and simmer for 15 minutes,
then add the chopped coriander and simmer for a
further 5 minutes. Taste and adjust the seasoning
if necessary. Serve with basmati rice.

I'm sure you're wondering what the collar is. Well, it's a meaty, gelatinous part of the fish around the back of the head where the gills are. It isn't really bony as such, but more of a plate structure surrounded by flesh. As the flesh is quite meaty, it stands up to a bit of rapid curry cooking and doesn't disintegrate the way a fillet would. Ask your fishmonger to save you the collars from large fish like cod and halibut.

"I do enjoy a good fish head curry. When I worked at The Dorchester, the Bangladeshi kitchen porters would take all of our fish heads to make a delicious fish curry for their staff meals. There's a lot more meat left on the head of some of those larger species of fish than you might imagine."

## SALT-BAKED SEA BASS

1kg coarse sea salt or Sel de Guérande
1 whole sea bass, about 2.5kg, scaled and boned
a handful of fennel tops or a few sprigs of dill
freshly ground white pepper
extra-virgin olive oil or melted butter, to serve

SERVES 4–6

An hour before you want to start cooking the fish, add a cup of water to the salt and mix well. Spread a thin layer of the salt on a baking tray or ovenproof serving dish. Fill the fish's stomach with some of the herbs and season with pepper. Lay the bass on top of the salt and pack the remaining salt in a 1cm layer all over the fish, firmly patting it in place. Leave for an hour to drain.

Preheat the oven to 250°C/gas mark 9. Drain off any excess water from around the fish. Bake for 45 minutes, then remove from the oven.

If you are feeling confident, you can serve the fish in front of your guests. Otherwise, hide in the kitchen to cut it – perhaps after showing them it as it comes out of the oven. Have warmed plates ready and a large plate for the bits. Crack the salt a couple of times with the back of a heavy knife, then carefully scrape it away from the fish, removing as much as possible. Remove the head and tail, and cut the fish through the body into even portions, giving the underside a final check for salt before transferring them to warm plates.

Serve drizzled with some olive oil or melted butter and with the rest of the dill or the fennel.

" This traditional way of cooking firm-textured fish like bass, bream and snapper produces delicious results. It seals the entire fish in completely, so it cooks without any juices or flavour escaping. "

## RAY WITH WINKLES AND CEPS

4 ray wings, each about 200–250g, skinned
150–200g fresh winkles
sea salt and freshly ground white pepper
plain flour, for dusting
vegetable or corn oil, for frying
150g unsalted butter
150–160g ceps, cleaned and sliced
1 tbsp chopped flat-leaf parsley

SERVES 4

Trim the ray wings and set aside. Wash the winkles, place them in a saucepan and cover with salted water. Bring to the boil and simmer for 5–6 minutes, then drain and leave to cool. Using a cocktail stick, prise out the meat from the winkle shells and remove the little hard 'foot' attached to the meat, which is too tough to eat.

Season the ray wings and lightly flour them. Heat a thin film of oil in a heavy-based or non-stick frying pan and cook the wings for 3–5 minutes on each side until golden. Just before they are cooked, add a third of the butter to the pan and continue to fry for about a minute to give them a nice brown colour. When done, remove them from the pan and keep warm. If your pan isn't large enough to cook them all at once, brown them two at a time. The first two can be finished off in a hot oven, preheated to 200°C/gas mark 6, for about 10 minutes – the time it will take to cook the other two in the pan.

Wipe the pan out with some kitchen paper (or use a clean pan). Add half the remaining butter and cook the ceps over a medium heat for a few minutes, turning them until lightly coloured. Add the rest of the butter, the winkles and chopped parsley and heat for 1–2 minutes.

Place each ray wing on a warm plate and spoon the contents of the pan evenly over the top. Serve with some spinach and a good buttery mash.

Rays are among my favourite eating fish. They are commonly referred to as skate in fishmongers, which is currently an unsustainable species of the family. You may need to order a sustainable ray (spotted, cuckoo or starry) and fresh winkles from your fishmonger. If you can't find or forage ceps, replace them with another wild mushroom.

## LING WITH CREAMED PEAS, LEEKS AND BACON

4 thick fillets of ling, each about 200g, with skin on
sea salt and freshly ground black pepper
150g freshly podded peas (about 300g before
    podding), or frozen peas
100g butter
6 rashers of streaky bacon, derinded and
    finely chopped
1 medium or 2 small leeks, trimmed,
    cut into rough 1cm squares and washed
200ml double cream
2 tbsp vegetable oil

SERVES 4

Season the ling fillets with salt and pepper. Add the peas to a pan of boiling salted water and simmer for 4-5 minutes or until tender, then drain.

In the meantime, melt half of the butter in a heavy-based saucepan and add the bacon and leek. Cover and cook gently over a medium-low heat for 3-4 minutes, stirring every so often, until the leek is soft.

Roughly chop the peas and add them to the leek and bacon with the cream. Season with salt and pepper and simmer for a few minutes until the cream has reduced and is just coating the peas.

Meanwhile, heat the oil in a non-stick frying pan over a medium-high heat and add the ling fillets, skin side down. Cook for 3-4 minutes until nicely coloured, then turn the fillets and add the rest of the butter to the pan. Fry for a couple of minutes until the fish is just cooked through.

To serve, spoon the creamed peas, leeks and bacon onto warmed plates and place the fish on top.

Ling is not commonplace on fish counters, but it is a truly great choice. Firm-fleshed and full of flavour, it really takes to any kind of cooking – from grilling to deep-frying. I think you will be pleasantly surprised by the taste and texture of this third division fish.

## STEAMED FILLETS OF JOHN DORY WITH BABY LEEKS

4 fillets of John Dory, each about 160–180g,
    with skin on
sea salt and freshly ground white pepper
250g baby leeks
2–3 tbsp extra-virgin olive oil
½ tbsp chopped chives
½ tbsp chopped flat-leaf parsley
juice of ⅓ lemon

SERVES 4

Each fillet of John Dory conveniently divides itself into 3 smaller fillets lengthways along the fillet. With a sharp knife, separate the fillets, cutting through the skin.

Season the fillets with sea salt and freshly ground white pepper, lay them on a plate that fits in the steamer to catch the juices and steam them with a lid on for 5-6 minutes until just cooked. If you don't have a steamer, simply use a large pan with a tight-fitting lid and set the plate of fish on a trivet, or something else that will hold it clear of the water.

Meanwhile, plunge the baby leeks into a large pan of boiling salted water and simmer for 5 minutes. Drain in a colander and season with salt and freshly ground white pepper.

Mix any cooking juices from the fish with the olive oil, herbs and lemon juice. Arrange the John Dory fillets on warmed plates, intertwining them with the leeks. Spoon the oil and herb liquid over the top.

"The beautiful looks of the John Dory are reflected in its eating. It even has a distinguishable beauty spot on the flesh, which is apparently the reason for its being named *Saint-Pierre* in France and *pez de San Pedro* in Spain – the most common explanation for this is that the distinctive marks were left by St Peter's fingers when he threw the fish back into the water after hearing it making noises of distress."

# GRILLED SARDINES WITH ESSAOUIRA SALAD

2 large green peppers

3 ripe tomatoes, skinned, deseeded and cut into rough 1cm dice

4 spring onions, trimmed and chopped

6 tbsp extra-virgin olive oil, plus more for brushing

2 tbsp white wine vinegar

1 small garlic clove, peeled and crushed

peel from 1 large or 2 small preserved lemons, cut into small dice

sea salt and freshly ground black pepper

8 sardines, cleaned

2 tsp ras el hanout

2 tbsp chopped coriander leaves

crusty bread, to serve

SERVES 4

Cut the peppers into 4 lengthways, remove and discard the stalk and seeds, and put the strips on a grill tray. Grill them, skin side up, for about 10 minutes or until the skin is blistering and blackening. Place in a bowl, cover with cling film and leave for about 10 minutes. Remove the skin with your fingers or by scraping with a knife.

Cut the peppers into rough 1cm cubes and put them in a bowl with the tomatoes, spring onions, olive oil, vinegar, garlic and preserved lemon. Season with salt and pepper, and mix well. Taste the salad and add a little of the juice from the preserved lemon to taste.

Preheat the grill to its hottest temperature. Brush the sardines with oil and rub ½ teaspoon of ras el hanout into the skin of each. Season the fish with some sea salt and freshly ground black pepper. Grill the fish for about 3 minutes on each side until the skin begins to crisp.

Sprinkle with coriander and serve with the salad and crusty bread.

“This is typical of the salad served on the quayside in Essaouira, on Morocco's Atlantic coast. It works really well with oily fish, like sardines or mackerel, as the acidity of the preserved lemon cuts the oiliness of the fish in a refreshingly tart way.”

Ras el hanout is a rich and complex Moroccan spice mix that is slightly different wherever you buy it, but tends to feature ginger, cumin, anise, cinnamon, nutmeg, cloves, cardamom, mace and turmeric, together with crushed dried flowers like lavender and rose. Good delis and ethnic foods stores will sell versions of it.

# PORK-STUFFED SEA BREAM WITH GINGER SAUCE

4 sea bream, each about 350–400g, or 1 or 2 large
 ones, cleaned and scaled
vegetable oil, for brushing

FOR THE STUFFING
200g minced pork belly
4 spring onions, trimmed and finely chopped
3 garlic cloves, peeled and crushed
1 lemongrass stalk, finely chopped
2 tbsp chopped coriander
1 tbsp chopped fresh root ginger or galangal
1 red chilli, deseeded and finely chopped
sea salt and freshly ground black pepper

FOR THE GINGER SAUCE
2 tbsp finely chopped fresh root ginger
2 garlic cloves, peeled and crushed
1 red chilli, deseeded and finely chopped
1 tbsp light (untoasted) sesame oil or groundnut oil
2 tbsp fish sauce
1 tbsp light soy sauce
1 tsp cornflour

SERVES 4

Preheat the oven to 220ºC/gas mark 7. Make the stuffing by mixing all of the ingredients together.

Fill the cavities of the fish with the stuffing, season both sides of the fish with salt and pepper and brush with vegetable oil.

Cook in the oven for about 30 minutes, or until the point of a skewer or small knife comes out hot when inserted into the centre of the fish.

While the fish is cooking, make the sauce: gently cook the ginger, garlic and chilli in the oil for 2–3 minutes until soft. Add the fish sauce, soy sauce and 150ml water, and bring to the boil. Simmer gently for 5 minutes. Dilute the cornflour in a little water and stir into the sauce. Simmer for 2 minutes and then remove from the heat. The sauce should be a thick coating consistency; if not, simmer a little longer until it thickens.

To serve, pour the sauce over the fish or to one side of it.

❝In Oriental cooking, the mixing of pork and fish is quite common. Here it gives quite an unusual twist to a neutral-tasting fish. Fatty pork like belly takes on Asian flavours well and makes a perfect dinner party sharing dish for serving together with some other Oriental-style dishes.❞

If you don't fancy meat in the stuffing, you could replace the pork with chopped raw prawns or even a mix of chopped vegetables like shiitake mushrooms and spring onions. Instead of the ginger sauce, you could use a black bean sauce.

# BAKED HERRINGS WITH MUSTARD AND OATS

40g butter
2 shallots, peeled and finely chopped
finely grated zest of ½ lemon
40g fresh white breadcrumbs
40g oat flakes
1 tbsp chopped flat-leaf parsley
sea salt and freshly ground black pepper
4 herring fillets, each about 150g, or 8 smaller ones
1 tbsp grain mustard

SERVES 4

Preheat the oven to 180°C/gas mark 6. Melt the butter in a pan and gently cook the shallots for a couple of minutes until soft. Transfer to a food processor with the lemon zest, breadcrumbs, oats and parsley. Season with salt and pepper and process for about 20 seconds.

Check over the herring fillets and remove any small bones, then place on a baking tray, skin-side up. Spread the mustard evenly over the fillets and spoon the oat mixture on top, pressing it down with the back of the spoon. Bake for 15–20 minutes until cooked. Serve with hot buttered new potatoes.

# HERRINGS WITH MUSTARD SAUCE

vegetable oil, for frying
8 small herring fillets, each about 60g, or 4 larger ones
a good knob of butter

FOR THE SAUCE
2 shallots, peeled and finely chopped
3 tbsp white wine
1 tbsp cider vinegar
100ml fish stock (see page 293)
2 tsp English mustard, or to taste
150ml double cream
1 tbsp chopped flat-leaf parsley
sea salt and freshly ground white pepper

SERVES 4

First make the sauce: simmer the shallots in the white wine and vinegar until the liquid has evaporated, then add the fish stock and mustard, and simmer until you have a couple of tablespoons of liquid left. Add the cream and simmer until the sauce has thickened and reduced by about half. Add the parsley, season and simmer gently for another minute.

Meanwhile, heat a little vegetable oil in, preferably, a non-stick pan, season the herring fillets and fry them, skin side down first, for 2–3 minutes on each side, adding the butter towards the end of cooking.

Spoon the sauce on to warmed plates and arrange the herring fillets on top.

“Herrings were plentiful and cheap around our
coastlines in times past, especially along the East
Anglian coast. In the twelfth century, Great Yarmouth
became the centre of the herring trade and the fish
were cured in barrels of salt, pickled, and smoked as
bloaters. Nowadays, herring fishing is restricted in the
North Sea because of overfishing, so these fish are a
less common sight on fishmongers' slabs.”

## PAN-FRIED MACKEREL WITH GREEN TOMATO AND LOVAGE RELISH

4 large mackerel fillets, or 8 smaller ones, trimmed
1–2 tbsp plain flour, for dusting
1 tbsp vegetable or corn oil

FOR THE RELISH
4 large green tomatoes
4 tbsp cold-pressed rapeseed oil
1 onion, peeled and finely chopped
1 tbsp cider vinegar
1 tbsp caster sugar
sea salt and freshly ground black pepper
a few lovage leaves, shredded

SERVES 4

First make the relish. Halve the tomatoes, squeeze out the seeds, then roughly chop the flesh. Heat the rapeseed oil in a pan and gently cook the onion for 4–5 minutes, stirring regularly, until softened but not coloured. Add the vinegar and sugar and simmer, stirring, for a minute.

Add the chopped tomatoes to the pan, season with salt and pepper, and continue cooking for 2–3 minutes, stirring regularly. Remove from the heat, stir in the lovage and leave to cool.

Check the mackerel fillets for any pin bones, then score the skin side 3 or 4 times. Season with salt and pepper and lightly flour the skin side only. Heat the oil in a non-stick frying pan. Cook the fillets, skin side down first, for 3–4 minutes on each side depending on the size of the fillets.

Serve at once, with some of the relish.

66 Green tomatoes have an acidity that works perfectly with the oiliness of mackerel. If you're a tomato grower, you may well have some green tomatoes on your vines that you could tempt off for this relish, or perhaps you grow one of the heritage varieties designed to be eaten green. If not, your greengrocer might be able to oblige. 99

## FILLET OF SEA TROUT WITH CRUSHED PEAS AND GIROLLES

4 sea trout fillets, each about 150g, any
    pin bones removed
1 tbsp cold-pressed rapeseed oil
a few knobs of butter
150–160g girolles, cleaned
1 tbsp chopped flat-leaf parsley

FOR THE CRUSHED PEAS
150g podded fresh or frozen peas
sea salt and freshly ground black pepper
a pinch of sugar
100g butter
1 shallot, peeled and roughly chopped
120–150ml fish stock (see page 293)

SERVES 4

First prepare the crushed peas. Cook the peas in boiling salted water with the sugar until almost tender, then drain. Melt half the butter in a pan and gently cook the shallot for a few minutes without colouring. Add the peas and stock, season and simmer over a medium heat for 3–4 minutes until most of the stock has evaporated. Tip into a food processor and whiz briefly to a coarse purée, then return to the pan and add the rest of the butter.

Season the fish with salt and pepper. Heat the oil and a knob of butter in a heavy-based frying pan and cook the fish, skin side first, for 2–3 minutes on each side, depending on thickness.

Meanwhile, heat 2 knobs of butter in another frying pan over a medium heat. Add the girolles and cook for 4–5 minutes until tender, seasoning and adding the parsley halfway through.

To serve, warm the crushed peas if necessary, then spoon onto warm plates. Place the fish fillets on top and spoon the girolles and parsley over and around.

“Peas and fish are a perfect match, and scattering a few girolles or other seasonal wild mushrooms on top makes it even better. I like to crush the peas with a little fish stock so they act rather like a sauce. If you can't find girolles, then any other wild mushroom will do.”

# FILLET OF SEA TROUT WITH MOUSSERONS

4 sea trout fillets, each about 160–180g, any
   residual bones removed
sea salt and freshly ground black pepper
vegetable oil, for frying
plain flour, for dusting (optional)
2 tbsp olive oil
3 large shallots, peeled and finely chopped
40g streaky bacon or pancetta, finely diced
125g mousserons
50g butter
2 tbsp chopped flat-leaf parsley

SERVES 4

Season the fish with salt and pepper. Heat the
vegetable oil in a large frying pan, preferably non-
stick (otherwise lightly flour the skin of the fish) and
gently cook the fish portions, skin side first, over a
medium heat for 3–4 minutes on each side, keeping
them slightly pink in the middle and crisping the
skin a little.

Meanwhile, heat the olive oil in another pan
and gently cook the shallots and bacon for 3–4
minutes without allowing them to colour. Add the
mousserons and butter, lightly season with salt and
pepper and cook over a low heat for another 3–4
minutes or until the mushrooms have softened.

Add the parsley, heat through for a minute, then
spoon the mixture on to warmed plates and serve
the sea trout portions on top.

Mousserons are a tiny version of the
St George's mushroom and have a
delicate but earthy flavour that will
match the trout; if you can't find them,
then chanterelles would be a good
substitute here.

# FILLET OF SEA TROUT WITH CUCUMBER SAUCE

1 tbsp vegetable or corn oil
sea salt and freshly ground black pepper
4 sea trout fillets, each about 150g, any residual
   bones removed

FOR THE SAUCE
2 small shallots, peeled and finely chopped
4 tbsp fish stock (see page 293)
4 tbsp double cream
1 small cucumber, halved lengthways, the seeds
   scooped out and the flesh cut into small (5mm) dice
a good knob of butter
1 tbsp finely chopped chives

SERVES 4

Heat the oil in a heavy-based or non-stick frying
pan. Season the fillets and cook for 3–4 minutes on
each side, skin side down first. The cooking time
will depend on the thickness of the fish; fillets from
a smaller fish will take about half the time.

Meanwhile, make the sauce: in a saucepan, gently
simmer the shallots in the fish stock until the liquid
has almost all evaporated. Then add the cream
and cucumber, season and simmer for a couple of
minutes until the sauce has thickened. Stir in the
butter and chives. Season to taste.

Spoon on to warmed plates and place the pieces of
fish on top.

66 Sea trout has a texture that is slightly
more delicate than that of salmon, but
it can be used in much the same way.
As with salmon, the flavour of wild and
farmed fish can vary somewhat. The sea
trout you find in the shops tends only
to be wild, although I have seen a few
farmed versions at the markets. The
flavour is slightly earthy and delicate,
and it doesn't take much cooking. 99

# PAN-FRIED DABS WITH PRAWNS

200–250g prawns, cooked and peeled, shells reserved
8 dabs, fins trimmed and dark skin removed
sea salt and freshly ground black pepper
plain flour, for dusting
2–3 tbsp vegetable or cold-pressed rapeseed oil
150g unsalted butter
2 tbsp chopped flat-leaf parsley
juice of 1 lemon

SERVES 4

Place the prawn shells in a saucepan and add enough water to just cover them. Bring to the boil, lower the heat and simmer for about 10 minutes until the liquid has reduced right down, then strain through a fine sieve into a bowl; set aside.

Season the dabs and lightly flour them. Heat the oil in two large frying pans (or use one pan and cook them in two batches). Add the dabs to the pan(s) and fry over a medium heat for about 2–3 minutes on each side until they begin to colour. Add half the butter and continue to cook for another 2–3 minutes. Remove from the pan and keep warm.

Add the prawn stock to the empty fish pan with the peeled prawns, then add the rest of the butter and the parsley. Season lightly and keep on a low heat for a minute, then add the lemon juice.

Arrange the dabs on warm plates and spoon the prawns and butter over them. Serve at once.

**66** Dabs are one of those fish that you rarely find at fishmongers. I imagine that most of them get dumped or used for pot bait... and there lies the problem with fishing. As consumers, we don't get to see the fish that go back, yet small flat fish like dabs, sand soles, megrim, etc., make good eating and their flesh is easily removed from the bone. Adding prawns turns a humble fish like dab into a luxury. **99**

# SAND SOLES WITH BUTTERED ALEXANDERS AND WILD GARLIC

250–300g young alexanders stalks with the leaves removed
sea salt and freshly ground black pepper
8 sand soles, each about 160–200g, black skin removed and fins trimmed
3 tbsp vegetable or cold-pressed rapeseed oil
120g butter
a handful of three-cornered garlic or wild garlic leaves

SERVES 4

Cut the alexander stalks into 8–9cm pieces and boil in salted water for 5–6 minutes, or until tender, then drain.

While the alexanders are cooking, season the soles. You will probably need to cook them in 2 or 3 batches, and then keep them just warm or reheat them when they are all cooked. Heat some vegetable oil in a (preferably) non-stick frying pan and cook the soles, skin side down first, for 3–4 minutes on each side, adding a knob of butter to the pan towards the end of cooking.

Melt the remaining butter in another pan, tear the garlic leaves into smaller pieces and cook gently in the butter for a minute or so until wilted. Add the alexanders, reheat for a minute or so and season. Spoon over the soles and serve.

You can use any type of sole for this dish, or any fish come to that, but I find the sand sole – which is of the Dover sole or common sole family, but generally about half the size of them – perfect for it. By the way, the latter is called Dover sole purely because large amounts of the fish used to get landed in Dover, but they were not necessarily from that area. Ask your fishmonger to skin the dark side and trim the fins.

# MONKFISH WITH COCKLES AND MUSSELS

4 monkfish fillets, each about 200g
sea salt and freshly ground black pepper
1–2 tbsp vegetable or cold-pressed rapeseed oil
150g cockles or clams, rinsed
125g mussels, scrubbed and any beards removed
50ml white wine
1 tbsp chopped flat-leaf parsley
75g unsalted butter, diced

SERVES 4

If the monkfish pieces are very thick, preheat the oven to 230°C/gas mark 8 and heat a roasting pan. Whatever their thickness, lightly season the monkfish with salt and pepper. Heat a little oil in a large non-stick frying pan and fry the fillets for about 3 minutes on each side, until they are nicely coloured. Transfer very thick fillets to the hot roasting pan and finish cooking in the hot oven for another 5-10 minutes, or until cooked.

Meanwhile, give the cockles and mussels a final rinse, discarding any mussels that stay open when given a sharp tap. Put them into a large pan with the white wine and cover with a tight-fitting lid. Cook over a high heat for 3-4 minutes until they open, shaking the pan frequently and giving them an occasional stir. Drain in a colander, reserving the liquid, then pour the liquid back into the pan.

Add the parsley and butter to the pan and keep stirring until the butter has melted. Return the molluscs to the pan, discarding any that haven't opened, adjust the seasoning and stir well.

To serve, carefully remove the monkfish from the pan with a fish slice and place on warm plates. Add the mussels and cockles, then spoon the parsley butter over the top to serve.

**"**Cockles in vinegar in little polystyrene pots bring back memories of being by the seaside. Fresh cockles, though, are sweet and delicious. Otherwise, simply use clams or more mussels instead. Monkfish is becoming increasingly expensive owing to the demand, but any firm white fish will work well here.**"**

If you can find live cockles, they will need washing well to remove any sand. The best way to do this is to keep them under cold running water for an hour, giving them an occasional stir with your hand, allowing them to release as much sand as possible.

# MONKFISH CHEEK AND FENNEL PIE

1 litre fish stock (see page 293)
2 fennel bulbs, trimmed
450–500g monkfish cheeks, trimmed and halved
   if large
70g butter
60g plain flour
sea salt and freshly ground black pepper
2 tbsp chopped flat-leaf parsley
2 tbsp double cream

FOR THE TOPPING
1–1.2kg potatoes (for mashing), peeled and quartered
50–60g butter
a little milk
2–3 tbsp fresh white breadcrumbs

SERVES 4

❝ Monkfish, cod and ray cheeks are a bit easier to get hold of these days, with the increased demand from restaurants. A few years ago you may have got a slightly odd look from your fishmonger if you had asked for them. ❞

Bring the fish stock to the boil in a saucepan. Meanwhile, quarter the fennel bulbs, cut into 2cm chunks and separate the layers. Add to the stock and simmer for 6–7 minutes until tender, then remove the fennel with a slotted spoon and leave to cool on a plate.

Add the monkfish cheeks to the stock and simmer for 2–3 minutes, then drain in a colander over a bowl to reserve the stock.

Melt the butter in a heavy-based saucepan, stir in the flour and cook, stirring, over a low heat for about 30 seconds. Gradually whisk in the hot stock, keeping the sauce smooth. Season, then simmer gently for about 30–40 minutes. The sauce should be really quite thick by now; if not, let it simmer for a little longer.

Meanwhile, for the topping, cook the potatoes in a pan of salted water until tender. Drain well and return to the pan over a low heat to dry out for 30 seconds or so. Take off the heat and mash thoroughly, incorporating all the butter and a little milk. Season with salt and pepper to taste.

Preheat the oven to 200°C/gas mark 6. Stir the monkfish cheeks, fennel, chopped parsley and cream into the sauce. Re-season if necessary, then transfer to a large pie dish or individual ones.

Spoon or pipe the mashed potato onto the pies and scatter over the breadcrumbs. Bake for 30 minutes (or 20 minutes for individual pies) until the topping is golden brown and the filling is hot.

# BARBECUED HUSS WITH CRISPY SHALLOTS

1–1.2kg huss, skinned

FOR THE BARBECUE MARINADE
2 tbsp cold-pressed rapeseed oil
3 medium shallots, peeled and roughly chopped
4 garlic cloves, peeled and crushed
30–40g fresh root ginger, scraped and finely grated
1 small red chilli, with seeds, roughly chopped
1 tsp fennel seeds
1 tsp cumin seeds
2 tsp tomato purée
1 tbsp clear honey
1½ tsp dark brown molasses sugar or brown sugar
1½ tsp Worcestershire sauce
1 tbsp HP sauce
1 tbsp tomato ketchup
juice of 2 limes
sea salt and freshly ground black pepper

FOR THE CRISPY SHALLOTS
vegetable oil, for deep-frying
2 tbsp self-raising flour
100–120ml milk
4 large shallots, peeled and thinly sliced

SERVES 4

To prepare the marinade, heat the rapeseed oil in a heavy-based saucepan and gently cook the shallots, garlic, ginger, chilli and fennel and cumin seeds for 2–3 minutes. Add the rest of the ingredients, stir in 100ml water and season lightly. Bring to the boil, reduce the heat and simmer for 3–4 minutes. Let cool slightly, then process the marinade in a blender until smooth. Transfer to a bowl and leave to cool completely.

Split the huss lengthways down the middle through the bone, then cut into 10–12cm lengths. Place the fish pieces in a shallow dish, pour the marinade over them and turn to coat. Cover the dish with cling film and leave to marinate in the fridge for 2–3 hours.

Preheat the oven to 200°C/gas mark 6. Remove the huss from the dish and lay on a roasting tray, reserving the marinade. Spoon a couple of tablespoonfuls of the marinade over the fish and place in the oven. Bake for 15–20 minutes until just cooked through, basting with extra marinade a few times during cooking.

Meanwhile, for the crispy shallots, heat an 8cm depth of oil in a deep-fat fryer or other suitable deep, heavy pan to 160–180°C. Have 2 bowls ready, one with the flour and the other with the milk. Season the flour with salt and pepper.

Coat the shallots in the seasoned flour, shaking off any excess, then pass them through the milk and again through the flour, shaking off the excess. Deep-fry the shallots in 2 or 3 batches, for 2–3 minutes until golden, turning them every so often to ensure they colour evenly. Remove with a slotted spoon and drain on kitchen paper.

Place a huss fillet on each warmed plate and top with the crispy shallots to serve.

**"** What's posh about dogfish you may ask; quite rightly so, but a few years ago you might have said the same of monkfish. Confusingly, both dogfish and smooth hound or tope are generally sold as huss, known to fishermen as dogfish and sold as rock salmon in fish and chip shops. Otherwise they are completely forgotten about. The fairly firm flesh will withstand a bit of braising and marinating. **"**

Tracey Emin *Chicken Sapp* 08

# POULTRY AND GAME

## POT-ROAST GOOSNARGH CHICKEN WITH ROOT VEGETABLES

1 free-range Goosnargh chicken, about 1.2–1.5kg
a few knobs of butter
1 medium onion, peeled and quartered
2 medium carrots, washed and cut into rough chunks
1 small swede, washed and cut into rough chunks
2 small parsnips, washed and cut into rough chunks
a few sprigs of thyme
½ tbsp flour
a good splash of white wine
500ml chicken stock (see page 293)

FOR THE STUFFING
a good knob of butter
1 medium onion, peeled and finely chopped
60g chicken livers, cleaned
2 tbsp chopped flat-leaf parsley
2 tsp chopped thyme leaves
60g fresh white breadcrumbs
sea salt and freshly ground black pepper

SERVES 4

Preheat the oven to 230°C/gas mark 8. To make the stuffing, melt the butter in the pan and gently cook the onion for 2 minutes, then add the chicken livers and cook for a couple of minutes on each side. Remove the pan from the heat. Remove the livers from the pan and chop into small pieces, then mix with the onions, parsley, thyme and breadcrumbs, and season. Spoon the stuffing into the cavity of the chicken; rub the outside with butter and season.

To cook the chicken, put the vegetables in a roasting tray with the thyme and place the bird on top. Cook for 15 minutes, then turn the oven down to 200°C/gas mark 6 and cook for another 45–50 minutes, basting every so often.

Remove the chicken and the vegetables from the roasting tray and put the tray on a low heat on the oven top. Stir in the flour, then gradually add the wine and chicken stock, stirring well to avoid lumps from forming. Bring to the boil and simmer for about 10 minutes, until the gravy has thickened, then strain through a fine-meshed sieve.

Joint the chicken, or carve the breast and halve the legs. Serve with the vegetables and some roast potatoes, preferably cooked in goose or duck fat.

## ROAST CHICKEN WITH NEW SEASON GARLIC SAUCE

1 free-range chicken, about 1.5kg, with livers
sea salt and freshly ground black pepper
a few sprigs each of thyme and rosemary
a few generous knobs of butter

FOR THE STUFFING
60g butter
1 medium onion, peeled and finely chopped
100g chicken livers, chopped
2 tsp chopped thyme leaves
80–100g fresh white breadcrumbs
2 tbsp chopped flat-leaf parsley, plus extra to serve

TO SERVE
baked new season garlic sauce (see page 298)
straw potatoes (see page 240)

SERVES 3–4

Preheat the oven to 200°C/gas mark 6. Season the chicken inside and out with salt and pepper. Put the herbs into the cavity. Rub butter all over the breast and legs.

For the stuffing, melt the butter in a pan. Add the onion, livers and thyme, season and cook over a medium heat for 2–3 minutes. Off the heat, mix in the breadcrumbs, parsley and seasoning. Either use to stuff your bird or cook separately in an ovenproof dish wrapped in foil for the last 30–40 minutes.

Put the chicken into a large roasting tin and roast in the oven, basting regularly and adding the livers to the roasting tin for the last 6 minutes or so. Test the chicken after 1¼ hours by inserting a skewer into the thickest part of the thigh. The juices should run clear; if not roast for a little longer.

Lift the chicken onto a warmed platter and rest in a warm place for 15 minutes. Sprinkle with some more chopped parsley and serve with the roasted livers, stuffing, garlic sauce and straw potatoes.

The best way to cook a quality chicken is simply, and on the bone. Try varying the vegetables according to the season, and in the summer, serve the bird with a simple garden salad or a selection of beans.

"This dish was inspired by several visits to L'Ami
Louis in Paris, where the food is simple and honest,
respecting the quality ingredients used. We buy
Swainson House Farm chickens, which have an
amazing gamey flavour."

# CHICKEN AND LOBSTER PIE

2 cooked lobsters, each about 500g
500g boneless skinless free-range chicken thighs
1 tbsp chopped flat-leaf parsley
½ tbsp chopped tarragon leaves
350–400g ready-made all-butter puff pastry
plain flour, for dusting
1 egg, beaten

FOR THE LOBSTER SAUCE
1 tbsp vegetable oil
reserved lobster shells
4 shallots, peeled and roughly chopped
1 garlic clove, peeled and chopped
60g butter
60g plain flour
a good pinch of saffron strands
a few sprigs of tarragon
½ tbsp tomato purée
60ml white wine
500ml fish stock (see page 293)
500ml chicken stock (see page 293)
400ml double cream
sea salt and freshly ground black pepper
1–2 tsp cornflour (if needed)

SERVES 4

 

**"** This is a bit of a take on my rabbit and crayfish pie that was successful on BBC2's *Great British Menu* a few years back. Shellfish like lobster and prawns really do go well with the delicate flavour of chicken. For slow-cooked chicken dishes I use thighs rather than breast meat as they stay much more moist and succulent. **"**

Remove the meat from the lobster tails and claws and cut roughly into 1cm pieces. Reserve one lobster head (if making a large pie). Break the rest of the shells up a bit, using a heavy knife. Cut the chicken thighs in half, or into thirds if large. Cover and refrigerate the lobster and chicken meat.

To make the sauce, heat the oil in a heavy-based saucepan and fry the lobster shells, shallots and garlic over a medium heat for about 5 minutes until they begin to colour lightly. Add the butter and, once melted, stir in the flour. Add the saffron, tarragon and tomato purée, then gradually stir in the white wine and the fish and chicken stocks.

Bring to the boil, lower the heat and simmer for about 30 minutes until the sauce has reduced by about half, then add the cream. Season lightly with salt and pepper, bring back to the boil and simmer very gently for about 20 minutes until the sauce has reduced by half again. (A simmer plate or heat-diffuser mat is useful here.)

Strain the sauce through a colander into a clean pan, moving the shells with a spoon to ensure all the sauce goes through.

Tip about one-tenth of the shells into a blender and add about a cupful of the strained sauce. Blend until smooth, then strain through a fine-meshed sieve into the pan.

Bring the sauce back to the boil, add the chicken and simmer for 5 minutes. The sauce should be a thick coating consistency by now; if not, simmer a little longer (or dilute a little cornflour in water and stir into the sauce). Leave to cool.

Stir the lobster and chopped parsley and tarragon into the cooled sauce. Adjust the seasoning if necessary. Fill a large pie dish or 4 individual ones with the mixture.

Roll out the pastry on a lightly floured surface to a 5mm thickness. Trim to about 2cm larger all round than the pie dish (or cut discs large enough to cover individual dishes). Brush the edges of the pastry with a little of the beaten egg. Lay the pastry over the filling, pressing the egg-washed sides onto the rim of the dish(es).

If making a large pie, cut a cross in the centre and insert the reserved lobster head, so it sits proud. Cut a small slit in the top of individual pies to allow steam to escape. Rest in a cool place for 30 minutes.

Preheat the oven to 200°C/gas mark 6. Brush the pastry lid with beaten egg and bake the pie for 40–50 minutes or until golden brown (allow 10–15 minutes less for individual pies). Let the pie stand for a few minutes before serving.

# KENTISH PUDDING

FOR THE SUET PASTRY
275g self-raising flour, plus extra for dusting
140g suet
½ tsp salt

FOR THE FILLING
750g boneless skinless free-range chicken thighs, halved
sea salt and freshly ground black pepper
3 tbsp flour, plus extra for dusting
50g butter, plus extra for greasing
1 large onion, peeled and finely chopped
100g rindless smoked streaky bacon, cut into 2cm pieces
250g button mushrooms, halved
4 tbsp white wine
350ml chicken stock (see page 293)
2 tbsp chopped flat-leaf parsley

SERVES 4–6

For the pastry, mix the flour, suet and salt in a bowl, then mix to a soft dough with about 100ml cold water. Roll out until large enough to line a 2 litre pudding basin. Cut a quarter out of the circle for the lid and to ease the lining of the bowl. Grease the basin well with butter, drop the larger piece of pastry into it and join the edges where the quarter was removed. Trim the edges around the bowl.

Season the chicken and dust with flour. Melt 15g of the butter in a large frying pan and cook the chicken for 2–3 minutes on each side without allowing it to colour. Remove from the pan and put to one side. Melt the rest of the butter in the pan, add the onion and bacon, and cook gently until soft, then add the mushrooms and cook for another 2–3 minutes, stirring well, until they soften. Add the flour, stir well, then slowly stir in the wine and stock and bring to the boil, stirring. Remove from the heat and leave to cool.

Add the chicken and parsley to the sauce, mix well, adjust the seasoning and tip into the basin. Roll out the remaining pastry for the lid. Lay over the filling and press the edges to seal, trimming as necessary.

Cover with a piece of pleated foil and secure under the rim with string, making a handle so it can be lifted. Lower into a pan containing enough boiling water to come halfway up the side. Cover with a lid and simmer very gently for 4 hours, topping up with boiling water. Lift out, remove the foil and serve.

# CHICKEN, HAM AND LEEK PIE

600ml chicken stock (see page 293)
500g skinless free-range chicken thigh fillets
3 large leeks, trimmed, roughly chopped and rinsed
40g butter
40g plain flour, plus extra for dusting
sea salt and freshly ground white pepper
100ml double cream
200g good-quality ham, trimmed of fat (see page 80)
2 tbsp chopped flat-leaf parsley
350–400g ready-made all-butter puff pastry
1 egg, beaten

SERVES 4

Pour the stock into a shallow pan and bring to the boil. Lower the heat, add the chicken and poach gently for 10 minutes. Remove with a slotted spoon and put to one side. Add the leeks to the chicken stock and simmer gently for 10 minutes. Drain in a colander over a bowl to retain the stock.

Melt the butter in a heavy-based pan, add the flour and stir well. Gradually add the reserved stock, stirring constantly to avoid lumps. Bring to the boil, season with a little salt and pepper, and simmer gently for 5 minutes, stirring every so often. Add the cream, bring back to the boil and simmer for 5 minutes. The sauce should be quite thick by now; if not, simmer a little longer, then leave to cool.

Cut the ham roughly into 2cm cubes. Add to the cooled sauce with the leeks, chicken and parsley. Adjust the seasoning, then spoon into 4 individual pie dishes, or one large one to 1cm from the top.

Roll the puff pastry out on a floured surface to a 5mm thickness. Cut out top(s) for the pie(s) about 2cm larger all the way round than the dish(es). Brush the edges of the pastry with a little of the beaten egg. Lay the pastry over the top of the pie dish(es), pressing the egg-washed sides against the rim. Cut a small slit in the top of each pie to allow steam to escape and brush with beaten egg. Leave to rest in a cool place for 30 minutes.

Preheat the oven to 200°C/gas mark 6. Cook for 40–50 minutes until the pastry is golden (allow 10–15 minutes less for individual pies). Serve hot.

# ROAST MICHAELMAS GOOSE WITH APPLE SAUCE

20g butter
1 goose, about 4–5kg, preferably with giblets
sea salt and freshly ground black pepper

FOR THE STUFFING
60g butter
2 onions, peeled and finely chopped
1 tbsp chopped fresh sage
100g fresh white breadcrumbs
1 tbsp chopped flat-leaf parsley

FOR THE APPLE SAUCE
1kg cooking apples, peeled, cored and roughly
   chopped
2 tbsp caster sugar
50g butter

SERVES 5–6

Preheat the oven to 160°C/gas mark 3. For the stuffing, melt the butter in a pan and gently cook the onions and sage for 2–3 minutes without letting them colour. Remove from the heat and stir in the breadcrumbs.

Meanwhile, add the butter to a hot frying pan, season the goose livers and fry for 2–3 minutes on each side. Remove from the heat and let cool a little. Roughly chop the livers into smallish pieces and mix into the stuffing with the parsley, then season to taste.

Remove the legs from the goose by pulling them away from the bone and cutting at the joint. Remove any fat and skin from underneath the goose on the backbone and put the legs in a snug-fitting oven tray. Season the legs and cook for 2½ hours, basting every so often. Drain off the fat and save for when you next want to roast potatoes. Keep the legs warm until required, or put them back in the oven for the last 15 minutes of the rest of the goose's cooking time.

Increase the oven setting to 220°C/gas mark 7. Spoon the stuffing into the cavity of the bird and season the breasts, spoon over a little of the fat that the legs released whilst cooking and put them in a roasting tray with the breasts facing down and cook for 50 minutes, draining off surplus fat from time to time.

Turn the oven down 200°C/gas mark 6, then turn the bird onto its back and cook for 30 minutes. This will produce a bird that is pink; allow longer for medium-cooked. Leave to rest for 20–30 minutes.

Remove the breasts from the bone with a sharp knife and slice thinly across, skin side down. The leg meat can just be carved off the bone, or cut into chunks.

While the bird is resting, put the apples, sugar and butter in a pan. Cover and cook gently, stirring every so often, for 15–20 minutes, until the apples start to disintegrate. You can keep the sauce chunky, or blend it. Taste and add more sugar if needed, although it shouldn't be too sweet. Serve the meat with a bowl of the sauce.

I would suggest getting a couple of birds for more than 8–10 people. I've tried lots of different ways with goose over the years and found that, unlike duck, the legs need extra slow and longer cooking, so the breasts can get just cooked to medium and you end up with slow-cooked crisp legs. I recommend getting your bird to room temperature before cooking to ensure a crispy, succulent bird.

"Wild duck and elderberries are a perfect seasonal
marriage, and the tartness of the little berries makes
a delicious sauce. There are several types of wild duck
that could be used for this dish – teal, widgeon and
mallard. Most people wouldn't give elderberries the
time of day, but they are well worth the effort and,
in the autumn, I freeze them to use in a dressing for
salads, or to drop into a sauce for other game."

# ROAST MALLARD
# WITH ELDERBERRIES

2 plump wild ducks
1 small onion, peeled and roughly chopped
1 carrot, washed and roughly chopped
2 celery stalks, washed and roughly chopped
a few sprigs of thyme
a few knobs of butter
sea salt and freshly ground black pepper
1½ tsp plain flour
100ml red wine
½ tsp redcurrant jelly
500ml chicken stock (see page 293)
80–100g elderberries, stems removed

SERVES 4

Preheat the oven to 230°C/gas mark 8. Put the ducks in a roasting tray with the vegetables and thyme, rub with a little butter and season. Roast the birds for 30 minutes, then remove from the tray and leave on a plate to rest and catch the juices.

Add the flour to the tray and stir over a medium heat for a minute or so. Pour in the wine and stir. Add the jelly and gradually add the stock. Simmer for 10 minutes until it has reduced by half and thickened. Strain through a fine-meshed sieve into a saucepan, add the elderberries and any juices from the duck, bring to the boil (boil for a little longer if it needs thickening) and remove.

To serve the duck, either chop each in half with a heavy kitchen knife and serve them on the bone, or remove the legs and then cut the breasts away from the bone and slice them into about 6 pieces. Serve with the elderberry sauce and accompany with some buttered autumn cabbage or mashed parsnip.

# DUCK HASH WITH
# A FRIED DUCK'S EGG

4 medium duck legs
½ head of garlic
sea salt and freshly ground black pepper
1 bouquet garni
250–300g duck fat, melted
2 medium onions, peeled and roughly diced
350g new potatoes, peeled and cooked
1 tbsp Worcestershire sauce, or to taste
2 tbsp fresh white breadcrumbs
2–3 tbsp cold-pressed rapeseed oil
4 duck's eggs

SERVES 4

Preheat the oven to 160°C/gas mark 3. Place the legs in a heavy ovenproof pan in which they fit snugly and scatter over the garlic and 1½ tsp salt. Add the bouquet garni. Pour the fat over the legs to cover. Slowly bring to a simmer, then put the lid on.

Transfer to the oven and cook for about 1½ hours until the meat is just coming away from the bone. Leave to cool for an hour, then take out the duck legs. Strain the fat into a jar (store in the fridge).

Heat a spoonful of duck fat in a heavy-based pan and add the onions. Cover and cook for 5–6 minutes until soft and lightly coloured. Tip into a bowl.

Cut the potatoes roughly into 1cm chunks. Heat 1 tbsp duck fat in a heavy-based frying pan until very hot. Fry the potatoes in batches over a high heat until lightly coloured. Drain and add to the onions. Strip the meat from the legs and cut into rough 1cm chunks with the skin. Add to the potatoes and mix well. Season and add Worcestershire sauce to taste.

Divide into 4 and shape into patties, about 8cm in diameter. Refrigerate for a few hours or overnight.

Coat the patties all over with breadcrumbs. Heat 1–2 tbsp of rapeseed oil in a non-stick frying pan and fry the patties for 3–4 minutes on each side until golden and crisp. Keep warm in the oven.

Heat 1–2 tbsp of rapeseed oil in a frying pan and gently fry the duck eggs for 2–3 minutes, seasoning the whites lightly. Place a duck hash patty on each warmed plate, slide a fried egg on top and serve.

# BRAISED DUCK WITH PEAS

2 good-quality ducks, each about 1.5–2kg,
    such as Gressingham
sea salt and freshly ground black pepper
200ml sweet cider
600ml basic gravy (see page 294)
600ml chicken stock (see page 293)
a few sprigs of thyme
1 bay leaf
2 tbsp double cream
200g podded fresh or frozen peas, freshly cooked

SERVES 4

Preheat the oven to 220ºC/gas mark 7. With a heavy chopping knife, cut the ducks in half. Cut the parson's nose off and trim away any excess fat and the backbone where there isn't any meat. Chop the knuckle from the legs and trim the wing bones, if necessary. Season the birds with salt and pepper, then roast them, skin-side down, in a roasting tin for 30 minutes. Transfer the ducks to a colander over a bowl to drain off the fat.

Turn the oven down to 160ºC/gas mark 3. Carefully cut the duck halves in half, where the breast joins the leg.

Put the duck pieces into a casserole dish with the cider, gravy, chicken stock, thyme and bay leaf. Cover with a lid and braise for 1¼ hours. Remove the duck pieces from the liquid with a slotted spoon, put them on a warm plate and cover with foil. Set aside.

Transfer the cooking liquid to a saucepan, skim off any fat and simmer until reduced and thickened. Return the duck to the liquid, add the cream and peas just to warm through, then check the seasoning and serve.

Try to buy good-quality ducks like Gressingham or Barbary, as they are reared with less fat and a higher meat content. When fresh peas are in season, make sure you use them – you'll need to buy about 600g of peas in the pod.

# ROAST PHEASANT BREASTS WITH CHESTNUT STUFFING

4 plump boneless pheasant breasts, with skin on
100g freshly shelled or vacuum-packed chestnuts, roughly chopped
2 shallots, peeled and finely chopped
40g fresh white breadcrumbs
1 tbsp chopped flat-leaf parsley
25g butter, melted
sea salt and freshly ground black pepper
1 tbsp vegetable oil

TO SERVE
creamed Brussels sprouts (see page 227)
150ml basic gravy (see page 294)

SERVES 4

Preheat the oven to 180°C/gas mark 6. Lay the pheasant breasts on a board, skin-side down. Remove the fillet and put to one side. With the tip of a sharp knife, cut two incisions away from the centre of the breast to form a pocket. (Basically you are transferring some of the meat away from the middle of the breast to make room for the stuffing.)

Mix the chestnuts, shallots, breadcrumbs, parsley and melted butter together and season with salt and pepper. Divide the stuffing between the 4 breasts. Flatten the fillet a little with the side of your hand and lay it over the stuffing. Fold the breast meat that you cut previously back into the centre to completely seal in the stuffing.

Heat the oil in a roasting tray in the oven for a few minutes. Season the pheasant breasts, then place in the hot tray and cook in the oven for 5-7 minutes on each side, or until cooked to your liking.

Remove the breasts from the oven and carve into slices. Serve on a bed of creamed Brussels sprouts, with the gravy.

66 Removing the breasts gives a more succulent result, as the cooking can then be better controlled. Stuffing can also disguise any dryness. Try to buy smaller, younger birds earlier in the season, as these will be more tender. 99

# WOOD PIGEON WITH ELDERBERRIES

4 wood pigeons
sea salt and freshly ground black pepper
4 sprigs of thyme
100g butter
2 tsp plain flour
60ml port
150ml chicken stock (see page 293)
1 small cup of elderberries

SERVES 4

Preheat the oven to 220°C/gas mark 7. Season the pigeons inside and out and put a sprig of thyme inside each cavity with a generous knob of butter. Rub the rest of the butter over the pigeon breasts, then roast the birds for 7-8 minutes in a roasting tray. Transfer to a warm platter and set aside.

Add the flour to the roasting tray. Stir in the port, then gradually stir in the stock to avoid any lumps from forming. Bring to the boil, stirring, and simmer over a medium heat for 4-5 minutes or until it has reduced and thickened. Meanwhile, cut the birds in half and cut away the backbone, leaving just the breasts on the bone with the legs attached (take the breasts off the bone if you wish).

Place the pigeon halves in the sauce and add the elderberries. Cover with a lid and simmer for 3-4 minutes, turning the birds after a minute and keeping them a little pink. Serve with buttered greens or braised cabbage if you like.

66 Like other game birds, a wood pigeon can easily be overcooked, which is as disastrous as a 'well done' fillet steak. I strongly recommend that whatever you serve with your pigeon, you get it ready almost to the point of serving before you pop the birds into the oven. Don't get caught rushing around putting accompaniments together, as the bird will continue to cook as it rests. 99

# CLASSIC ROAST GROUSE WITH BREAD SAUCE

4 young grouse, livers and hearts reserved
6 knobs of butter
4 sage leaves
2 shallots, peeled and finely chopped
a few knobs of lard
4 slices of white bread, crusts removed
a splash of red wine
100ml of basic gravy (see page 294)

FOR THE BREAD SAUCE
1 small onion, peeled and halved
50g butter
3 cloves
1 bay leaf
500ml milk
a pinch of freshly grated nutmeg
100g fresh white breadcrumbs
sea salt and freshly ground black pepper

SERVES 4

Start by making the bread sauce: finely chop half the onion and, in a pan over a medium heat, cook the onion gently in half the butter until soft. Stud the other half of the onion with the cloves, pushing them through the bay leaf to anchor it. Put the milk, nutmeg and onion in the saucepan with the cooked onion and bring to the boil. Season and simmer for 10–15 minutes. Remove from the heat and leave the sauce to infuse for 30 minutes or so.

Preheat the oven to 220°C/gas mark 7. Season the grouse inside and out, rub the breasts with butter and put a knob inside each cavity, along with a sage leaf. Roast for 15–20 minutes, for medium rare, basting every so often.

Meanwhile, melt a good knob of butter in a small frying pan and gently cook the shallots without colouring for a few minutes. Season the grouse livers and hearts, add to the pan and cook over a high heat for a couple of minutes. Tip into a small food processor and whiz to a coarse paste, or finely chop by hand.

Melt the lard in a roasting pan on the hob and fry the bread until nicely browned on one side. Remove from the heat, turn the bread over and spread the browned side with the coarse paste; keep hot.

Remove the grouse from the pan, transfer to a warm platter and set aside in a warm place to rest. Place the roasting pan over a medium heat and pour in the wine and gravy, stirring with a wooden spoon to deglaze and scrape up the sediment. Let bubble for a minute or so.

While the grouse is resting, finish the sauce: discard the studded onion, add the breadcrumbs and return to a low heat. Simmer gently for 10 minutes, stirring occasionally. Pour one-third of the sauce into a blender and process, then return to the pan and add the remaining butter. Stir until the sauce has amalgamated; check the seasoning and adjust if necessary.

Serve the grouse, on or off the bone, with the croûtes, pan gravy, bread sauce and any other accompaniments of your choice.

❝ Grouse has a fine flavour that, in my view, is best appreciated if the bird isn't hung for too long. I like to roast it quickly in a hot oven with a knob of butter inside to keep it moist, rather than covered with rashers of bacon that interfere with the flavour of the bird. If you really want bacon, then I suggest you cook it separately. I know it's difficult to change one's eating habits, especially if you've been brought up on game, but that's my theory on the pure grouse eating pleasure. ❞

"Once a rarity, now the bohemian of the poultry yard, the guinea fowl has a delicious flavour somewhere between pheasant and the best flavoured chicken you can buy. Unfortunately, it still doesn't grace many home tables. This is a real pity, as its moist, creamy yellow flesh is delicious and will withstand most robust garnishes."

# GUINEA FOWL WITH SAVOY CABBAGE AND WILD MUSHROOMS

6 garlic cloves, peeled
a few sprigs of thyme
2 guinea fowl, each about 1.1kg
125g butter
sea salt and freshly ground black pepper
4 tbsp red wine
4 tbsp port
150ml chicken stock (see page 293)
1kg Savoy cabbage, trimmed, cored and chopped
200g wild mushrooms, cleaned, trimmed and halved
1 tbsp chopped flat-leaf parsley

SERVES 4

Preheat the oven to 220°C/gas mark 7. Divide the garlic and thyme between the cavities of the two birds. Rub the breasts with 25g of the butter and season well. Place in a roasting tray and roast for 1 hour, basting occasionally.

Transfer the guinea fowl to a plate, cover with foil and set aside to rest. Put the tray on a medium heat on the hob, add the wine and port, and stir well to scrape up any residue on the bottom of the tin. Add the stock and simmer for 3–4 minutes until reduced and thickened, then strain through a fine sieve.

While the birds are resting, cook the cabbage in boiling salted water for about 5 minutes, until tender. Drain and add 50g of the butter, season with salt and pepper and cover with a lid.

Meanwhile, heat the rest of the butter in a frying pan, add the mushrooms and parsley, season and sauté over a medium heat until tender. Timing will depend on the type of mushrooms; for example, chanterelles take only 30–40 seconds, whereas girolles will take a couple of minutes.

To serve, remove the legs from the guinea fowl and cut the breasts away from the bone with a sharp knife. Arrange the cabbage on the plates, put the leg and breast meat on top, then pour over the sauce. Spoon the mushrooms on top and serve.

# SNIPE 'BUTCHER'S TREAT'

4 oven-ready snipe
sea salt and freshly ground black pepper
4 large baking potatoes
a few good knobs of butter
4 sage leaves
a few sprigs of thyme

SERVES 4

Preheat the oven to 230°C/gas mark 8. Season the snipe with salt and pepper.

Cut a small slice off a long side of the potatoes so that they sit level on a baking tray. Cut about a 1cm slice off the tops for the lid and carefully hollow out the flesh, using a small sharp knife, a grapefruit knife or melon baller, leaving about a 1cm-thick shell of potato. (You can cook and mash the potato flesh to serve with the snipe or season and butter the flesh and roast it with some chopped onion and bacon while the snipe is cooking.)

Put a little butter in the bottom of each potato, place the seasoned snipe on top, then add more butter on top with the sage and thyme. Replace the lid and bake for about an hour. Serve immediately.

66 Whenever I'm up at my friend and game suppliers – Ben and Silvy Weatheralls' in Dumfriesshire – I'm always inspired by something to do with game, however simple or complicated it may be. On one of my trips, Ben recited a recipe from a book by Prue Coates, *Prue's New Country Cooking*, which sounded just genius. Here's my adaptation. A snipe doesn't have a lot of meat on the bone so this is a great idea and a fun way to serve these tiny game birds. 99

# CHRISTMAS LUNCH OF SMALL GAME BIRDS

16 or so small game birds (see right)
sea salt and freshly ground black pepper
32 sage leaves
a few knobs of butter

TO SERVE
basic gravy (see page 294)
rowan jelly
bread sauce (see page 164)

SERVES 8

Preheat the oven to 230°C/gas mark 8. Season the birds inside and out with salt and pepper and place the sage leaves in the cavities. Rub the breasts with the butter. Place in one or two large roasting trays and roast for about 15 minutes, keeping them pink and basting with the butter from time to time. If you are cooking widgeon, allow an extra 10 minutes or so, as they tend to be twice the size.

Serve the game birds on wooden boards or a platter, with gravy or a rowan jelly. Buttered sprout tops tossed with chanterelles or lightly roasted chestnuts work a treat and bread sauce is a must.

66 Game birds like teal, snipe, woodcock, widgeon, pintail and even pigeon are a great way to entertain your guests at Christmas. What's more they don't take much longer than 15 minutes in a hot oven to cook so you can pop them in while you are having your starter. Allow for a couple of birds per person. You can buy your birds trussed or tied, or just as they are, and if you're using snipe and woodcock then the beak can be used to truss the birds through the legs for an even more dramatic presentation. 99

If your birds come with the livers, these can be fried quickly and spread onto toast. I'd also recommend serving a gravy or a jelly, such as hedgerow, cranberry, rowan, quince or rosehip.

# GAME PIE

1kg boneless game meat

200ml red wine

1 garlic clove, peeled and crushed

1 tsp chopped thyme

4 juniper berries, crushed

1 bay leaf

2 tbsp vegetable oil

2 tbsp plain flour, plus extra for dusting

sea salt and freshly ground black pepper

25g butter

1 large onion, peeled and finely chopped

1 tsp tomato purée

1 litre dark meat stock (see page 292)

1–2 tsp cornflour (optional)

350–400g ready-made all-butter puff pastry

1 egg, beaten

SERVES 4

"Game for pies is traditionally a mixture of game birds, rabbit, hare and diced venison. As these take different times to cook, I find the best solution is to use a mixture of game bird thighs and tender cuts from the leg of venison. You'll need to marinate the meat a couple of days in advance."

About 2 days ahead, cut the game roughly into 3cm cubes and put into a stainless steel (or other non-reactive) bowl with the red wine, garlic, thyme, juniper berries and bay leaf. Cover with cling film and marinate in the fridge for 2 days.

Drain the meat in a colander over a bowl, reserving the marinade, and dry the meat pieces on kitchen paper. Heat the oil in a large heavy-based frying pan until almost smoking. Meanwhile, lightly flour the meat with ½ tablespoon of the flour, seasoned with salt and pepper. Fry the meat in 2 or 3 batches over a high heat until nicely browned, then remove and set aside.

Heat the butter in the pan and gently fry the onion until soft. Add the remaining flour and tomato purée and stir over a low heat for a minute. Slowly stir in the marinade and the stock. Bring to the boil, add the meat, cover and simmer gently for 1–2 hours, or until the meat is tender. Or cook in the oven at 160°C/gas mark 3. Start checking the meat after 1 hour; it's difficult to put an exact time on braised meats. Once it is cooked, the sauce should have thickened to the consistency of gravy. (If not, thicken with the cornflour mixed with a little cold water and simmer briefly, stirring.)

Allow the game mixture to cool, then use to fill a large pie dish, to about 1cm from the rim, discarding the bay leaf.

Roll out the pastry on a floured surface to a 5mm thickness and cut out a lid, about 2cm larger all round than the pie dish. Brush the pastry edges with a little beaten egg. Lay the pastry on top of the dish, pushing the sides against the rim. Cut a small slit in the top to allow steam to escape and brush with beaten egg. Leave to rest in a cool place for 30 minutes. Meanwhile, preheat the oven to 200°C/gas mark 6. Cook the pie for 40–50 minutes, until the pastry is crisp and golden.

# GAME FAGGOTS WITH ONION SAUCE

1 tbsp vegetable oil

2 small onions, peeled and finely chopped

2 garlic cloves, peeled and crushed

2 tsp chopped thyme leaves

3 juniper berries, crushed

200g coarsely minced pork belly

250g coarsely minced pork or game liver

350g coarsely minced game meat, such as pheasant, wild duck, pigeon, etc.

100g fresh white breadcrumbs

1 egg, beaten

sea salt and freshly ground black pepper

½ tsp ground mace

200g caul fat (lamb or pig's), soaked for an hour in cold water

creamed Brussels sprouts, to serve (see page 227)

FOR THE ONION SAUCE

1 tbsp vegetable oil

2 medium onions, peeled and finely chopped

a good knob of butter

3 tsp plain flour

1 tsp tomato purée

250ml dark meat stock (see page 292)

SERVES 4

Preheat the oven to 220°C/gas mark 7. Heat the oil in a pan and gently cook the onions and garlic with the thyme and juniper for 2-3 minutes until softened. Add the pork belly and continue cooking for 3-4 minutes, stirring well. Remove from the heat and leave to cool.

Add the liver, game meat, breadcrumbs and egg to the cooled pork mixture and season well with salt, pepper and the mace. Shape into 150g balls (bigger than a golf ball, but smaller than a tennis ball), then wrap in a double layer of caul fat. Place in a deep baking tray with join side down and roast for 20 minutes or so until the faggots are nicely coloured. Drain off the fat.

Meanwhile, make the sauce. Heat the oil in a heavy-based pan, add the onions, cover and cook gently for 8-10 minutes until lightly coloured - you may need to add a splash of water if they start to catch on the bottom of the pan. Add the butter, then the flour and tomato purée and stir well over a low heat for a minute. Gradually add the stock, stirring well to avoid lumps from forming. Season with salt and pepper, bring to the boil and simmer gently for 20 minutes.

Turn the oven down to 180°C/gas mark 4. Put the faggots into an ovenproof dish and pour on the sauce. Cover with a lid or foil, and continue cooking for 30 minutes. Serve with creamed Brussels sprouts and cabbage.

I use the mincing attachment of my food mixer to mince the meat, but you could easily use the chopping blade of a food processor.

“ I've enjoyed the spiced livery flavour of faggots ever since I was a kid. They are good cheap winter fodder, ideal for using up bits and pieces (in this case, game). Generally they're eaten with peas, though in the winter I prefer mashed potato, neeps or coarsely mashed parsnips. To wrap the faggots, you'll need some lamb or pork caul fat, which a butcher should be able to get for you. ”

## GAME SALAD WITH BLAEBERRIES

500g selection of game bird breasts and fillets, such as
    grouse, pigeon and venison fillets, rabbit saddles, etc.
sea salt and freshly ground black pepper
a good knob of butter
50–60g small salad and herb leaves, such as celery
    leaves, pea shoots, chives, chickweed, etc.
30–60g blaeberries or blueberries, washed

FOR THE DRESSING
6 tbsp cold-pressed rapeseed or olive oil
2 tbsp sherry vinegar or red wine vinegar

SERVES 2–4

Season the game and pan-fry very briefly in the
butter, so that they stay pink. Transfer them to a
warmed plate and leave to rest, saving the juices.

Make the dressing by mixing the oil and vinegar
with any cooking juices, and season to taste.

Toss the dressing with the leaves and arrange on
plates. Slice the game thinly and scatter over the
leaves and the berries.

## SILLFIELD FARM WILD BOAR AND ALE STEW

1kg wild boar meat, cut roughly into 3cm chunks
sea salt and freshly ground black pepper
1½ tbsp plain flour, plus more for dusting
2 tbsp vegetable oil
200–250g wild boar pancetta, ordinary pancetta, or a
    piece of smoked streaky bacon, cut into 3cm chunks
1 onion, peeled and roughly chopped
2 garlic cloves, peeled and crushed
1 tsp chopped fresh thyme leaves
1 tsp tomato purée
500ml dark ale or bitter
2 litres dark meat stock (see page 292)
2 wild boar sausages, each about 100g, or 4 small ones

SERVES 4

Preheat the oven to 180°C/gas mark 4. Season the
wild boar meat and lightly dust with flour, shaking
off any excess. Heat half of the oil in a heavy frying
pan and brown the pieces of boar, a few at a time.
Fry the pancetta in the same fat and put into an
ovenproof dish with the boar.

In another pan, gently cook the onion, garlic and
thyme in the rest of the oil for 3–4 minutes until
they begin to colour. Add the flour and purée, and
stir well over a medium heat for 2–3 minutes.

Gradually add the ale, stirring well to avoid lumps
from forming. Add the stock, bring to the boil,
season and add to the dish with the boar meat and
pancetta. Cover and cook in the oven for 1½ hours.

Meanwhile, twist each sausage in half and cut
across. Grill them under a hot grill for about 2–3
minutes on each side, then add to the stew for the
last half hour in the oven. Check the pieces of boar
to see if they are tender; if not, return to the oven
for another 30 minutes or so. Serve with mashed
potatoes or other root vegetables.

❝It's difficult to know what to do with
boar and there are few cuts that are
tender enough to cook as you would
pork. In France, this would be cooked
in red wine for a hunting party.❞

# BRAISED VENISON WITH CARROTS

1.5kg trimmed venison meat, from a single muscle
750ml red wine
2 garlic cloves, peeled and crushed
1 tsp chopped thyme leaves
1 bay leaf
3 juniper berries, crushed
3 tbsp plain flour
sea salt and freshly ground black pepper
vegetable oil, for frying
60g butter
2 onions, peeled and finely chopped
2 tbsp tomato purée
1.5 litres dark meat stock (see page 292)
1–2 tsp cornflour (optional)

FOR THE CARROTS
200–250g small carrots, such as Chantenay, peeled
a couple of good knobs of butter
1 tsp caster sugar
1 tbsp chopped flat-leaf parsley

SERVES 4

About 2 days ahead, cut the venison into 3–4cm chunks and place in a stainless steel or ceramic bowl with the red wine, garlic, thyme, bay leaf and juniper. Cover and leave to marinate in the fridge for 2 days.

Drain the meat in a colander, reserving the marinade, and dry the meat pieces on some kitchen paper. Flour the meat lightly, using a tablespoon of the flour, and season with salt and pepper. Heat 2 tablespoons of oil in a heavy-based frying pan and fry the meat, a few pieces at a time, over a high heat until nicely browned. Put aside.

Heat the butter in a large, heavy-based saucepan and gently fry the onions for a few minutes until soft. Add the remaining flour and the tomato purée, and stir over a low heat for a minute. Slowly add the reserved marinade, stirring constantly to avoid lumps from forming. Bring to the boil and simmer until it has reduced by half.

Add the stock and the pieces of venison and bring back to a simmer. Cover with a lid and simmer very gently over a low heat for about 1½ hours until the meat is tender. It's difficult to put an exact time on braising meat; you may find it needs an extra half an hour. Once the meat is cooked, the sauce should have thickened sufficiently. If not, mix the cornflour with a little cold water, stir into the sauce and simmer, stirring, for a few minutes.

Meanwhile, put the carrots in a pan and just cover with water. Add the butter, sugar and seasoning and simmer rapidly until the carrots are tender. Drain off any excess cooking liquid, leaving a little to glaze them, then toss with the chopped parsley.

Divide the stew among warm bowls and top with the glazed carrots. Serve at once.

“ Try to use a singular cut from a seamed haunch, shoulder, neck or shank for this recipe, as the cooking time will then be consistent. If you buy ready-diced meat, it may be a mixture of cuts and there is a risk that some pieces will be tender, while others won't be cooked. You'll need to marinate the meat a couple of days in advance. ”

## PEPPERED VENISON CHOPS WITH SWEET AND SOUR RED ONIONS

4 large red onions
a couple of good knobs of butter
1 tbsp malt vinegar
1 tbsp redcurrant jelly
sea salt and freshly ground black pepper
8 venison chops, each about 120–150g
vegetable oil, for brushing

SERVES 4

Preheat the oven to 200°C/gas mark 6. Place the whole red onions on a baking tray and bake for about an hour or so, or until soft. Leave to cool for a while, then remove the skins, quarter the onions and separate into 'petals'.

Melt the butter in a frying pan over a low heat, add the onions, vinegar and redcurrant jelly, season with salt and pepper and cook gently for 4–5 minutes or so until the liquid has evaporated and the onions are nice and glossy.

Meanwhile, heat a ridged griddle or heavy-based frying pan. Season the chops with salt and liberally with coarsely ground pepper. Brush the griddle pan with a little oil and cook the chops for 4–5 minutes on each side, keeping them nice and pink.

Spoon the red onions onto warm serving plates and place the venison chops on top. Serve at once.

Chops are a nice, easy way to cook venison. Perhaps surprisingly, since it's a pretty economical way to prepare a large saddle, chops are not a standard venison cut, so you may need to order them from a butcher or game dealer.

## FILLET OF VENISON WITH HAGGIS AND BASHED NEEPS

4 trimmed venison saddle fillets or under-fillets, each about 150g
100ml red wine
6 juniper berries, crushed
a few sprigs of thyme, chopped
sea salt and freshly ground black pepper
500g swedes or turnips, peeled and roughly chopped, plus the leaves, if available, destalked and chopped
90g butter
150ml dark meat stock (see page 292)
vegetable oil, for frying
150g–200g good-quality cooked haggis, skinned and meat crumbled or spooned into pieces

SERVES 4

The day before, place the fillets in a non-reactive dish with the wine, juniper and thyme. Cover with cling film and refrigerate overnight. The next day, drain the meat in a colander, reserving the marinade. Dry the fillets on some kitchen paper and season.

For the neeps, cover the swedes with water and season. Bring to the boil and simmer gently for 10-15 minutes until soft enough to mash. Drain in a colander, then coarsely mash with a potato masher. Adjust the seasoning and stir in 60g of the butter.

Meanwhile, cook the leaves in a separate pan of boiling salted water until just tender. Drain and toss in with the neeps. Keep warm.

Also while the neeps are cooking, put the marinade into a saucepan and boil rapidly until reduced to a tablespoonful. Add the stock and any juices from the venison. Boil for about 5 minutes, or until the sauce has thickened. Strain through a fine-meshed sieve and whisk in the remaining butter.

Heat some oil in a heavy frying pan and cook the fillets for 2–3 minutes on each side for medium-rare or a few minutes longer for medium. Rest on a plate to catch the juices, covered with foil to keep warm.

Reheat the neeps if necessary and fold the haggis into them. Spoon into the centre of each plate. Slice each venison fillet into 4 or 5 pieces and arrange on the neep mixture, then pour over the sauce.

# BRAISED WILD RABBIT WITH ST GEORGE'S MUSHROOMS

8–12 rabbit legs (use both front and back legs)
sea salt and freshly ground black pepper
40g plain flour, plus extra for dusting
vegetable oil, for frying
80g butter
6 shallots, peeled and finely chopped
2 garlic cloves, peeled and crushed
100ml white wine or cider
1.5 litres chicken stock (see page 293)
200–250g St George's mushrooms, cleaned and sliced
3 tbsp double cream
2 tbsp chopped flat-leaf parsley

SERVES 4

Chop the large back legs in half at the joint, using a heavy knife. Lightly season and dust the legs with some flour.

Heat a little oil in a heavy-based frying pan and lightly fry the rabbit legs for 2 minutes on each side, without colouring them too much. Remove and set aside.

Meanwhile, melt about 40g of the butter in a large heavy-based saucepan and gently cook the shallots with the garlic for 2–3 minutes until soft. Add the flour and stir well. Gradually add the wine or cider, stirring well to avoid any lumps from forming, and then add the chicken stock. Bring to the boil, stirring often.

Add the rabbit legs to the saucepan and season lightly. Lower the heat, put the lid on and simmer gently for 1¼ hours or until the rabbit is very tender.

Meanwhile, melt the rest of the butter in the now empty frying pan. Add the mushrooms, season lightly and cook gently for 4–5 minutes until softened. Add to the rabbit legs with the cream and the parsley and simmer for another 5–6 minutes. Check the seasoning.

Serve with some mashed potato and seasonal vegetables.

❝A rabbit makes for a cheap springtime meal and along with some seasonal, earthy mushrooms, the legs from two or three rabbits will easily serve four. Don't braise the rabbits' tender little saddle fillets with the legs; instead save them (in the freezer if you like) to pan-fry and use in a salad.❞

## JUGGED HARE

8 hare back legs
500ml red wine
4 juniper berries, chopped
1 bay leaf
a few sprigs of thyme
sea salt and freshly ground black pepper
1 tbsp flour, plus extra for dusting
vegetable oil, for frying
1 onion, peeled and finely chopped
50g butter
½ tbsp tomato purée
3 litres dark meat stock (see page 292)

SERVES 4–6

Cut the hare legs in half at the joint and then cut them once more through the middle of the thigh, so you end up with 3 pieces from each leg. Place in a non-reactive bowl or dish, together with the red wine, juniper, bay leaf and thyme. Cover with cling film and refrigerate for 24–48 hours.

Drain the hare in a colander over a bowl and pat the pieces dry with some kitchen paper. Season the meat and lightly dust with flour. Heat the oil in a heavy frying pan and fry the pieces, a few at a time, until well coloured, then put to one side on a plate.

Meanwhile, in a heavy-based saucepan, gently cook the onion in the butter for 3–4 minutes until soft. Add the tablespoon of flour and stir well over a medium heat until it begins to turn a sandy colour. Add the tomato purée, then slowly add the marinade, stirring well to avoid lumps from forming. Bring to the boil and simmer over a medium heat until the liquid has reduced by half.

Add the stock and hare, bring back to the boil, cover and simmer gently for 1 hour or cook in an oven preheated to 160°C/gas mark 3. Remove a piece of the meat to check if it's tender; if not, continue cooking for another 30 minutes or so.

Once the meat is tender, remove the meat from the sauce and simmer the sauce until it has thickened to a gravy-like consistency, then return the pieces of meat to warm through. Adjust the seasoning, if necessary. Serve with mashed or roasted root vegetables – beetroot is particularly good with it.

## SADDLE OF HARE WITH BEETROOT MASH

the saddle fillets from 2 large hares
a couple of good knobs of butter
1 large red onion, peeled and chopped
150–170g red beetroot, peeled and finely chopped
1 tsp chopped thyme leaves
1 tbsp cider vinegar
1 tsp redcurrant jelly
150ml chicken stock (see page 293)
1–2 tbsp vegetable or corn oil

FOR THE BEETROOT MASH
300g yellow or white beetroot, peeled and quartered
sea salt and freshly ground black pepper
a couple of good knobs of butter

SERVES 4

For the mash, cook the beetroot in simmering, salted water for 40 minutes or until very tender.

Set the fillets aside to bring to room temperature. Heat a knob of butter in a saucepan and add the onion, red beetroot and thyme. Cover and cook over a very low heat for 30 minutes, stirring occasionally and adding a splash of water if the pan is too dry.

When the beetroot for the mash are cooked, drain and coarsely mash with a potato masher. Return to the pan, mix in the butter and season to taste; keep warm. Add the vinegar and jelly to the red beetroot, season and cook for another 5 minutes or so without the lid on, stirring every so often. Add the stock and continue simmering until there are just 2 or 3 spoonfuls of liquor left in the pan; keep warm.

Season the hare fillets with salt and pepper. Heat the oil in a frying pan and cook the fillets for 3–5 minutes over a fairly high heat, turning them every so often and keeping them quite rare. The thickness of the fillets will determine the cooking time, but it's important not to overcook them.

To serve, spoon the red onion and beetroot mix onto warm serving plates with the cooking liquor. Cut each fillet into 3–4 slices and arrange on top. Spoon the mash alongside and serve.

You should get two decent portions from a saddle once filleted, saving the rest of the hare for a casserole or pie.

“I wasn't much of a hare fan when I was young. It was something to do with the way they would just appear from nowhere, hanging in my grandparents' porch. Hare were plentiful in Dorset, so often ended up as dog food instead of in a traditional West Country dish. These days, though, I'm a big fan of its unique flavour, whether it be braised or in a rich sauce with pasta.”

**MEAT**

## GRILLED VEAL CHOP WITH OFFAL SALAD

200–250g veal offal, such as liver, kidney, heart,
   sweetbreads, etc., trimmed
4 veal chops or cutlets, each about 300g
sea salt and freshly ground black pepper
vegetable or corn oil, for brushing
2 tbsp cold-pressed rapeseed oil
a couple of good knobs of butter
a couple of handfuls of small tasty salad leaves,
   such as pea shoots, buckler leaf sorrel, rocket,
   purslane, etc.
Tewkesbury mustard dressing (see page 301)

SERVES 4

Cut the offal into 1cm chunks and set aside.

Heat a griddle or heavy-based frying pan. Season
the veal chops and brush with oil. Cook for about
5 minutes on each side, depending on thickness,
keeping them nice and pink. Put to one side.

Meanwhile, heat the rapeseed oil in a heavy-based
frying pan. Add the butter and heat until foaming,
then season the offal pieces and add them to the
pan. Fry briskly over a high heat for 2–3 minutes
until nicely coloured, but keeping them pink in the
middle. Remove from the pan and put to one side.

Meanwhile, in a bowl, toss together the salad leaves
and dressing. Add the offal, toss briefly and arrange
on serving plates alongside the chops.

**“** British veal is well worth a try. Serving
the offal in a leafy salad alongside
makes this dish of chops that much
more interesting. **”**

## BUTCHER'S STEAK WITH BONE MARROW AND WILD MUSHROOMS

4 butcher's steaks, each about 200g
2 × 8cm lengths of bone marrow, halved lengthways
a couple of good knobs of butter
4 small shallots, peeled and finely chopped
2 garlic cloves, peeled and crushed
50–60g fresh white breadcrumbs
2 tbsp chopped flat-leaf parsley
sea salt and freshly ground black pepper
1 tbsp vegetable oil, for brushing
120–150g wild mushrooms, such as winter chanterelles

SERVES 4

Place the steaks on a plate and leave to reach room
temperature. Preheat the oven to 200°C/gas mark 6.

To prepare the bone marrow, heat a little of the
butter in a pan and gently cook the shallots and
garlic for 2–3 minutes until softened, then remove
from the heat. Scoop the bone marrow out of the
bones with a spoon and chop roughly. Toss with
the shallot mix, breadcrumbs, parsley and some
seasoning. Spoon the mixture back into the bones,
place on a baking tray and bake for about 12–15
minutes until lightly coloured.

Meanwhile, heat a griddle or heavy frying pan.
Season and lightly oil the steaks and cook in the
hot pan for 3–4 minutes on each side, keeping them
fairly rare, then set aside to rest in a warm place.

Meanwhile, heat the rest of the butter in a heavy
frying pan until foaming. Add the chanterelles,
season and cook over a high heat for just 30
seconds. (More meaty wild mushrooms will take
longer; allow a few minutes.)

To serve, cut each steak into about 5 slices and
arrange on warm plates with the stuffed bone
marrow alongside. Spoon the mushrooms over the
steaks and serve.

To save yourself the bother, ask your
butcher to saw the bone marrow shaft
in half lengthways for you.

"This cut is well regarded in France and known as *onglet*. In the US it is called hanger steak and it is on most decent brasserie menus. Here, it is usually cooked as a stewing steak rather than a proper steak. Old school butchers knew how good it was, though, saving it for themselves once the beast was butchered – hence the name. It lies just below the kidneys, near the flank and has a wonderful flavour."

# ROAST BEEF AND YORKSHIRE PUDDING

beef dripping or vegetable oil, for roasting
1 rib-eye of beef, about 1–1.5kg
sea salt and freshly ground black pepper
2 onions, peeled and halved
2 carrots, scrubbed or peeled and halved

FOR THE YORKSHIRE PUDDING
250g plain flour
4 medium eggs, beaten
500–600ml milk

TO SERVE
100ml red or white wine
200ml basic gravy (see page 294)

SERVES 4–6

Preheat the oven to 220°c/gas mark 7. Put a little dripping or oil into a large roasting tin and heat in the oven for 10 minutes. Season the beef and roast for 15 minutes, then turn it over to seal the meat and keep the juices in. Put the onions and carrots under the beef to act as a trivet (or use a steel trivet); this helps the beef to cook evenly and flavours the gravy. Allow 30 minutes per kg for rare; add another 10 minutes per kg for medium; or an extra 20 minutes per kg for well done. Baste the meat regularly with the pan juices.

Meanwhile, make the Yorkshire batter. Put the flour into a bowl and add a good pinch of salt. Whisk in the eggs and a little of the milk to form a paste. Mix in the rest of the milk, trying not to beat the batter too much, to give a thick pouring consistency.

About 25 minutes before the beef will be ready, pour some of the hot fat from the beef into a large roasting tin and heat in the oven for 5 minutes until smoking. Pour the batter into the roasting tin and bake for 30 minutes, until well risen and crisp on the outside.

Rest the beef for 15 minutes before carving. To serve, deglaze the roasting pan with the wine and add the gravy. Simmer, stirring to remove any residue, for 1–2 minutes. Serve the beef cut into thick slices, with the Yorkshire pudding and gravy.

“A rib of beef, on or off the bone, is by far the best roasting joint as far as I'm concerned. It has some fat, but this really enhances the flavour. If cooking on the bone, you need a very large joint for 4–6 people, and space in the oven for Yorkshire pudding and potatoes, which may not be convenient at home. Instead I would recommend rib-eye, which is readily available these days.”

Here the Yorkshire pudding is cooked whole, the old-fashioned way, so it's still a bit gooey in the middle. If you prefer crisp little puddings, cook the batter in individual Yorkshire pudding moulds at 230°c/gas mark 8 while the beef is resting.

# BARBECUED CROSS-CUT RIBS

1–2 tbsp vegetable oil
12–16 cross-cut beef ribs

FOR THE BARBECUE SAUCE
a couple of generous knobs of butter
4 large shallots, peeled and finely chopped
4 garlic cloves, peeled and crushed
200ml cider
200ml dark meat stock (see page 292)
60–80g tomato ketchup
60–80g HP sauce or Oxford sauce
½ tbsp Tewkesbury mustard
1 tbsp clear honey
1 small chilli, finely chopped
4 tbsp tomato purée
40ml Henderson's relish or Worcestershire sauce
sea salt and freshly ground black pepper

SERVES 4

Preheat the oven to 150°C/gas mark 2. For the barbecue sauce, simply mix all the ingredients together in a bowl, seasoning with salt and pepper to taste.

Heat 1 tbsp oil in a large, heavy-based frying pan over a medium-high heat. When hot, fry the ribs in batches for 2-3 minutes on each side until they are nicely coloured, adding more oil to the pan as necessary. Once browned, transfer the ribs to a large ovenproof dish.

Pour the barbecue sauce over the ribs and toss to coat all over. Cook in the oven for about an hour or until the ribs are tender and glazed, and the meat is just falling away from the bone.

**"**This recipe, using my favourite cross-cut ribs, leans more towards American barbecue cooking, although it is prepared with British ingredients. Serve the ribs with a simple salad or perhaps the blue Monday salad on page 66.**"**

Deep-fried green tomatoes also make a great accompaniment, should you happen to have some unripe tomatoes in the garden (see page 12).

# BEEF AND OYSTER PIE

1kg trimmed flank or shin of beef
3 tbsp plain flour, plus extra for dusting
sea salt and freshly ground black pepper
vegetable oil, for frying
30g butter
1 medium onion, peeled and finely chopped
1 garlic clove, peeled and crushed
1 tsp tomato purée
200ml dark ale, such as Hix Oyster Ale or Guinness
1.5 litres dark meat stock (see page 292)
1 tsp chopped thyme leaves
1 small bay leaf
1–2 tsp cornflour (optional)
12 large oysters, 8 shucked, 4 left in the half-shell

FOR THE PASTRY

225g self-raising flour, plus extra for dusting
1 tsp salt
85g shredded beef suet
60g butter, chilled and coarsely grated
1 medium egg, beaten

FOR THE PARSLEY CRUST

a generous knob of butter
2 tbsp fresh white breadcrumbs
1 tbsp chopped flat-leaf parsley

SERVES 4

66 Pies are a great way to use the less expensive, yet full-flavoured meat cuts, such as flank and shin of beef, mutton shoulder and neck, and ox cheeks. Tucking in a few oysters adds a touch of luxury. 99

Cut the meat roughly into 3cm cubes. Season half of the flour with salt and pepper and use to lightly flour the meat. Heat a little oil in a large, heavy-based frying pan and fry the meat in 2 or 3 batches over a high heat until nicely browned. Set aside on a plate.

Melt the butter in a large, heavy-based pan or flameproof casserole and fry the onion and garlic for a few minutes until lightly coloured. Add the remaining flour and tomato purée. Stir over a low heat for a minute or so, then slowly add the ale and stock, stirring to avoid lumps from forming.

Add the beef with the thyme and bay leaf. Bring back to a simmer, cover and simmer very gently (ideally using a heat-diffuser mat or a simmer plate) for about 2 hours until the meat is tender. When the meat is cooked, the sauce should have thickened to a gravy-like consistency. If not, mix the cornflour to a paste with 1 tbsp water, stir into the sauce and simmer, stirring, for a few minutes. Leave to cool.

To make the pastry, mix the flour, salt, suet and butter together in a large bowl and make a well in the centre. Mix in enough water (about 150ml) to form a smooth dough and knead for a minute.

Spoon the cooled filling into 4 individual pie dishes (or 1 large dish) to about 1cm from the rim. Roll the pastry out on a floured surface to a 7–8mm thickness. Cut out 4 discs to make pie lids (or one large lid for a big pie), about 2cm larger all the way around the pie dish(es). Brush the edges of the pastry with a little of the beaten egg.

Lay the pastry over the filling, pressing the egg-washed sides onto the rim of the dish(es). Cut a 2cm circle in the centre but leave in position on top of the pie(s). Let rest in a cool place for 30 minutes.

Preheat the oven to 200°C/gas mark 6. Brush the pie(s) with beaten egg and bake for 30–35 minutes (or 40–50 minutes for a large one) until the pastry is golden. Meanwhile, for the parsley crust, melt the butter in a pan, mix in the breadcrumbs and parsley, and season with salt and pepper.

Once the pie(s) are ready, remove the pastry circle(s) in the centre and pop in the shucked oysters. Return to the oven for 10 minutes. In the meantime, heat the grill. Scatter the parsley crust over the oysters in their half-shell and grill until golden. Place over the hole in the pie and serve.

# CORNISH PASTIES

FOR THE PASTRY
500g plain flour, plus extra for dusting
2 tsp salt
125g butter, chilled and diced
125g lard, chilled and diced
a little milk, to mix
1 medium egg, beaten

FOR THE FILLING
200g swede, peeled
200g large potatoes, peeled
sea salt and freshly ground black pepper
250ml dark meat stock (see page 292)
500g rump or frying steak
1 tbsp vegetable oil
1 large onion, peeled and finely chopped
1 tbsp Worcestershire sauce
1 tsp chopped thyme leaves

MAKES 6–8

To make the filling, cut the swede and potatoes roughly into 2cm pieces and cook separately in boiling salted water until just tender. Drain and leave to cool. Meanwhile, boil the dark meat stock in a pan to reduce right down to 2–3 tablespoons. Trim any fat from the steak, then cut into 5mm pieces, or coarsely mince.

Heat the oil in a large heavy-based pan and gently cook the onion until translucent, then add the meat and cook over a high heat, turning, until evenly browned. Add the reduced stock, Worcestershire sauce, thyme and some seasoning, and cook over a medium heat until the stock has almost totally reduced. Set aside to cool.

To make the pastry, mix the flour and salt together, then rub in the butter and lard with your fingers, or using a food processor, until the texture of fine breadcrumbs. Mix in enough milk to give a smooth dough which leaves the sides of the bowl clean.

Roll out the pastry on a lightly floured surface to a 3mm thickness and cut out 6 circles, about 18cm in diameter, using a plate or bowl as a template.

Add the vegetables to the cooled meat, mix well and adjust the seasoning. Spoon the filling evenly along the middle of the pastry discs, then brush around the edges with beaten egg. Bring the edges of the pastry up over the filling and crimp the edges together with your fingers. Brush with beaten egg and cut a small slit in the top for steam to escape. Chill for about 30 minutes. Meanwhile, preheat the oven to 200°C/gas mark 6.

Bake for 20 minutes, then turn the oven down to 180°C/gas mark 4 and cook for another 20 minutes or so until golden. If they are browning too fast, cover them with foil or greaseproof paper.

" Cornwall's famous pasties were originally made for miners, farmers and children to take to work or school, though fillings would vary depending on the wealth of the household. Some would only contain swede, potato and onion, plus some leek, and perhaps ham off-cuts. "

## SLOW-ROAST BREAST OF VEAL WITH ONION AND ROSEMARY SAUCE

1 breast of veal, about 1.5–2kg
sea salt and freshly ground black pepper
3–4 tbsp cold-pressed rapeseed oil
100g butter, in pieces
1 tbsp fennel seeds, lightly pounded with a pestle and mortar or chopped
a handful of rosemary leaves
10–12 garlic cloves, peeled and roughly chopped

FOR THE SAUCE
a couple of generous knobs of butter
3 medium onions, peeled and finely chopped
½ tbsp chopped rosemary leaves
200ml double cream

SERVES 4

Preheat the oven to 180°C/gas mark 4. Season the veal breast. Heat a little of the oil in a frying pan and brown the veal breast on both sides over a high heat. Transfer to a roasting tray, spoon over the rest of the oil and dot with the butter. Sprinkle the fennel, rosemary and garlic over the meat. Cover with foil and cook in the oven for an hour.

Remove the foil, baste the joint with the pan juices and continue cooking, uncovered, for another hour or until the veal is very tender, basting occasionally.

Meanwhile, to make the sauce, melt the butter in a pan and add the onions. Cover and cook very gently without colouring over a low heat for 5–6 minutes, stirring every so often, until they are very soft. Add the rosemary and cream, season and simmer until the liquor has reduced by about half. Ladle out a third of the sauce into a blender and purée until smooth, then return to the pan. Re-season if necessary and keep warm.

Either serve the veal as a whole joint and carve it at the table, serving the sauce separately, or carve it in the kitchen and serve on warmed plates with the sauce poured over.

Breast of veal isn't often cooked whole – it is most frequently sold minced or diced as pie veal – but it is delicious slow-cooked. A 1.5–2kg breast on the bone should be enough to feed four.

## BOILED SALT BEEF WITH CARROTS AND DUMPLINGS

1kg salted silverside or brisket, soaked overnight in cold water
4 small onions, each about 80–100g, peeled
12 young carrots, trimmed and scraped
10 black peppercorns
a few sprigs of thyme
2 cloves
2 blades of mace
1 bay leaf

FOR THE HORSERADISH DUMPLINGS
125g plain flour, sieved, plus extra for dusting
1 tsp baking powder
½ tsp salt
65g shredded beef suet
1 tbsp chopped flat-leaf parsley
1 tbsp freshly grated horseradish

SERVES 4

Drain the beef and rinse under cold water. Put in a large pan with the vegetables and flavourings. Cover with water to about 5-6cm above the beef. Bring to the boil. Skim and simmer, covered, for 30 minutes.

Remove the carrots and put to one side. Simmer for another 30 minutes, or until the onions are cooked, remove them and put with the carrots. Continue cooking the beef for an hour or so. Cooking times will vary depending on the size of the beef; if it's prepacked, cooking times will normally be given. When the beef is cooked, remove it from the pan and keep warm, reserving the cooking liquor.

Meanwhile, make the dumplings: mix all the ingredients with enough cold water to form a sticky dough. Flour your hands and roll into 12 little balls. Transfer some of the cooking liquid to another pan and poach the dumplings for 10 minutes. Remove the dumplings and discard the dumpling liquid.

Simmer the rest of the cooking liquor until reduced by half, or until it has a good strong flavour. Skim off any fat. It shouldn't need seasoning.

To serve, reheat the vegetables and dumplings in the reduced liquid. Slice the beef and arrange in a deep plate with the dumplings and vegetables and spoon over the liquid.

" This dish was a great favourite in London pubs, taverns and eating houses: many old London music hall songs refer to boiled beef and carrots, and it is still one of the city's best dishes. We often serve it on the menu in our restaurants, as it is actually very light. It can be made with other vegetables, like young leeks and turnips, according to what's in season. "

# SPICED BEEF

1.5-2kg piece of boned and rolled brisket, topside,
    or thick flank
80g sea salt
10g saltpetre
15g black peppercorns, coarsely ground
15g ground allspice
15g juniper berries, ground
50g dark brown sugar, like muscovado

SERVES 4–6

66 Sometimes referred to as 'huntsman's
beef', this was a popular dish all over
Britain. For centuries, beef would have
been preserved by salting and this is
more than likely a development of this
process when spices – at one time an
expensive commodity – were imported. 99

About two weeks before you need it, put the beef in a close-fitting casserole dish, stainless steel saucepan or plastic container. Mix all of the remaining ingredients together and rub into the beef. Cover and leave in the fridge for 10-12 days, turning it once or twice a day.

Preheat the oven to 150°C/gas mark 2. Wipe the marinade off the beef, rinse out the casserole dish, then put the beef back into it or an ovenproof pot with lid. Put a couple of layers of foil over the dish, then fit the lid tightly. Cook for 3 hours, then remove from the oven and leave to cool for 3 hours.

Remove the beef and wipe dry with kitchen paper. Wrap the beef in cling film and put into a clean dish with a weight on top and refrigerate for 24 hours.

Rewrap and keep in the fridge for up to 3 weeks. Serve thinly sliced, with pickles or in a sandwich.

Saltpetre is a crystalline powder used for curing meats. It can be difficult to get hold of nowadays, as it is normally only used for charcuterie, but you should be able to find it online or in some independent chemists.

# BRAISED OXTAIL WITH SUMMER VEGETABLES

1.5kg oxtail, cut into 2–3cm pieces and trimmed of fat
sea salt and freshly ground black pepper
50g plain flour, plus extra for dusting
a little vegetable oil, for oiling
60g butter, plus an extra generous knob
1 onion, peeled and finely chopped
2 garlic cloves, peeled and crushed
1 tsp chopped thyme leaves
2 tsp tomato purée
100ml red wine
2 litres dark meat stock (see page 292)
250g small carrots, such as Chantenay, trimmed
60g podded peas
90–100g podded broad beans
½ tbsp chopped flat-leaf parsley

SERVES 4

Preheat the oven to 220°C/gas mark 7. Season the oxtail and dust lightly with flour. Place in a lightly oiled roasting tray and roast for 30 minutes, turning halfway through to colour nicely on both sides. Lower the oven to 160°C/gas mark 3.

Meanwhile, heat the butter in a large ovenproof pan. Add the onion, garlic and thyme and cook gently for 3–4 minutes until soft, stirring. Add the flour and purée and stir. Slowly add the wine and stock, stirring to avoid lumps from forming. Bring to the boil. Add the oxtail and coat in the liquor.

Cover with a tight-fitting lid and put in the oven for 2 hours. It should be tender and easily removed from the bone; if not, cook for a further hour.

Skim the fat off the sauce. If the sauce is not thick enough, strain it into another pan and simmer briskly until reduced and thickened, skimming every so often, then pour back over the meat.

Shortly before serving, cook the carrots, peas and broad beans separately in boiling salted water until tender. Remove the tough skins from larger beans.

To serve, melt a knob of butter in a pan, add the carrots, peas and beans and toss over a low heat to glaze, then season and add the parsley. Divide the oxtail between warmed plates, spoon over the sauce and serve with the glazed vegetables.

# COW HEEL AND BLACK PEAS

475g beef shin, cut into rough 3cm cubes
sea salt and freshly ground black pepper
1 tbsp vegetable oil
2 large onions, peeled and sliced
1 cow heel on the bone, cut into 8–10 pieces
400g black peas, soaked overnight
3 litres dark meat stock (see page 292)

SERVES 6–8

Lightly season the pieces of beef and fry on a high heat in the vegetable oil for 3–4 minutes until browned all over. Remove the meat from the pan and put to one side. Add the onions and cook over a low heat for 2–3 minutes until softened.

Put the beef, onions, cow heel, peas and stock into a large heavy saucepan, bring to the boil and simmer gently for 2½ hours until the beef is tender. The cow heel should have broken down by now and the liquid reduced and thickened. Adjust the seasoning, if necessary, and serve.

If you have any left after the meal, it can be set in a container and eaten like brawn.

"This recipe is from some friends of mine, Annette and Barry Broadhurst. They serve this and tripe at their annual festive bash, which happens between Christmas and New Year, along with the usual festive goodies, and it's quite delicious. The trickiest part of the dish is finding the black peas (try an Asian supermarket), also known as maple peas or carlings, which are more traditionally eaten at Easter, rather like pease pudding."

# DUBLIN CODDLE

8 good-quality pork sausages
8 rashers of rindless streaky bacon
2–3 tbsp vegetable oil, for frying
3 small onions, peeled and thinly sliced
1 tsp chopped tansy, sage or rosemary
6 baking potatoes, peeled and thinly sliced
1 litre (or enough to cover) dark meat or chicken
    stock (see pages 292–293)
250ml dry cider

SERVES 4

Preheat the oven to 220°C/ gas mark 7 and heat
the grill to hot. Grill the sausages and bacon until
cooked and put to one side.

Heat a heavy frying pan with some vegetable oil and
fry the onions for 5–10 minutes over a medium heat
until lightly coloured. Mix in the herbs and now
you're ready to assemble the coddle.

Take an ovenproof casserole dish that has a lid or
similar, cover the bottom with a layer of potatoes,
followed by the onions with a little stock and cider,
then another layer of potatoes and onions. Continue
until all the onions and potatoes have been used,
finishing the top with a layer of nicely overlapping
potato slices.

Cook in the oven for 35–45 minutes, then arrange
the sausages and bacon on the potatoes. Pour the
rest of the cider over and cook for another 15–20
minutes. Turn the oven off and keep warm until
needed or serve immediately.

Versions of this dish seem to crop up all
over the world. If you want to transport
a hot feast for, say, a fishing or hunting
trip, then this is perfect, just pop it into
one of those takeaway containers or
even in stacking tiffin boxes.

# BACON CHOP WITH RED CABBAGE AND PRUNES

4 bacon chops, each about 180–200g
a couple of good knobs of butter
1 large red onion, peeled and thinly sliced
1 small head of red cabbage, quartered, root removed
    and very finely shredded
sea salt and freshly ground black pepper
1 tsp redcurrant jelly
8 no-need-to-soak prunes, pitted and shredded
vegetable oil, for frying

SERVES 4

Add the bacon chops to a pan of cold water, bring
to the boil and blanch for 6–7 minutes, then drain.

Heat the butter in a large saucepan, add the red
onion and cook gently for 3–4 minutes until soft.
Add the cabbage, season with salt and pepper and
cover with the lid. Cook over a very low heat for 10
minutes, stirring every so often. Add the redcurrant
jelly and prunes and continue to cook, covered, for a
further 10–15 minutes, stirring every so often, until
the cabbage is soft. Taste and adjust the seasoning
if necessary and keep warm.

Heat a little oil in a large heavy-based frying pan
and fry the bacon chops for about 4–5 minutes on
each side until golden brown and tender. Remove
and drain on kitchen paper.

Spoon the red cabbage and prunes onto warm
serving plates and place a bacon chop alongside.
Serve at once.

Home-cured bacon chops would be
ideal here, but otherwise ask your
butcher if he can lay his hands on a
piece of smoked streaky or back bacon
with the bone in. Thick pieces of bacon
like this tend to be a bit on the salty
side, so I recommend blanching first.

“I tried this at home one night after I had been on an experimental bacon curing session. Red cabbage and raisins is a classic pairing, so I thought why not add prunes as they have something of an affiliation with bacon in classic French cooking. It worked a treat!”

# SLOW-COOKED PORK BELLY WITH AUTUMN SQUASH

1 piece of boneless pork belly with rind, about 1–1.5kg
sea salt and freshly ground black pepper
a few sprigs of rosemary, chopped
1 tbsp crushed fennel seeds
cold-pressed rapeseed oil, for basting
1kg mixed squashes, such as acorn, onion and
    butternut
apple sauce, to serve

SERVES 4

Preheat the oven to 230°C/gas mark 8. Put the pork belly in a large roasting tray with the rind down and pour in about a 2cm depth of water. Place on the hob and bring to the boil, then lower the heat and simmer for a couple of minutes. Remove from the heat and pour off the water. Using a Stanley knife or a razor-sharp knife, score lines about 5mm apart across the pork belly rind.

Season the pork belly with salt and pepper, then rub the rosemary and fennel seeds into the scored rind and over the flesh. Spoon over a little rapeseed oil and roast for 30 minutes. Turn the oven down to 180°C/gas mark 4 and cook for a further 1½ hours, basting the meat every so often and draining off excess fat from the tin.

Meanwhile, prepare the squashes. Peel those with thicker skins. Cut all of them into even-sized chunks and wedges, discarding the seeds and fibrous bits. Season the squash and tip into the roasting tray around the pork. Spoon over some of the pork fat in the tray and roast for about another hour, basting every so often.

To serve, cut the pork into 1cm thick slices and arrange on warm plates or a large serving dish with the roasted squash. Accompany with the apple sauce.

66 Pork belly is one of the tastiest cuts to slow roast, especially if you can get your hands on a rare breed like Saddleback, Old Spot or Middle White. Their bellies may look a little more fatty, but the fat renders down during cooking, to give you a very fine piece of roast meat. Ask your butcher to remove the bones, which can be cooked as spare ribs or used as a trivet to cook the pork on. 99

# POT-ROAST GLOUCESTERSHIRE OLD SPOT PORK LOIN WITH SCRUMPY

1 piece of Gloucestershire Old Spot pork loin, boned, about 1.5–2kg
sea salt and freshly ground black pepper
1 onion, peeled and roughly chopped
1 carrot, peeled and roughly chopped
1 celery stalk, roughly chopped
a few sprigs of thyme
300ml scrumpy or dry cider

FOR THE CELERIAC AND APPLE MASH
1 celeriac, peeled and roughly chopped
60g butter
3 cooking apples, peeled, cored and roughly chopped
1 tbsp brown sugar

SERVES 4

❝A well-sourced piece of pork really needs very little doing to it, and a good layer of fat should not put you off, because that's where a lot of the flavour lies. The fat melts away during slow cooking, so you can drain off excess as the cooking progresses and use it another time.❞

Preheat the oven to 220°C/gas mark 7. Remove the pork rind with a razor-sharp knife. Score the fat in a criss-cross with the knife, season and cook the pork in a roasting tray for 30 minutes, turning halfway. Lower the oven to 160°C/gas mark 3, add the vegetables and thyme and return to the oven. Spoon some cider over the meat every so often until it's all used, and drain away any excess fat into a container during cooking. Cook fat side up for the last 45 minutes.

Towards the end of that time, make the celeriac and apple mash: cook the celeriac in boiling salted water for 10-12 minutes until tender. Drain and coarsely mash.

While the celeriac is cooking, melt the butter in a pan, add the apples and sugar, cover and cook for 10-12 minutes, stirring occasionally, until the apples are falling apart. If the mixture is wet, remove the lid and cook for a few minutes more over a low heat until it dries a little. Mix with the celeriac mash and season to taste.

Cut the pork into thick slices and serve with the mash.

If you wish, you can make a gravy by adding half a tablespoon of flour to the vegetables in the roasting pan and then stirring in some chicken stock and simmering for 15 minutes or so. With a cut like this I prefer to keep it natural, as the meat is moist and the mash really does the job of a sauce here.

# CAWL

1 smoked ham hock, soaked overnight and rinsed well

1 neck of lamb or mutton, cut into chunks

2 onions, peeled and roughly chopped

10 black peppercorns

2 garlic cloves, peeled and sliced

a few sprigs of thyme

1 bay leaf

3 carrots, peeled and cut into rough chunks

2 medium leeks, halved, roughly chopped and
   well rinsed

1 small swede, peeled and cut into rough chunks

2 tbsp roughly chopped flat-leaf parsley

sea salt and freshly ground black pepper

SERVES 4

"There is no precise translation for the word 'cawl'; in Welsh, it signifies a soup or broth, but is actually much more of a meal in itself, a classic one-pot dish, originally cooked in an iron pot over an open fire. Recipes for cawl vary from region to region, village to village, even house to house, and ingredients will be added according to what's in season. In some cases, the broth would be served first and the meat and vegetables served as the main course, rather like a French pot-au-feu. I often make a soupy broth like this at home if I have cooked a ham hock, as I just hate wasting anything that I can turn into another dish."

Put the ham hock, lamb, onions, peppercorns, garlic, thyme and bay leaf into a large pan, cover well with cold water and bring to the boil. Skim and simmer for 1½ hours.

Add the carrots, leeks and swede, and continue cooking for another hour, or until the meat is tender.

Add the parsley, taste and adjust the seasoning and simmer for a further 10 minutes.

Remove the ham from the bone in chunks and serve with pieces of lamb and vegetables, and the liquid.

# HAM HOCK WITH PEASE PUDDING AND TEWKESBURY MUSTARD SAUCE

4 small unsmoked ham hocks or knuckles, about
   800g each, soaked overnight in cold water
   to remove any excess salt
1 onion, peeled and roughly chopped
2 carrots, peeled and roughly chopped
1 bay leaf
5 cloves
1 tsp black peppercorns
120g dried yellow split peas, soaked overnight
   in cold water
a generous knob of butter

FOR THE MUSTARD SAUCE
30g butter
2 large shallots, peeled and finely chopped
20g plain flour
1 tbsp Tewkesbury mustard, or more to taste
sea salt and freshly ground white pepper
2 tbsp double cream
1 tbsp chopped flat-leaf parsley

SERVES 4

Drain the ham hocks, rinse in cold water and put them into a large cooking pot with the onion, carrots, bay leaf, cloves and peppercorns. Add enough cold water to cover generously and bring to the boil. Skim any scum off the surface and simmer gently, covered, for 1 hour.

Drain the split peas, tie them loosely in a piece of muslin and add to the cooking pot. Top up with more water if necessary. Continue to simmer for another hour, then lift out the bag of peas and check that they have turned into a chunky purée by pressing the bag between your fingers. Check the hocks as well to see whether the meat is tender and coming away from the bone. If either the meat or peas are not quite ready, simmer for a little longer. Once done, leave to cool.

To make the sauce, melt the butter in a heavy-based pan and add the shallots. Cook gently over a low heat for a few minutes until soft. Add the flour and mustard and cook, stirring, for a minute, then gradually add 300ml of the ham cooking liquor, stirring with a whisk to avoid forming any lumps. Bring to the boil and season.

Simmer the sauce for about 20 minutes, stirring every so often. It should be quite thick by now; if not, simmer a little longer. Stir in the cream and parsley. Taste and adjust the seasoning if necessary and add a little more mustard if you think it is needed. Simmer for another minute or so; keep warm.

Once the ham hocks are cool enough to handle, lift them out of the pan, reserving the liquor, and cut off the outer layer of fat with a knife. Carefully remove the smaller bone by twisting and pulling it out, leaving the larger bone attached. (If the hocks are a bit large you can cut off some of the meat at this stage for a salad, soup or sandwiches if you like.)

To serve, reheat the ham hocks in the reserved cooking liquor. Meanwhile, reheat the pease pudding with the butter, adding a little water if it seems too thick. Season with pepper to taste and a little salt if needed.

Drain the ham hocks and place in warmed deep plates with a portion of pease pudding. Spoon the mustard sauce over the meat and serve.

**"** This is old-fashioned cooking at its best. Your butcher should be able to supply you with some ham hocks or knuckles relatively cheaply. They have a fantastic flavour and you'll end up with a flavourful stock base for a soup. **"**

"A few years ago I bought some lovely metal skewers (pictured) from my favourite cookshop in Paris – E. Dehillerin in rue Coquillière. They are perfect for this robust pork dish, which we serve in the restaurant on bespoke wooden boards with grooves to catch the juices."

# MIXED GRILL OF PORK

150g minced pork (with about 20% fat)
100g black pudding, finely chopped
sea salt and freshly ground black pepper
200–250g pork loin fillet or tenderloin
200–250g shoulder or neck fillet of pork
2 pig's kidneys, trimmed
150g pig's liver
vegetable oil, for brushing
a generous knob of butter
a few sprigs of rosemary
crackling, to serve
350g apple sauce, to serve

SERVES 4

In a bowl, mix the minced pork with the black pudding and season well. Divide into 4 portions, flatten and shape into patties. Cover and place in the fridge. Cut the pork loin into 4 similar-sized chunks; do the same with the pork shoulder, kidneys and liver. Season all of the meat.

Heat a griddle pan or heavy frying pan and lightly oil it. Cook the pork patties and pieces of meat and offal in batches as necessary, for about 3–4 minutes on each side, keeping them slightly pink. The liver and kidney will need less time, just 1–2 minutes.

Heat the butter and rosemary in a separate pan until foaming and remove from the heat. Thread the meat onto skewers or simply arrange on warmed plates. Trickle the butter over the meat and serve, with some crackling and apple sauce.

This recipe involves lots of different bits of the pig, but you can really use whatever cuts and offal you fancy. You can also always cook some pork crackling to add to the boards.

# PORK PIES

FOR THE FILLING
1kg boned shoulder of pork (about 20–30% fat),
    cut into rough 1cm dice
sea salt and freshly ground black pepper

FOR THE HOT-WATER CRUST PASTRY
500g plain flour, plus extra for dusting
½ tsp salt
175g lard
1 egg, beaten

MAKES 6–8 SMALL PIES

First prepare the filling: keep aside some of the best bits of pork and mince or finely chop the rest. Season well and mix in the diced meat. Take a small teaspoonful of the mixture and fry it to check the seasoning, then adjust it if necessary. Preheat the oven to 200°C/gas mark 6.

For the pastry, mix the flour and salt in a bowl and make a well. Bring 200ml water and the lard to the boil in a saucepan, then gradually stir into the flour with a wooden spoon to form a smooth dough. Cover for 15 minutes or so, until it can be handled.

Divide the dough into 6-8 equal pieces. Take one of the balls of dough and divide it into 2 balls, one twice the size of the other. Roll the larger piece on a lightly floured table to about 12–14cm in diameter. Use the smaller piece to make another circle about half the size for the top. Put some of the filling in the centre of the larger circle, lay the smaller circle on top and raise the sides of the larger one up, then pinch the lid and the top of the sides together with your fingers. If it looks a bit of a mess, you can reshape it, as the pastry is quite pliable. Repeat with the rest of the pastry and filling.

Place on a baking tray and brush the pies all over with the egg. Cook them for 35-40 minutes. If they are colouring too much, cover them with foil and turn the oven down. Serve warm or cold.

I prefer to eat these warm rather than cold – they are more flavoursome and the pastry is crisper. You can also add seasonings like anchovy essence, mace or allspice and a bit of sage – it's entirely up to you. These are delicious with the piccalilli on page 54.

# PORK AND BLENHEIM ORANGE APPLE PIE

FOR THE HOT-WATER CRUST PASTRY
500g plain flour, plus extra for dusting
1 tsp salt
175g lard
1 egg, beaten

FOR THE FILLING
400g minced pork (about 30% fat), such as from
   the belly
1 tsp chopped thyme leaves
grated zest of 2 oranges
sea salt and freshly ground black pepper
3–4 Blenheim Orange apples or another tasty variety

FOR THE JELLY
6g of leaf gelatine (2 sheets)
150ml chicken stock (see page 293)

TO SERVE
piccalilli (see page 54) or redcurrant jelly

MAKES 1 LARGE OR 6 SMALL PIES

To make the pastry, mix the flour and salt together in a bowl and make a well in the centre. Bring 200ml water and the lard to the boil in a pan, then pour into the well and stir with a wooden spoon to form a smooth dough. Cover the dough with a cloth and leave for about 15 minutes until it is cool enough to handle.

Preheat the oven to 200ºC/gas mark 6. For the filling, in a bowl, mix the minced pork together with the thyme and orange zest. Season well. Peel, core and slice the apples.

If you are using a large pie mould (or perhaps two smaller moulds), roll out two-thirds of the pastry on a lightly floured surface and use to line the mould(s). Layer the pork mixture in the mould(s) alternating with one or two layers of apple slices. Roll out the rest of the pastry to make pie lid(s). Lay on top of the pie(s) and press the pastry edges together with your fingers to seal. If you intend to serve them cold (with jelly), cut a 1cm hole in the centre of the pastry lid.

If you are making individual pies, roll out a ball of dough on a lightly floured surface to a 12–14cm diameter. Roll out another round, about half the size, for the top. Spoon some pork filling into the centre of the larger round and put a few apple slices in the middle. Lay the smaller round on top. Now raise the sides of the larger round up to meet the lid and pinch the edges together with your fingers. If it looks a bit misshapen, you can reshape it as the pastry is quite pliable.

Brush the pie(s) all over with the egg and bake until a skewer inserted in the centre feels hot when removed – allow 35–40 minutes for individual pies; 50–55 minutes for larger pies. If the pie(s) are colouring too quickly, cover loosely with foil and turn the oven down.

Place the cooked pie(s) on a wire rack. If serving warm, leave to stand for 5–10 minutes.

If serving cold, allow the pie(s) to cool, then chill overnight. The following day, soak the gelatine leaves in cold water to cover for a few minutes. Meanwhile, bring the stock to a simmer. Remove the stock from the heat, squeeze the gelatine leaves to remove the excess water, then add to the hot stock and stir until fully dissolved. Leave to cool, but do not let it set. Pour the jelly into the pies to reach the top and return to the fridge to set. To serve, carefully remove the pie(s) from the moulds if using. Serve warm or cold, ideally with homemade piccalilli or redcurrant jelly if you prefer.

"Homemade pies are so much better than shop-bought ones and you can bespoke the filling to suit what's in season. Don't be put off if you haven't got a mincer at home – just chop the meat up very finely by hand, or ask a helpful butcher to mince it for you. I used Blenheim Orange apples, which I scrumped from Simon Kelner's back garden right next to Blenheim palace, but you could use any other flavourful seasonal apple. I have included a method for jellying the pie(s) so that you can serve them cold if you like."

## TRIPE AND ONIONS

40g butter
4 medium onions, peeled and thinly sliced
1 tsp chopped fresh thyme
30g plain flour
4 tbsp white wine or dry cider
1 litre chicken stock (see page 293)
1kg fresh tripe, preferably natural and untreated,
    washed and cut into 6–8cm pieces
sea salt and freshly ground white pepper
2 tbsp double cream
mashed potato, to serve

SERVES 4

Melt the butter in a heavy-based pan, add the
onions and thyme, cover and cook gently until
the onions are soft. If they begin to colour, add a
tablespoon of water to the pan and stir well.

Stir in the flour and cook over a low heat for another
minute. Gradually add the wine or cider and the
stock, stirring constantly. Bring to the boil, add the
tripe and seasoning and simmer gently for 1 hour
until tender. Add a little more stock or water if the
sauce gets too thick. Different types of tripe will
have different cooking times, so keep an eye on it
and cook it for a bit longer or shorter as necessary.

Finish by stirring in the cream and adjust the
seasoning if necessary. Serve with mashed potato.

## GRILLED OX LIVER WITH CREAMED MUSTARD ONIONS

4 slices of ox liver, each about 120g and 5mm thick
50g butter
4 large onions, peeled and thinly sliced
sea salt and freshly ground black pepper
2 tsp English mustard
4 tbsp double cream
vegetable oil, for brushing

SERVES 4

Trim the ox liver, removing any sinews. Melt half
the butter in a heavy pan, add the onions and cook
gently with the lid on for about 8-10 minutes until
they are really soft, stirring every so often. Season
and stir in the mustard. Add 2 to 3 tablespoons of
water and simmer until evaporated. Pour in the
cream and simmer very gently, stirring every so
often, until it just binds the onions. Cover with a
lid and keep warm.

Heat a griddle pan until almost smoking. Season
the liver and brush with oil. Griddle for about 30
seconds on each side so that it stays nice and pink,
then serve on top of the creamed onions.

The creamed onions here make a great
accompaniment to other offal, such
as lamb's or calf's kidneys, as well as
simply grilled steaks. They are also
good with salt beef.

“Being a chef, I'd always been obsessed with cooking expensive calf's liver from Holland. I then discovered that ordinary beef liver has similar eating qualities – it doesn't need to be stewed for hours, as our parents and grandparents used to. In fact most offal can cope with brief flash-frying or grilling. You will pay next to nothing for ox liver, as butchers tend to think it has little value.”

# BRAISED FAGGOTS WITH PEAS

2 medium onions, peeled and finely chopped

1 tbsp vegetable oil

1 garlic clove, peeled and crushed

½ tsp ground mace

1 tsp chopped fresh sage

1 tsp chopped fresh thyme

400g pork liver, coarsely minced or chopped
in a food processor

250g pork mince, with a good proportion of fat

100–150g fresh white breadcrumbs

100–120g caul fat, well washed (optional)

olive oil, for roasting

FOR THE PEAS AND GRAVY

100g dried green peas, soaked in plenty of cold
water overnight and drained

sea salt and freshly ground black pepper

2 large onions, peeled and finely chopped

1 tbsp vegetable oil

30g butter

30g plain flour

½ tsp tomato purée

1 litre dark meat stock (see page 292)

a few drops of Worcestershire sauce

SERVES 4

First prepare the peas and gravy: drain the peas, rinse them well and cook in lightly salted water for about 45 minutes, or until tender. It's difficult to put an exact cooking time on dried pulses, as you never know how long they've been dried, so you may have to be patient on cooking times.

Meanwhile, gently cook the onions in the oil in a covered pan for 5 minutes or so until soft. Turn up the heat and allow the onions to colour. Add the butter and then stir in the flour, and cook over a low heat for a minute or so. Add the tomato purée, stir well and gradually add the stock, stirring well to avoid any lumps. Bring to the boil, season with Worcestershire sauce, salt and pepper and simmer for 1 hour on a low heat. Remove from the heat and add the peas.

Also, while the peas are cooking, start to prepare the faggots: gently cook the onions over a low heat in the oil, together with the garlic, mace, sage and thyme, for about 4-5 minutes. Remove from the heat and leave to cool.

Mix the pork liver and minced pork together with the breadcrumbs and cooked onion mixture, and season with salt and pepper. Divide the mixture into 4 balls and refrigerate for 30-40 minutes.

If you are not using caul fat, wrap each faggot in cling film a couple of times and steam them over a pan of simmering water in a steamer or a colander for 20 minutes, then leave to cool.

If you have caul fat, rinse it well under cold running water for about 10 minutes and pat dry on some kitchen paper. Lay it out on a table and cut it into 12 rough squares big enough to wrap around each ball of meat a couple of times, then carefully wrap them up in it.

Preheat the oven to 220°C/gas mark 7. Lightly oil a deep roasting tray and put the faggots in it, with the join of the caul fat on the undersides. Roast for about 20-30 minutes, until they are lightly coloured. Then drain off any excess oil from the tin and pour in the peas and gravy. Turn the oven setting down to 160°C/gas mark 3, cover with foil or a lid and braise them for about 1 hour. If you are not using caul fat, unwrap the faggots and roast and braise as above. Serve the faggots with the peas spooned over and around them.

The wrapping of caul fat, the lacy-thin marbled membrane that lines the pig's stomach, keeps the filling wonderfully moist. It's not a general stock item for most butchers nowadays, so you will need to pre-order some.

# ROAST CAULIFLOWER WITH DEVILLED LAMB'S KIDNEYS

1 small cauliflower, trimmed
sea salt and freshly ground black pepper
100g butter
plain flour, for dusting
14 lamb's kidneys, halved and sinews removed

FOR THE SAUCE
4 shallots, peeled and finely chopped
6–10 black peppercorns, coarsely crushed
a good pinch of cayenne pepper
3 tbsp cider vinegar
40g butter
2 tsp plain flour
200ml dark meat stock (see page 292)
1 tsp English mustard
2 tbsp double cream
8 small gherkins, finely chopped

SERVES 4

Preheat the oven to 200°C/gas mark 6. Cook the cauliflower whole in boiling salted water for about 8 minutes. Drain in a colander, then place under cold running water for a few minutes until cool, then drain well. Trim the ends from the cauliflower and cut into four 1.5cm thick slices.

Melt half of the butter in a frying pan until foaming. Meanwhile, dust the cauliflower with flour and season well. Pan-fry, in two batches if necessary, over a high heat for a couple of minutes on each side until nicely coloured. Then place in the oven to finish cooking for 10 minutes (if your pan isn't ovenproof or big enough, transfer the cauliflower to a roasting pan).

Meanwhile, make the sauce. Put the shallots, peppercorns and cayenne in a saucepan with the vinegar and 3 tablespoons of water. Simmer gently until the liquid has almost totally evaporated, then add the butter and stir in the flour. Gradually add the stock, stirring to prevent lumps from forming. Season lightly and add the mustard. Simmer gently for 10–12 minutes. Add the cream and continue to simmer until the sauce is of a thick, gravy-like consistency. Add the gherkins and keep warm.

When ready to serve, season the kidneys. Melt the rest of the butter in a heavy-based frying pan. When hot, add the kidneys and cook over a high heat for a couple of minutes on each side, keeping them pink. Drain and add to the sauce. Simmer for 20 seconds or so.

Pat the cauliflower dry with some kitchen paper, then place a slab on each warm serving plate. Spoon the kidneys and sauce on top and serve straight away.

"Pan-roasting a slab of cauliflower is an ingenious way to serve it. Ray Driver, my old sous chef at Le Caprice, came up with the idea some years ago and it went down a treat. You can use a piece of cauliflower like this as a base for all sorts of meaty dishes, but I reckon its caramelised sweetness is best suited to offal."

# LIVERPOOL LOBSCOUSE

50g beef dripping or 3 tbsp vegetable oil
750g neck of lamb fillet or shin of beef, cut into rough
    2cm cubes
sea salt and freshly ground black pepper
1 large onion, peeled and chopped
3 carrots, peeled and roughly chopped
500g medium potatoes, quartered
200g dried peas, soaked in cold water overnight,
    drained and rinsed
a few sprigs of thyme
2 litres dark meat stock (see page 292)
50g pearl barley

SERVES 4–6

Melt the dripping or heat the oil in a heavy-based
saucepan. Season the meat and fry quickly on a
high heat until nicely coloured all over.

Add the rest of the ingredients, bring to the boil,
lightly season and simmer gently for 2–2½ hours
until the meat is tender. Serve.

**"** I just love the name of this dish. Perhaps the original
version, made with salted meat, was eaten by seamen
in the days of sail ships and they dreamt of eating
lobster. The more down-to-earth reality is that it's a
sort of typical poor man's meat and vegetable stew
with pulses to bulk it out – and it's why Liverpudlians
are known as Scousers. The modern-day version of
this dish can be made with any stewing meat, ideally
cuts like shin of beef and neck of lamb to give the
broth a rich flavour. It is incredibly easy, economical
and tasty too. Serve it with some buttery cabbage or
mashed root vegetables. **"**

# LAMB'S SWEETBREADS WITH RUNNER BEANS, BACON AND MUSHROOMS

300–400g lamb's sweetbreads
sea salt and freshly ground black pepper
250–300g runner beans, trimmed
100g butter
120g unsmoked streaky bacon, cut into 5mm cubes
150g girolles or other wild mushrooms, cleaned
1 tbsp cold-pressed rapeseed oil

FOR THE DRESSING
1 small red onion, peeled and finely chopped
3 tbsp cider vinegar
1 tsp Tewkesbury mustard
4 tbsp cold-pressed rapeseed oil

SERVES 4

Put the sweetbreads into a pan of cold salted water,
bring to the boil and lower the heat. Simmer for 2–3
minutes, then drain and leave to cool.

Meanwhile, for the dressing, put the onion, vinegar
and 2 tablespoons of water into a pan and simmer
for 2–3 minutes or until it has reduced by half.
Remove from the heat and whisk in the mustard
and oil. Season with salt and pepper and set aside.

Very finely shred the runner beans lengthways on
a slight angle. Add to a saucepan of boiling salted
water and cook for 30 seconds, then drain in a
colander. Refresh briefly under the cold tap, drain
and pat dry with kitchen paper.

Trim the sweetbreads of any fat and membrane,
then season them. Melt half the butter in a frying
pan and cook the sweetbreads, stirring frequently,
over a fairly high heat for 4–5 minutes until golden.
Drain on kitchen paper and keep warm.

Melt the rest of the butter in the frying pan. Add the
bacon and fry over a medium heat for 2–3 minutes.
Add the mushrooms and cook for 4–5 minutes until
tender, turning every so often and lightly season.

Meanwhile, toss the runner beans in the rapeseed
oil, then add to the dressing to warm and season.

To serve, divide the runner beans between warmed
serving plates and scatter the sweetbreads and
mushrooms over the top. Serve at once.

“This is a lovely light main course, or you could serve it in smaller portions as a starter. Try to buy the plumper sweetbreads from above the heart if you possibly can, as those of the thymus glands in the neck can be a little scraggy.”

# LAMB CUTLETS REFORM

60–70g fresh white breadcrumbs
50g cooked ham (see page 80), very finely chopped
1 tbsp chopped flat-leaf parsley
8 lamb cutlets, French-trimmed and flattened slightly
2 eggs, beaten
vegetable oil, for frying
a good knob of butter

FOR THE SAUCE
2 large shallots, peeled and finely chopped
1 garlic clove, peeled and crushed
a good pinch of cayenne pepper
60g butter
2 tsp plain flour
½ tsp tomato purée
2 tbsp tarragon vinegar
1 tbsp redcurrant jelly
300ml dark meat stock (see page 292)
sea salt and freshly ground black pepper
40g sliced tongue or ham, cut into thin 3cm strips
1 small cooked beetroot, about 70g, peeled and cut into similar-sized strips
2 large gherkins, cut into similar-sized strips
the white of 1 large hard-boiled egg, shredded into similar-sized strips

SERVES 4

First make the sauce: gently cook the shallots, garlic and cayenne pepper in half the butter for 2–3 minutes, stirring every so often. Add the flour and tomato purée, and stir well. Add the vinegar and redcurrant jelly, and simmer for a minute, then gradually add the stock, bring to the boil and simmer very gently for 15 minutes. Season to taste and whisk in the remaining butter.

While the sauce is simmering, mix together the breadcrumbs, ham and parsley. Season the lamb cutlets and pass them through the egg and then the breadcrumbs. Heat a couple of tablespoons of oil in a frying pan over a medium heat and cook the cutlets for 3–4 minutes on each side until golden, adding the butter towards the end of cooking.

Add the sliced tongue, beetroot, gherkin and egg white to the sauce, or mix and serve separately.

# LAMB CHOPS WITH CUCUMBER AND MINT

2 cucumbers
8 lamb loin chops, each about 120–150g
sea salt and freshly ground black pepper
vegetable or corn oil, for brushing
2 tbsp cold-pressed rapeseed oil
2 large shallots, peeled and thinly sliced
a small handful of mint leaves, shredded

SERVES 4

Cut the cucumbers in half lengthways and scoop out the seeds with a teaspoon. Cut each half on an angle into 1–2cm thick slices.

Heat a griddle or heavy-based frying pan over a medium-high heat. Season the lamb chops with salt and pepper, brush with oil and cook for about 5 minutes on each side, keeping them pink.

Meanwhile, heat the rapeseed oil in another frying pan and add the shallots. Fry, stirring, for a minute, then add the cucumber slices. Season with salt and pepper and sauté over a fairly high heat for 2–3 minutes until tender. Take off the heat and stir in the shredded mint.

Divide the cucumber between warmed plates and place the lamb chops on top to serve.

"Cooking cucumbers may seem a bit odd, but it's really no different to cooking courgettes or marrow, and I reckon they have even more flavour."

# MUTTON AND TURNIP HOTPOT

1–1.5kg mutton neck chops
sea salt and freshly ground black pepper
plain flour, for dusting
6 lamb's kidneys, halved and trimmed (optional)
4–5 tbsp vegetable oil
450–500g onions, peeled and thinly sliced
60g unsalted butter, plus exta, melted, for brushing
800ml dark meat stock (see page 292)
1 tsp chopped fresh rosemary
500g large potatoes
500g large turnips

SERVES 4–6

&#10075;&#10075;This is basically a Lancashire hotpot, incorporating turnips as well as potatoes. There are various versions of this traditional dish, but the main ingredient is usually a flavoursome cut of lamb, such as the neck, which is traditionally cut on the bone like chops. I prefer to use mutton, as the end flavour is far better – almost gamey. Kidneys and black pudding are sometimes added to a classic hotpot and, back in the days when they were cheap, a few oysters would have been put under the potato topping near the end of cooking.&#10076;&#10076;

Preheat the oven to 220°C/gas mark 7. Season the mutton chops with salt and pepper and dust with flour. Do the same with the kidneys if you're including them. Heat a heavy-based frying pan and add 2 tablespoons of oil. Fry the chops, a few at a time, over a high heat until nicely coloured, then remove to a colander to drain. If using kidneys, fry them briefly to colour; drain and set aside.

Wipe out the pan, then add another 2 tablespoons of oil and fry the onions over a high heat until they begin to colour. Add the butter and continue to cook for a few minutes until they soften. Dust the onions with a tablespoonful of flour, stir well, then gradually add the stock, stirring to avoid lumps. Sprinkle in the rosemary. Bring to the boil, season, then lower the heat and simmer for about 10 minutes. Peel the potatoes and turnips and cut into 3mm slices.

To assemble, take a deep casserole dish with a lid. Cover the bottom with a layer of potatoes and turnips followed by a layer of meat moistened with a little sauce, then another layer of potatoes and turnips. Continue in this way until the meat and most of the sauce have been used, ending with turnips and finally an overlapping layer of potato slices. Brush the top with a little of the sauce.

Cover and cook in the hot oven for about 30 minutes. Now turn the oven down to 140°C/gas mark 1 and cook slowly for a further 2 hours or until the meat is tender.

Remove the lid and turn the oven back up to 220°C/ gas mark 7. Brush the potato topping with a little melted butter and return to the oven for 15 minutes or so to allow the potatoes to brown.

## BEST END AND BRAISED NECK OF BLACK WELSH MOUNTAIN LAMB

4 neck of lamb steaks, each about 200g, cut through
   the neck about 2cm thick
sea salt and freshly ground black pepper
1 tbsp flour
2 tbsp vegetable oil
a good knob of butter
1 small onion, peeled and finely chopped
1 garlic clove, peeled and crushed
1 tsp chopped fresh rosemary
½ tsp tomato purée
1 litre dark meat stock (see page 292)
1 small leek, trimmed, well rinsed and finely chopped
1 celery stalk, peeled if necessary, finely diced
1 small carrot, peeled and finely diced
8-bone rack of lamb

SERVES 4

Season the neck chops with salt and pepper and lightly flour them with about ½ tablespoon of the flour. Fry them in the oil for about 2–3 minutes on each side over a high heat until nicely coloured.

Melt the butter in a medium heavy-based saucepan and add the onion, garlic and rosemary, and cook over a low heat for 2–3 minutes, stirring occasionally. Stir in the rest of the flour and the tomato purée, then stir in the stock a little at a time.

Add the pieces of lamb, bring to the boil, cover and simmer gently for an hour. Add the leek, celery and carrot, and continue to simmer for another hour, or until the meat is tender. It's difficult to put a cooking time on a cut like this it may well take another 30–40 minutes.

While this is cooking, preheat the oven to 220°C/gas mark 7. Season the best end of lamb and roast it fat side down for 15 minutes, then turn it over and cook for another 10 minutes. Remove and leave to rest in a warm place.

While the rack of lamb is cooking, remove the lamb neck from the cooking liquid, skim off any fat and reduce the liquid until it has reduced and thickened.

Carve the best end between the bones, plate the neck and spoon over the sauce, then arrange 2 cutlets on each.

# STUFFED BREAST OF LAMB

1 breast of lamb, boned
splash of cider or water
120–150g lamb's sweetbreads
2 lamb's kidneys
a couple of generous knobs of butter
1 tbsp chopped flat-leaf parsley

FOR THE STUFFING
1 onion, peeled and finely chopped
2 garlic cloves, peeled and crushed
1 tsp chopped thyme leaves
1 tsp chopped fresh rosemary
2 tbsp olive oil
120g lamb mince
100g lamb's liver, coarsely minced or chopped
3–4 lamb's sweetbreads, cut into small dice
2 lamb's kidneys, sinews removed and cut into
    small dice
50g fresh white breadcrumbs
sea salt and freshly ground black pepper

TO SERVE
cooked spring greens
mashed potato

SERVES 4–6

Preheat the oven to 220°C/gas mark 7. To make the stuffing, gently cook the onion, garlic, thyme and rosemary in the olive oil for 3–4 minutes until soft. Transfer to a bowl, add the rest of the ingredients, season generously and mix well.

Lay the breast of lamb, skin side down, on a work surface or board and spoon the stuffing down the centre, then roll it up tightly. Tie with string at 3–4cm intervals, season and lay in a roasting tray. Roast in the oven for 20 minutes, then lower the setting to 180°C/gas mark 4 and cook for another 1½ hours. Set aside to rest for about 10 minutes. Deglaze the roasting tray with a little cider or water and reserve the juices.

Meanwhile, blanch the sweetbreads in lightly salted water for 1 minute, then drain. Remove any sinew or fat and cut the larger ones in half. Remove any sinews from the kidneys and cut into similar-sized pieces. Season both with salt and pepper.

Heat the butter in a heavy-based frying pan until foaming. Add the sweetbreads and kidneys and fry for 3–4 minutes over a high heat until nicely coloured. Add the parsley and remove from the heat.

To serve, slice the breast of lamb into 2cm thick slices and arrange on plates, then spoon the offal around the meat and pour over the pan juices. Serve with spring greens and mash. Serve any leftover roast as lamb baps or sandwiches.

“Breast of lamb is one of those cuts that invariably ends up in the butcher's bin these days. I doubt whether many butchers even bother trimming the small amount of meat to put it through the mincer. However, there are a few good things you can do with the breast. The simplest way to cook it is to slow-roast it until crisp, then slice it up and snack on it as is, scatter it into a salad or make it into scrumpets (see page 52).”

# MUTTON CHOP CURRY

FOR THE ROASTED CURRY SPICE MIX
1 tbsp fenugreek seeds
1 tbsp fennel seeds
1 tbsp fenugreek leaves
1 tbsp cumin seeds
1–2 tbsp dried chilli flakes
½ tbsp caraway seeds
½ tbsp nigella seeds
1 tbsp turmeric
8 cloves
1 tbsp mustard seeds
½ tbsp cardamom seeds (from green cardamom pods)
1 tbsp ground cumin
1 tsp ground cinnamon
1 tbsp ground coriander

FOR THE CURRY
12 mutton chops or cutlets
2–3 tbsp natural yoghurt
75g ghee (or half oil, half butter mix)
2 medium red onions, peeled and finely chopped
3 garlic cloves, peeled and crushed
a small piece of fresh root ginger, peeled and finely grated
a good pinch of saffron strands
a good handful of curry leaves
2 tbsp roasted curry spice mix (see above)
1 tbsp tomato purée
500ml dark meat stock (see page 292)
sea salt and freshly ground black pepper
a few sprigs of coriander, roughly chopped
1 tbsp vegetable oil
cooked basmati rice, to serve

SERVES 4–6

To prepare the spice mix, grind all of the spices, except the ground cumin, cinnamon and coriander, in a spice grinder or with a mortar and pestle. Then mix them with the ready-ground spices and sprinkle into a heavy-based frying pan. Cook over a medium heat, stirring constantly, until they turn dark brown; don't let them burn. Tip onto a plate and leave to cool, then store in a sealed jar until needed.

Coat the mutton chops with the yoghurt and leave to marinate for a couple of hours.

Meanwhile, heat two-thirds of the ghee in a pan and gently cook the onions with the garlic, ginger, saffron and a few of the curry leaves for 3–4 minutes until softened. Add the roasted curry spice mix and tomato purée and stir well. Pour in the stock and bring to the boil, then lower the heat and let the sauce simmer for 20 minutes.

Transfer the sauce to a blender and process until smooth, then strain it through a fine-meshed sieve into a clean pan, pushing as much through as possible. Return to a low heat and simmer until the sauce has reduced and thickened.

Heat the remaining ghee in a frying pan. Remove the excess yoghurt from the chops and season them, then fry until lightly coloured on both sides. Pour the sauce over the chops and simmer gently for 15–20 minutes, stirring occasionally. Add the coriander and simmer for another couple of minutes.

Meanwhile, heat the oil in a frying pan and briefly fry the rest of the curry leaves. Scatter over the curry and serve with the basmati rice.

"The Hix Oyster & Chop House menu wouldn't be the same without a mutton chop or halibut collar curry. For some reason, most restaurants and butchers struggle to sell mutton but we can't seem to cook enough of it. Out of the traditional mutton season, use Blackface or Herdwick, which have different lambing seasons."

This recipe makes a larger quantity of spice mix than you will need. Keep the remainder in a sealed jar – you'll have enough for a few batches of curry.

# VEGETABLES

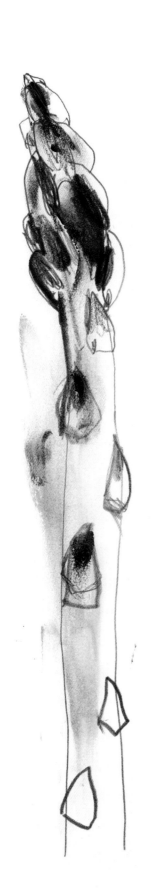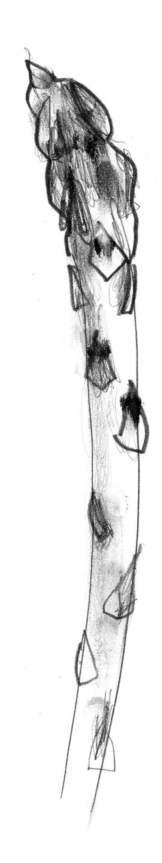

## ASPARAGUS TART

300–350g ready-made all-butter puff pastry
plain flour, for dusting
1 egg, beaten
1kg medium asparagus
sea salt and freshly ground black pepper
30g mature cheese, such as Cheddar, grated
50g butter, plus extra for greasing

SERVES 4

Roll out the puff pastry on a lightly floured surface to a 3mm thickness and let it rest for 15 minutes. Cut 4 pastry rectangles, 14cm × 11cm and prick them all over with a fork, then lay on a baking tray.

From the remaining pastry, cut 1cm wide strips, as long as you can. Brush the edges of the rectangles with egg and lay the pastry strips on top, trimming them as necessary, to form a rim on all four sides. Mark these raised edges by pressing half-moons with the blade of a knife, or using a pastry crimper, then brush with egg. Rest in the fridge for 1 hour.

In the meantime, cut off the woody ends of the asparagus spears and discard. Then cut 10cm below the tips, reserving the tips and stalks. Bring two pans of salted water to the boil. Cook the tips for 3–4 minutes until tender, then drain and refresh in cold water to stop them discolouring.

Cook the stalk trimmings in the other pan for 7–8 minutes until soft, then drain and whiz in a blender or food processor with the cheese and butter to a coarse purée. Season with salt and pepper to taste.

Preheat the oven to 160°C/gas mark 3. Bake the pastry cases for 7 minutes, then remove. Turn the oven up to 200°C/gas mark 6. Spread about a tablespoonful of the asparagus purée in the middle of each tart. Don't put in too much (save what you have left to use as a dip). Then lay the asparagus tips, as close together as you can, on the purée.

Cut some pieces of foil just large enough to cover the asparagus (but not the pastry edges) and butter them. Season the asparagus with salt and pepper and lay the foil, buttered-side down, on top. Bake the tarts for 15 minutes and serve immediately.

## ASPARAGUS WITH HOLLANDAISE SAUCE

1kg medium to thick asparagus

FOR THE HOLLANDAISE
3 tbsp white wine vinegar
1 small shallot, peeled and chopped
a few sprigs of tarragon
1 bay leaf
5 black peppercorns
200g butter
3 egg yolks
sea salt and freshly ground white pepper

SERVES 4–6

To prepare the asparagus, cut off the woody ends. If you are using thick asparagus you can peel the stalks with a fine swivel vegetable peeler, starting about 5cm down from the tips. You do not need to do this if using smaller, thinner stalks. Set aside.

To make the hollandaise, put the vinegar, shallot, tarragon, bay leaf, peppercorns and 3 tablespoons of water in a pan and boil until reduced to 2 teaspoons. Strain and cool. Melt the butter in a small pan and simmer for 5 minutes. Allow to cool a little, then pour off the clarified butter into a bowl, leaving the sediment behind.

Put the yolks into a small bowl with half of the reduced vinegar and stand the bowl over a pan of gently simmering water. Whisk until it begins to thicken and become frothy. Slowly trickle in the butter, whisking constantly; if added too quickly the sauce will separate. When you've added two thirds of the butter, add some or all of the remaining vinegar reduction to taste. Then add the rest of the butter. The vinegar should just cut the oiliness of the butter. Season, cover with cling film and leave in a warm, not hot, place until needed. Reheat over a bowl of hot water and lightly whisk to serve.

Add the asparagus to a pan of gently simmering salted water and cook until tender, allowing about 4–5 minutes for finger-thick spears. Drain and serve with the hollandaise sauce.

Make the most of the short English asparagus season, which starts in early May and lasts about 6 weeks.

## FRIED SQUASH OR COURGETTE FLOWERS

8 large courgette, squash or pumpkin flowers,
   with their stalks
120g gluten-free self-raising flour, plus extra for dusting
20–30g mature Cheddar cheese, finely grated
sea salt and freshly ground black pepper
vegetable or corn oil, for deep-frying

SERVES 4

Check that the flowers are clean and free from insects. To make the batter, place the flour in a bowl and slowly whisk in 200ml ice-cold water to form a thickish batter. Add the grated cheese and seasoning and give it a final whisk.

Heat an 8cm depth of oil in a deep-fat fryer or other suitable deep, heavy pan to 160–180°C, or until a little batter dropped into the oil turns golden brown after a minute or so.

Have a shallow bowl of flour ready. One at a time, dip the flowers into the flour, shaking off any excess, then dip into the batter to coat and drop into the hot oil. Deep-fry 3 or 4 flowers at a time, moving them around in the oil with a spoon, for 2–3 minutes until they are crisp and light golden.

Remove the courgette flowers with a slotted spoon and put on a plate lined with kitchen paper to drain. Season lightly with salt and serve.

“Courgettes and other members of the squash family produce great flowers that can be harvested continually for 2 or 3 months during the summer and cooked as a snack, starter or accompaniment. The flowers are best harvested when the sun is out and when they have fully opened. On menus you often see stuffed courgette flowers, but the filling adds moisture, which tends to make the batter go soggy.”

## DEEP-FRIED ONIONS IN CIDER BATTER

2 white onions, peeled
2 red onions, peeled
1 bunch of spring onions
120g gluten-free self-raising flour
150–200ml cider
sea salt and freshly ground black pepper
vegetable or corn oil, for frying
plain flour, for dusting
onion salt, to serve

SERVES 4

Cut the white onions into 5mm thick rings; halve the red onions, then cut into 5mm thick slices. Separate into individual rings and slices. Trim the spring onions, but leave whole.

To make the batter, sift the flour into a bowl and whisk in enough of the cider to form a smooth coating batter. Season with salt and pepper.

Heat an 8cm depth of oil in a deep-fat fryer or other suitable deep, heavy pan to 160–180°C, or until a little batter dropped into the oil turns golden after a minute or so. Season the flour for dusting well.

You'll need to cook the onions in 2 or 3 batches. Toss the first batch in the seasoned flour to coat, shaking off any excess. Now pass the onions through the batter and drop into the hot oil. Deep-fry for about 3–4 minutes until nicely coloured, turning them occasionally with a slotted spoon.

Remove and drain on kitchen paper, then scatter with onion salt. Eat straight away or keep hot while you cook the rest, then serve.

“I do love deep-fried onions. Rather like deep-fried calamari or scampi, they are incredibly comforting. A must-have side dish with grilled steak, they could easily replace the chips.”

## ROASTED JERUSALEM ARTICHOKES AND SHALLOTS WITH ROSEMARY

12 large shallots
500g Jerusalem artichokes, scrubbed
2–3 tbsp cold-pressed rapeseed oil
sea salt and freshly ground black pepper
a few sprigs of rosemary
a couple good knobs of butter

SERVES 4

Preheat the oven to 180°C/gas mark 4. Lay the shallots on a baking tray and roast them in their skins for 45-50 minutes until tender. Remove from the oven and leave until cool enough to handle.

Meanwhile, toss the Jerusalem artichokes in the rapeseed oil in a roasting tray and season with salt and pepper. Bake for about 30-40 minutes, turning them every so often until almost tender.

Pop the shallots out of their skins by cutting a sliver off the root end and pushing them out. Toss the shallots and rosemary in with the artichokes and bake for 15 minutes, turning them occasionally. Transfer to a serving dish, add the butter and gently mix. Serve immediately.

## WELSH ONION CAKE (TEISEN NIONOD)

800g large potatoes, thinly sliced
100g butter, melted, plus extra for brushing
sea salt and freshly ground black pepper
500g onions, peeled and sliced

SERVES 4–6

Preheat the oven to 200°C/gas mark 6. Wash the potatoes briefly in water and dry on kitchen paper. Put them in a bowl, season with salt and pepper and mix in the melted butter.

Brush a shallow ovenproof serving dish with melted butter and layer the potatoes and onions alternately, beginning with the potatoes and finishing with a neat layer of overlapped potatoes on top.

Cover with foil or a lid and bake for 1 hour, then remove the foil, brush with a little more melted butter and cook for another 15-20 minutes to allow them to brown.

" When you roast a Jerusalem artichoke, its flavour becomes concentrated and it seems to take on a different character. Shallots, roasted in their skins, are the perfect partner and a handful of rosemary added towards the end of cooking just gives them another dimension. This is an excellent accompaniment to grilled or roast lamb. "

“This is a little bit like the famous French *pommes boulangère*, in which the potatoes are cooked in meat stock. If you are roasting a joint, I would strongly recommend you finish cooking it on top of the onion cake, so that the juices are absorbed into the potatoes and onions.”

# ROASTED BEETS WITH HORSERADISH

1kg small beetroot
sea salt and freshly ground black pepper
1–2 tbsp rapeseed or olive oil
a few sprigs of thyme
65g freshly grated horseradish
a knob of butter

SERVES 4

Cook the beetroot in their skins in a pan of boiling salted water for 1 hour, or until they are tender to the point of a knife. Drain in a colander and leave to cool. Preheat the oven to 200°C/gas mark 6.

Wearing rubber gloves to avoid staining your hands, remove the skin from the beetroot and trim the ends if necessary. If the beetroot are very small leave them whole, otherwise cut into quarters.

Heat the oil in a roasting tray in the oven for about 5 minutes. Add the beetroot and season with salt and pepper. Cook for 30 minutes, then scatter over the thyme leaves and continue cooking for another 15-20 minutes until nicely coloured.

Scatter the horseradish over the beetroot, add the butter and turn to coat, then return to the oven for 10 minutes. Serve hot.

# WINTER COLESLAW

1 small head or ½ a large head of red cabbage, trimmed
1 small head or ½ a large head of white cabbage, trimmed
2 large carrots, peeled and trimmed
1 small head of celeriac, peeled
1 medium kohlrabi or turnip, peeled
1 medium red onion, peeled and finely sliced
sea salt and freshly ground black pepper
5–6 tbsp mayonnaise (see page 295)

SERVES 6–8

If using small cabbages, slice them in half. Cut the core out of the red and white cabbages. Shred the leaves as finely as possible, using a sharp chopping knife. Slice the carrots, celeriac and kohlrabi into thin matchsticks, by cutting them into 3-4cm lengths with a sharp knife, then into thin slices, then into sticks. (Alternatively, use a mandolin.)

In a large bowl, mix the cabbage with the onion and root vegetable matchsticks. Season with salt and pepper, add the mayonnaise and toss to mix. Leave to stand for about 20 minutes. Before serving, give the coleslaw a final mix and check the seasoning.

**66** There are other ways to treat beetroot, apart from pickling. It makes a delicious soup, is good in salads and can be cooked simply to serve as an accompaniment. Beetroot is easy to cook, although a bit messy to peel. If you can't get a hold of fresh, then the grated horseradish sold in jars will work well. **99**

**66** Cabbage and carrots are the classic coleslaw components, but by adding some shredded kohlrabi or turnip, and some red cabbage, you can take this rudimentary salad to a whole new level. Beyond hamburgers and crumbed chicken drumsticks, coleslaw goes with hot-smoked mackerel or salmon. **99**

## BUTTERED SAMPHIRE

300–400g samphire, woody stalks trimmed
butter, melted (as much as you like)
freshly ground black pepper

SERVES 4

Cook the samphire in boiling unsalted water (or steam it if you prefer) for 2–3 minutes until tender. Drain thoroughly in a colander.

Toss the samphire with melted butter and black pepper to taste, then serve immediately.

66 Marsh samphire, or sea asparagus, can be found on the salt marshes around the coast during the summer months. It has a natural salty taste of the sea, which makes it a perfect accompaniment for fish. 99

## CREAMED SPINACH

750–800g large spinach leaves, thick stalks removed
   and washed
sea salt and freshly ground black pepper
200ml double cream

SERVES 4–6

Plunge the spinach leaves into a pan of boiling salted water and cook for 2–3 minutes until tender. Drain in a colander, refresh under the cold tap and squeeze out any excess water.

Tip the spinach into a food processor and blend as smoothly or as coarsely as you wish. You can take it to this stage in advance if you like, then finish at the last minute.

Simmer the cream in a saucepan until reduced by about half, then stir in the spinach and season with salt and pepper to taste. Cook over a low heat for a minute or so, stirring every so often, until the spinach is hot. Serve immediately.

66 Creamed spinach makes a delicious comforting accompaniment to simply grilled meat or fish. It has a feeling of luxuriousness about it the moment you put it into your mouth. Cooked in this way it almost acts like a sauce. This also works really well with sea spinach. 99

# CREAMED BRUSSELS SPROUTS

500g large Brussels sprouts
sea salt and freshly ground black pepper
150ml double cream
50g butter

SERVES 4–6

Cook the sprouts in boiling salted water for 5–10 minutes or until just tender. Drain well and allow to cool slightly. Slice the sprouts thinly.

Boil the cream until reduced by half, then add the sprouts and seasoning. Simmer for 4–5 minutes over a low heat, stirring every so often. Stir through the butter and serve.

“This is a simple way to use up leftover Brussels sprouts, or you can prepare them from fresh. Serve as an accompaniment to poultry and game dishes.”

## PURPLE-SPROUTING BROCCOLI TART WITH BEENLEIGH BLUE

500g ready-made all-butter puff pastry
plain flour, for dusting
1 egg, beaten
700–800g small tender stems of purple-sprouting
     broccoli
sea salt and freshly ground black pepper
30g mature Cheddar, grated
50g butter
60–80g Beenleigh Blue cheese

SERVES 4

Roll out the pastry on a floured surface to a 3mm thickness and cut 4 rectangles, each about 14cm × 11cm. Prick them all over with a fork, then place on a large baking tray. Cut 1cm wide strips from the rest of the pastry. Brush the edges of the rectangles with egg. Lay the strips along all four sides and trim to form a neat raised border. Crimp these edges with a pastry crimper, or press half-moons along them with the blade of a knife. Brush the edges with egg. Leave to rest in the fridge for 1 hour.

Trim 10cm down from the tip of the broccoli, saving the stalks for later. Bring two pans of salted water to the boil. Cook the tips and leaves for 3–4 minutes until tender. Drain and refresh in cold water to stop them discolouring; drain well and set aside.

Cook the stalks in the other pan for 4–5 minutes or until soft, then drain and tip into a blender. Add the Cheddar, butter and salt and pepper, then whiz to a coarse purée. Taste and adjust the seasoning.

Preheat the oven to 160°C/gas mark 3. Cover the centres of the pastry cases with baking beans. Bake for 8–10 minutes. Remove from the oven and lift out the beans. Turn the oven up to 200°C/gas mark 6.

Spread about a tablespoon of the broccoli purée in the middle of each tart. Don't put too much in; save what's left for a dip or sauce. Lay the blanched broccoli, as close together as you can, over the purée and season with salt and pepper. Lay some buttered foil loosely on top, to cover the broccoli but not the pastry edges. Bake the tarts for about 10 minutes, then remove the foil and crumble the Beenleigh Blue over the broccoli. Serve immediately.

## PURPLE-SPROUTING BROCCOLI WITH PICKLED WALNUTS AND ROASTED GARLIC

1 head of new season garlic
4–5 pickled walnuts
700–800g tender stems of purple-sprouting broccoli
sea salt and freshly ground black pepper
a couple of good knobs of butter

SERVES 4

Preheat the oven to 200°C/gas mark 6. Wrap the garlic in foil and bake for 45 minutes, then unwrap and leave until cool enough to handle. Separate the cloves of garlic and remove the skin. Cut each of the pickled walnuts into 3 or 4 pieces.

Add the broccoli to a pan of boiling salted water and cook for 3–4 minutes or until tender. Meanwhile, heat the butter in a pan with the garlic and add some seasoning.

Drain the broccoli as soon as it is ready. Transfer to a warm serving dish and spoon over the garlicky butter. Scatter the pickled walnuts over the broccoli and serve.

" Be sure to buy slender, young stems of broccoli as thicker stalks tend to be woody. Also be aware that there are fakes on the market trying to pass themselves off as purple-sprouting, which won't taste like the real thing. "

# BUTTERED GREENS WITH KENTISH COBNUTS

1kg spring greens or Savoy cabbage or a mixture of
  the two, trimmed and stalk removed
sea salt and freshly ground black pepper
100g shelled cobnuts
65g butter

**SERVES 4**

Cut the spring greens or cabbage roughly into 3cm squares. Cook in plenty of boiling salted water for 4–5 minutes until tender, then drain in a colander.

Meanwhile, preheat the grill to medium. Roughly chop the cobnuts and toast lightly. Drain the greens well and toss with the toasted nuts and butter. Season with salt and pepper, then serve.

66 Kentish cobnuts are available during the autumn months. They give a nice texture to greens which can otherwise be a bit boring on their own. If you have missed the cobnut season, then chestnuts make a good alternative. 99

# BRAISED CELERY HEARTS

2 small celery heads with leaves
sea salt and freshly ground black pepper
500ml vegetable stock (see page 292)
300ml double cream

**SERVES 4**

Preheat the oven to 190°C/gas mark 5. Remove the outer stalks from the celery and save the leaves for the sauce.

Place the celery hearts in an ovenproof dish, season with salt and pepper and pour over all of the stock. Cover with a lid or foil and cook for 1 hour or until the celery hearts are tender when tested with the point of a knife. Drain in a colander, reserving the stock, then halve or quarter the celery hearts and set aside.

Transfer about half of the reserved stock to a saucepan and boil until it has reduced to just a few tablespoons. Add the cream, bring to the boil and simmer until the sauce has thickened and reduced by about half.

Chop the celery leaves very finely and add them to the sauce. Taste and adjust the seasoning and simmer for a couple of minutes. Add the celery hearts and warm through briefly, then serve.

"These can be served as an accompaniment to most meat and fish dishes, or even as a part of a buffet. Don't discard the outer stalks – use them to make a soup or flavour a casserole. If the celery is very small you won't need to discard the outer stalks, just peel them instead."

## MINTED PEAS WITH THEIR SHOOTS

300–400g freshly podded peas, about 1kg
    before podding
sea salt and freshly ground black pepper
1½ tsp caster sugar
a handful of mint sprigs, leaves stripped and
    stalks reserved
60g butter
a couple of handfuls of pea shoots

SERVES 4–6

For the peas, bring a pan of salted water to the boil
with the sugar and mint stalks added. Tip in the
peas and simmer for 4–5 minutes or until tender,
then drain and discard the mint stalks.

Melt the butter in a wide pan. Add the pea shoots,
quickly season with salt and pepper and toss for a
few seconds until they are just wilted.

Tip in the peas, toss to combine and add more
seasoning, if necessary, before serving.

66 Peas are an all-time great summer
vegetable that can involve the whole
family – whether it's harvesting from
the garden or a day out at a pick-your-
own farm. Pea shoots or tendrils are
often overlooked, yet I love using them
in salads or quickly tossing them in
butter to eat on their own or with the
peas themselves. 99

## AUTUMN GREENS WITH WILD MUSHROOMS

1 head of green cabbage, or a mixture of greens
sea salt and freshly ground black pepper
100g butter
1 small onion, peeled and finely chopped
2 garlic cloves, peeled and crushed
120–150g wild mushrooms, cleaned

SERVES 4

Cut the cabbage or greens roughly into 2–3cm
chunks and wash well. Add to a pan of boiling
salted water, bring back to the boil and cook for
3–5 minutes or until just tender. Drain thoroughly
in a colander.

Meanwhile, melt half of the butter in a frying
pan and gently cook the onion and garlic for
3–4 minutes to soften.

Add the rest of the butter to the pan. Once it has
melted, add the mushrooms and cook over a
medium heat for 4–5 minutes until tender, turning
frequently. Season after a couple of minutes.

Add the cabbage to the mushrooms and toss
them together over the heat until hot. Check the
seasoning and serve at once.

66 Cabbage and greens often benefit
from being spruced up with another
ingredient. A singular or a mix of wild
mushrooms does the trick. 99

# PEAS WITH BACON AND ONIONS

75g butter
150g piece of streaky bacon, cut into 5mm cubes or
    diced pancetta
400g shelled fresh or frozen peas
sea salt and freshly ground black pepper
2 tsp sugar
1 bunch of spring onions, preferably the bulbous ones

**SERVES 4**

Melt 25g of the butter in a pan and gently cook the bacon over a low heat for 3-4 minutes without allowing it to colour.

Meanwhile, put the peas into a saucepan and just cover them with boiling water. Add 25g of the remaining butter, season well and add the sugar. Bring back to the boil and cook over a medium heat for 6-7 minutes (or only 2 minutes if frozen) or until tender. Drain in a colander set over a bowl to save the liquid.

Cut the spring onions into 2.5cm lengths, put into the empty pan and pour just enough of the reserved liquid over to cover them. Boil rapidly until most of the liquid has evaporated, then add the rest of the butter and mix with the peas and the bacon. Check the seasoning and serve.

66 This is similar to the French *petits pois
bonne femme*. If you are used to plain
old boiled peas, you'll find bacon and
spring onions give them a new lease
of life. Use fresh peas when they are in
season - you'll need about 1kg peas in
the pod to give this shelled weight. 99

# MARROW WITH BACON AND HERBS

1 young marrow, about 1kg
sea salt and freshly ground black pepper
2–3 tbsp cold-pressed rapeseed oil
a couple of good knobs of butter
1 medium onion, peeled and finely chopped
4 garlic cloves, peeled and crushed
4 rashers of streaky bacon, finely chopped
1 tsp chopped thyme leaves
60g fresh white breadcrumbs
3 tbsp chopped flat-leaf parsley
a few sprigs of tarragon, finely chopped

SERVES 4–6

Halve the marrow lengthways, then scoop out the seeds with a spoon and discard. Cut the marrow into 5mm thick slices. Lay these on a tray, scatter lightly with salt and leave for an hour. Drain the marrow in a colander and pat dry with kitchen paper.

Heat the rapeseed oil in a large frying pan. Season the marrow with pepper, add to the pan and cook over a high heat for 3–4 minutes, turning every so often until lightly coloured and tender.

Meanwhile, heat the butter in a heavy-based saucepan. Add the onion, garlic, bacon and thyme, and cook gently for 3–4 minutes until the onion is soft and the bacon is cooked. Stir in the breadcrumbs, parsley and tarragon, and season with salt and pepper to taste.

Preheat the grill to medium. Transfer the marrow to a serving dish (suitable for use under the grill). Scatter the breadcrumb mixture over and place under the grill until lightly browned. Serve immediately.

# RUNNER BEAN PUREE

500g runner beans, trimmed
sea salt and freshly ground black pepper
a few knobs of butter

SERVES 4–6

Roughly chop the runner beans. Bring a pan of salted water to the boil, drop in the beans and cook for 5–7 minutes until just tender, then drain.

Tip the beans into a blender or food processor and blend to a purée – as coarse or smooth as you like; you may need to add a little water.

Return the purée to the pan and place over a low heat. Add the butter, season with salt and pepper to taste, then serve.

"You may think it's a bit extravagant to purée runner beans but it is a great way to serve them if you have a glut in your garden, or if you just fancy a change. Try serving this side with grilled meat or deep-fried fish, or top a smaller portion with grilled scallops and scatter some blanched shredded runner beans over them for a lovely summery starter."

# PEASE PUDDING

450g dried yellow split peas
about 1 litre ham stock or chicken stock (see page 293)
1 medium egg, beaten
65g butter, plus extra to grease
sea salt and freshly ground black pepper

SERVES 4

Soak the dried split peas in cold water to cover overnight, then drain and rinse well.

Place the peas in a large pan. Add enough stock to cover them generously and simmer for 1 hour or so, until tender. Drain and tip into a large bowl.

Add the egg and butter to the peas and mix well, seasoning with salt and pepper. Transfer to a greased 1.2 litre pudding basin and cover the top with a sheet of foil, pleated in the centre. Secure under the rim with string.

Put the pudding basin into a steamer or saucepan containing enough boiling water to come halfway up the side of the basin and steam for 1 hour. Check the water level during cooking as you may have to top it up with more boiling water. Alternatively, cook it in a deep-roasting tin half-filled with boiling water in the oven at 180°C/gas mark 4 for 1 hour.

Lift the pudding basin from the pan, remove the foil and run a knife around the side of the pudding to loosen it. Turn out on to a warm plate and serve.

"Traditionally this Northern dish would be made by tying the dried peas in a muslin cloth and boiling them with a ham joint. If you have prepared a boiled ham, don't throw the stock away – use it here, or cook the two together. You can flake any pieces of cooked ham into the pudding for a bit of added texture."

# CAULIFLOWER CHEESE

1 medium cauliflower
1 litre milk
1 bay leaf
sea salt and freshly ground black pepper
60g butter
60g plain flour
100ml double cream
120g mature Cheddar cheese, grated
1–2 tbsp finely chopped flat-leaf parsley

SERVES 4

❝This is one of my all-time favourite dishes. It's great comfort food – perfect for family meals and TV suppers. I prefer to keep and use the leaves in a dish like this – they taste great and give a bit of colour, so there's no point in wasting them.❞

Cut the cauliflower into florets, reserving the leaves and stalk. Place the milk and bay leaf in a saucepan and bring to the boil. Season well. Add the florets and leaves, and simmer for about 7–8 minutes until tender. Drain in a colander over a bowl to reserve the milk.

Melt the butter in a heavy-based pan and stir in the flour. Stir over a low heat for about 30 seconds, then gradually stir in the reserved hot milk, using a whisk. Bring to a simmer and turn the heat down very low (use a heat diffuser if you have one). Continue to simmer very gently for 20 minutes, stirring every so often to ensure that the sauce doesn't catch on the bottom.

Add the cream and simmer for a couple of minutes. The sauce should be of a thick coating consistency by now; if not simmer for a little longer. Strain through a fine sieve into a bowl, whisk in three-quarters of the cheese, then taste and adjust the seasoning.

Preheat the oven to 220°C/gas mark 7 (or the grill to medium-high). Make sure the cauliflower is dry – you can use kitchen paper to pat it dry if necessary. Mix the cauliflower with half of the cheese sauce and transfer to an ovenproof dish. Spoon the rest of the sauce over and scatter the parsley and the rest of the cheese on top. Either bake in the oven for about 20 minutes until golden, or reheat and brown under the grill.

# BOXTY

150g peeled raw potatoes
250g cooked potatoes in their skins, peeled and
    mashed
200g plain flour
½ tsp bicarbonate of soda
200–300ml buttermilk or ordinary milk
a good pinch of salt
butter, for frying

SERVES 4–6

Grate the raw potatoes and mix with the mashed potatoes, flour and bicarbonate of soda, then add enough buttermilk to make a thick batter. Season with salt.

Heat a griddle or frying pan and grease it well with butter. Drop in a quarter of the mix to make large pancakes or smaller amounts for small ones. Cook for 5 minutes on each side until golden.

❝ There are two main types of boxty: in the pan, which are fluffy thickish pan-fried cakes, or cooked on the griddle, which are sometimes called boxty pancakes. Both can be served in many ways as a breakfast dish. Here, I served it with rashers of bacon drizzled with honey. ❞

## CHAMP

150–200ml milk
1 large bunch of scallions or spring onions, trimmed
　and chopped
500g cooked floury potatoes in their skins, peeled,
　mashed and slightly cooled
2 tbsp chopped chives
100g butter, or more if you wish
sea salt and freshly ground black pepper

SERVES 4–6

Bring the milk to the boil, add the scallions or
spring onions, and leave to infuse off the heat for
3–4 minutes.

Add to the mashed potatoes with the chives and
butter, season to taste and mix well.

**❝** A good, hearty and simple
winter dish, this is a great
accompaniment to boiled
ham or braised meats.**❞**

## STRAW POTATOES

4 large chipping potatoes, such as Yukon Gold, Spunta
　or Maris Piper, peeled
vegetable or corn oil, for deep-frying
10 garlic cloves, peeled and thinly sliced
sea salt

SERVES 4

Using a mandolin with a shredding attachment or a
sharp knife, cut the potatoes into long matchsticks,
about 3mm thick. Wash them well in a couple of
changes of cold water to remove the excess starch,
then drain and pat dry on some kitchen paper.

Heat an 8cm depth of oil in a deep-fat fryer or other
suitable deep, heavy pan to 120–140°C. Deep-fry
the potatoes in manageable batches (a couple of
handfuls at a time) for 2–3 minutes, then remove
with a slotted spoon and drain in a colander.

Increase the temperature of the oil to 160–180°C
and re-fry the potatoes with the garlic slices in
batches, moving them around in the pan, until
golden and crisp. Remove with a slotted spoon and
drain on kitchen paper. Sprinkle with sea salt and
serve immediately.

Alternatively, you can keep the straw potatoes
warm, uncovered, on a baking tray in a low oven
until ready to serve. They should stay crisp but if
not you can briefly re-fry them in hot oil to crisp
them up again.

These fine chips can be prepared
ahead and fried for the second time
just before serving. In between
blanching and re-frying place on a tray,
cover and refrigerate until required.

**❝** You can serve the chips with just about anything, from grilled and roasted meat, poultry and game to fish and shellfish – especially mussels. **❞**

## SPRING BUBBLE AND SQUEAK

125–150g cooked and peeled new potatoes
200g spring greens, cooked and drained
6 spring onions, trimmed
100g podded broad beans, cooked
100g podded peas, cooked
1 tbsp chopped flat-leaf parsley
sea salt and freshly ground black pepper
2 tbsp vegetable oil

SERVES 4

Chop the potatoes, greens, spring onions and beans and place in a bowl with the peas. Add the parsley, mix well and season with salt and pepper to taste.

Shape the mixture into 4 even-sized patties and flatten them slightly.

Heat the oil in a non-stick frying pan and cook the patties for 3-4 minutes on each side until golden. Drain on kitchen paper and serve straight away, or keep warm in a low oven until ready to serve.

## WHIPPED POTATOES WITH CHANTERELLES

300–400g waxy potatoes, such as Charlotte or Anya
sea salt and freshly ground black pepper
250g butter, cut into small pieces
100ml double cream
150–200g chanterelles, cleaned
1–2 tbsp chopped flat-leaf parsley

SERVES 4

Peel the potatoes and cook in boiling salted water until tender. Drain and mash finely – ideally using a potato ricer. If you use a masher, then push them through a sieve afterwards.

Put the potato into a pan with 200g of the butter, season with salt and pepper and stir over a low heat until the butter has melted. Add the cream and more seasoning if necessary and keep warm.

Melt the remaining butter in a large, heavy frying pan and heat until foaming. You may need to cook the chanterelles in two batches. Drop them into the pan with the parsley, season and cook over a high heat for a minute or so, turning every so often.

To serve, spoon the whipped potato in a thin layer on each warm plate and scatter the chanterelles over the top. Serve at once.

Chanterelles look particularly attractive in this dish, but you can use ceps, hedgehog fungus or girolles – whatever you can lay your hands on.

"Two simple earthy ingredients – potatoes and wild mushrooms – come together to make a perfect dinner party starter. The secret here is to be very generous with the butter in the whipped potatoes so they almost become sauce-like, and of course you don't need very much of them."

# HONEY-ROASTED PARSNIPS

700–800g parsnips
sea salt and freshly ground black pepper
65–75g beef dripping or lard
2 tbsp clear runny honey

SERVES 4–6

Top and tail the parsnips. If the skins are clean they don't need to be peeled, otherwise peel them. Quarter the parsnips lengthways and remove the hard core which runs down the centre. Cook the parsnip quarters in boiling salted water for 5 minutes, drain in a colander and leave to cool.

Preheat the oven to 200°C/gas mark 6 and heat a roasting tray in the oven. Melt the beef dripping or lard in the hot tray, then add the parsnips and season with salt and pepper. Roast for about 30 minutes, turning occasionally, until the parsnips are nicely coloured. (Alternatively, they can be roasted around a joint of meat.)

Add the honey, turn the parsnips to coat and return the tray to the oven for a further 5 minutes, basting once or twice with the honey and dripping until they are golden. Serve immediately.

"This is the perfect accompaniment to a roast joint. Lots of people don't like parsnips for some reason and in some countries they are fed to cattle. What a waste - they have a delicious natural fluffy texture and sweet flavour. I'm sure the cows think the same."

# PARSNIP DROP SCONES

1 large parsnip, about 200g
sea salt and freshly ground black pepper
80g self-raising flour
1 medium egg, beaten
milk, to mix
vegetable oil, for frying
a good knob of butter

SERVES 4

Peel, halve and core the parsnip, then chop roughly and cook in boiling salted water until tender. Drain thoroughly and mash well. Put the mashed parsnip into a bowl with the flour and beaten egg and mix well, then stir in enough milk to make a stiff batter. Season with salt and pepper.

Preheat the oven to 140°C/gas mark 1. Heat a little vegetable oil in a small non-stick omelette pan and ladle in enough batter to cover the bottom. (Or you could cook the drop scones two at a time in a larger frying pan.) Cook for 2–3 minutes on each side, adding a knob of butter as you turn them. Once they are nicely coloured and crisp, transfer to a warm plate and keep warm in the oven while you cook the rest. Serve immediately or keep warm in the oven until needed.

“These drop scones really aren't traditional at all, I've just made them up and found the sweetness of parsnip in this format works a treat. I often serve these with pan-fried under-fillets of venison.”

## BAKED PARSNIPS WITH LANCASHIRE CHEESE

750g parsnips, peeled
400ml double cream
400ml milk
a good pinch of freshly grated nutmeg
2 garlic cloves, peeled and crushed
sea salt and freshly ground black pepper
150g Lancashire cheese, grated
2 tbsp fresh white breadcrumbs
1 tbsp chopped flat-leaf parsley

SERVES 4–6

Preheat the oven to 160°C/gas mark 3. Cut the parsnips into rough 2–3cm chunks.

Pour the cream and milk into a saucepan, add the nutmeg and garlic, and season generously with salt and pepper. Bring to the boil, then remove from the heat and leave to cool slightly.

Put the parsnips into a shallow ovenproof (gratin-type) dish and mix with all but 1 tablespoon of the cheese. Pour the cream mixture over the top.

Stand the dish in a roasting tray and pour in enough boiling water to come halfway up the side of the dish; this will create a bain-marie. Cook in the oven for 1 hour or until the parsnips are cooked through.

Preheat the grill to medium. Mix the breadcrumbs with the parsley and remaining 1 tablespoon of grated cheese. Scatter over the parsnip bake and place under the grill for a few minutes until golden. Serve at once, or cover with foil and leave in a low oven until ready to serve.

❝This is an excellent alternative to a traditional *gratin dauphinois* that could also be made with turnip, squash or even swede. It's a great sharing dish to put in the middle of the table for guests to help themselves.❞

## ROOT VEGETABLES WITH GOOSE FAT, GARLIC AND THYME

12 garlic cloves, with skins still on
2–3 tbsp goose or duck fat
2 medium parsnips, peeled
1 small swede, peeled
2 medium-large turnips
sea salt and freshly ground black pepper
a few sprigs of thyme
1 tbsp chopped flat-leaf parsley

SERVES 4–6

Preheat the oven to 180°C/gas mark 4. Put the garlic cloves into a large roasting tray with the goose or duck fat and cook for about 30 minutes until they soften, turning occasionally.

Meanwhile, halve the parsnips and cut out the hard cores. Cut all the vegetables into rough 1cm cubes. Bring a pan of boiling salted water to the boil and blanch the vegetables for 2–3 minutes, then drain.

Add the blanched vegetables and the thyme to the roasting tray of garlic. Season generously and roast for about 15–20 minutes, turning every so often, until the vegetables are lightly coloured and tender. Stir in the parsley and serve.

❝A wintry selection of root vegetables is a great accompaniment to almost any main dish you might concoct, even fish dishes. In this mixture, the roots work in perfect harmony. Here I've used the obvious ones, but you could add salsify or kohlrabi - an alien-looking vegetable with a turnipy-radish taste.❞

# TURNIPS WITH CHERVIL

800g young turnips, peeled
2 tsp sugar
100g butter
sea salt and freshly ground black pepper
1 tbsp chopped chervil

SERVES 4

If the turnips are very small leave them whole, otherwise quarter them. Put the turnips into a pan and just cover with boiling water. Add the sugar and half of the butter, and season generously with salt and pepper. Bring back to the boil and cook over a medium heat for 7–8 minutes or until tender.

Drain the turnips in a colander, then toss with the remaining butter and the chervil. Taste and adjust the seasoning, then serve.

" Prepared and cooked in the right way, turnips, swede and parsnips truly are the best of the root vegetables. "

# PUDDINGS

## RHUBARB AND CUSTARD

400–500g rhubarb, trimmed and chopped
　　into 1cm pieces
120g caster sugar
FOR THE CUSTARD
300ml thick Jersey cream
½ vanilla pod
5 egg yolks
60g caster sugar
2 tsp cornflour
SERVES 4–6

Preheat the oven to 200°C/gas mark 6.

To make the custard, pour the cream into a small saucepan. Split the vanilla pod lengthways and scrape out the seeds using the point of a knife. Add the seeds and the empty pod to the cream. Slowly bring to the boil, then remove from the heat and set aside to infuse for about 10 minutes.

Meanwhile, mix the egg yolks, sugar and cornflour together in a bowl. Pick out the vanilla pod, then pour the cream onto the egg mixture, mixing well with a whisk as you do so. Return to the pan and cook gently over a very low heat, stirring constantly with a wooden spoon, for a few minutes until the custard thickens; don't let it boil or it will curdle. Remove from the heat and give it a final mix with a whisk. Immediately pour into a clean bowl and leave to cool.

Place the rhubarb in a baking tray or ovenproof dish and spoon over the sugar. Cover with foil and bake for about 30 minutes until the rhubarb is tender. Remove from the oven and carefully pour the cooking liquid into a saucepan. Boil the liquid until it has thickened and reduced by about half, then pour back over the rhubarb and leave to cool.

Serve the rhubarb warm or cold, topped with the thick warm or cold custard.

**❝**This is a classic pudding. Thick custard prepared with good-quality ingredients is what really makes it special.**❞**

## RHUBARB PIE

1kg rhubarb, trimmed and chopped into 2cm pieces
1 large cooking apple, peeled, cored and chopped
300g granulated sugar, plus a little extra for the top
1 egg white, beaten
thick custard or clotted Jersey cream, to serve

FOR THE SWEET PIE PASTRY
110g soft butter, plus extra for greasing
135g caster sugar
1 tsp baking powder
225g strong flour
a pinch of salt
125ml double cream
SERVES 6–8

Put the rhubarb, apple and sugar in a heavy pan, cover and cook on a medium heat for 3-4 minutes, stirring occasionally. Remove the lid and cook for 8-10 minutes over a fairly high heat, until the rhubarb is soft and most of the liquid has evaporated. Remove from the heat and leave to cool.

Preheat the oven to 200°C/gas mark 6. To make the pastry, cream the butter and sugar. Sieve the baking powder and flour together and stir into the butter mix with the salt, then slowly pour in the cream until well mixed. Chill for about 30 minutes before rolling.

Grease a 17–18cm diameter, 2–3cm deep tart tin with butter and roll two-thirds of the pastry to about 2-3mm thick. Line the tin with the pastry and trim the edges. Then line the tin with a circle of greaseproof paper and fill with baking beans. Bake for 15-20 minutes, or until the pastry is lightly coloured.

Meanwhile, roll the remaining pastry out to a circle just a little larger than the tart. If you like, you can cut the pastry into strips about 1cm wide to lay on top in a lattice pattern or just keep as a circle.

Remove the beans and paper from the tart and spoon the rhubarb mixture in. Cover with the pastry top, trim and press on to the edges of the pastry base with your thumb and forefinger. Brush the top with egg and scatter with sugar. Bake for 30-35 minutes or until the top is a golden crisp. Leave to cool to room temperature and serve with thick custard or cream.

“So, what do we have against rhubarb? Memories of school meals of stewed rhubarb and lumpy custard maybe, or when mum didn't quite put enough sugar into the pot. There is, however, undoubtedly a rhubarb revival happening, with lots of new and interesting recipes hittting the streets, along with well-made old classics.”

# WHITE PORT AND STRAWBERRY TRIFLE

FOR THE JELLY
100–120g strawberries, hulled and chopped
100g caster sugar
6g leaf gelatine (2 sheets)
200ml white port

FOR THE BASE
50g sponge cake
100ml white port
150g strawberries, hulled and sliced

FOR THE CUSTARD
300ml double cream
½ vanilla pod
5 medium egg yolks
60g caster sugar
2 tsp cornflour

FOR THE TOPPING
250ml double cream
50–60g strawberries, hulled and sliced
20–30g flaked almonds, lightly toasted, or crushed
    macaroons

SERVES 4

For the jelly, put the strawberries, 200ml water and the sugar into a saucepan. Bring to the boil, then lower the heat and simmer gently for a couple of minutes.

Meanwhile, soak the gelatine leaves in cold water for a few minutes to soften. Take the strawberry mixture off the heat. Squeeze the gelatine to remove the excess water, add to the strawberry mixture and stir until dissolved. Strain the mixture through a fine sieve into a bowl and leave to cool a little, then add the white port. Leave to cool.

For the trifle base, break the sponge into pieces and arrange in a layer in the bottom of a glass serving bowl or 4 individual glasses. Sprinkle the port evenly over the sponge and lay the strawberries on top. Pour over the cooled (but not set) jelly so it just covers the strawberries and put in the fridge for an hour or so to set.

Meanwhile, make the custard. Pour the cream into a heavy saucepan. Split the vanilla pod lengthways, scrape out the seeds with a knife and add the seeds and pod to the cream. Slowly bring to the boil, then remove from the heat and leave to infuse for about 10 minutes.

In a bowl, mix the egg yolks, sugar and cornflour together. Take out the vanilla pod and pour the cream onto the egg mix, whisking well. Return to the pan and cook gently over a low heat, stirring constantly with a wooden spoon until the custard thickens; don't let it boil. Pour into a bowl, cover the surface with a sheet of greaseproof paper to prevent a skin forming and leave to cool.

Once the jelly has set, spoon the cooled custard on top. Cover and refrigerate for half an hour or so until the custard has set.

For the topping, softly whip the cream, then spoon on top of the trifle. Decorate with the strawberry slices and almonds or crushed macaroons and serve.

66 This luxurious trifle was inspired by a trip to Portugal to visit one of our wine suppliers, Quinta de la Rosa, who also produces fine white port. I'm not sure why sherry is traditionally used in a trifle, perhaps it's to use up what's left after Christmas, but having enjoyed white port as an apéritif in Portugal, I thought I'd give it a go instead. It worked a treat. 99

# APPLE BREAD PUDDING

500ml medium cider
200g caster sugar, plus extra for dusting
½ tsp ground cinnamon
½ tsp ground mixed spice
60g sultanas
60g raisins
grated zest of ½ orange
500g brown or white bread, crusts removed
4 medium crisp dessert apples, such as Cox's
50g butter
4 medium eggs, beaten
thick Jersey cream or ice cream, to serve

SERVES 6–8

Put the cider, sugar, spices, sultanas, raisins and orange zest into a saucepan and bring to the boil. Meanwhile, break the bread into small pieces and place in a bowl. Tip the cider mixture over the bread and stir to mix. Cover the bowl with cling film and leave to stand overnight.

The next day, peel, quarter, core and slice the apples. Melt the butter in a large frying pan and fry the apples over a medium heat, stirring occasionally, for 3–4 minutes until lightly coloured. Set aside to cool.

Preheat the oven to 180°C/gas mark 4. Line the base and sides of a 20cm square baking tin, about 6cm, with greaseproof paper.

Fold the eggs into the bread mixture, then fold in the cooled apples. Spoon the mixture into the prepared tin and bake for about 30–40 minutes until firm. Dust the top with sugar while still hot. Serve warm with cream or ice cream.

**"** Bread pudding is of one of those recipes that you can tweak and add other ingredients to very easily. Here I've included apples and cider to give it a real taste of the West Country. **"**

# BOOZY BAKED WORCESTER APPLES

4 medium-sized dessert apples
1 small egg, beaten
thick custard or double cream, to serve

FOR THE PASTRY
250g plain flour, plus extra for dusting
a pinch of salt
½ tbsp caster sugar
60g lard
25g unsalted butter

FOR THE FILLING
30g walnuts, chopped
30g nibbed almonds
1 tbsp ground almonds
6 dates, chopped
1 tbsp raisins
2 tbsp brown sugar
3 tbsp cider brandy
a good pinch of mixed spice

SERVES 4

Preheat the oven to 200°C/gas mark 6. First make the pastry: mix the flour, salt and sugar in a bowl and make a well. In a pan, heat 100ml water with the lard and butter until they come to the boil, then pour on to the flour and stir with a wooden spoon to form a smooth dough. Leave the dough covered for about 15 minutes or so, until it can be handled.

Divide the dough into 4 balls. Roll each on a lightly floured table to about 14–16 cm in diameter and cut into circles large enough to cover the apples.

Cut the stalk end off each apple and remove the core, making a hole about 1.5 cm wide – enough to pour filling into. Mix the ingredients for the filling together and stuff into the apples. If any is left over, just spoon it on top.

Put an apple in the centre of each piece of pastry and bring the pastry up the sides of the apple, gathering it up and pinching it together, leaving the top of the apple and filling exposed. Place on a baking tray, brush with the egg and bake for 45 minutes, or until the pastry is golden. If the pastry starts browning too much, cover with foil. Serve hot with custard or cream.

An appropriate alcohol for these includes cider brandy, a drop of homemade sloe gin, or even a mixture of the two. If you have neither, then Cognac, Calvados, sherry or rum work well, and will give a good aroma when you break through the crust.

"These are a rather grown-up version of baked apples. The booze and filling is cleverly contained in the pastry, which also makes them easier to transport. The ideal apple for this would be Worcester Pearmain, but they are not always available so I would go for a dessert apple, like Cox's, Pink Lady or Braeburn."

# APPLE AND GUINNESS FRITTERS

150ml Guinness
110g gluten-free self-raising flour, plus extra for dusting
1 tbsp caster sugar, plus extra for dusting
vegetable oil, for deep-frying
4 well-flavoured eating apples, peeled, cored and sliced
  into rounds
thick cream, to serve

SERVES 4–6

Whisk the Guinness into the flour to form a thick batter, add the sugar and leave to stand for an hour.

Preheat about 8cm of oil to 160–180ºC in a large deep, heavy pan or electric deep-fat fryer.

Dust the slices of apple in flour and shake off the excess, then dip 4 or 5 slices at a time into the batter, shake off any excess, and then drop them into the hot fat. After a minute or so, turn them with a slotted spoon so they colour evenly. When they are golden all over, remove them from the oil and drain on kitchen paper. Repeat with the rest of the apples.

Dust with caster sugar and serve with thick cream.

# APPLE AND COBNUT TART

FOR THE PASTRY
2 medium egg yolks
225g unsalted butter, softened, plus extra for greasing
1 tbsp caster sugar
275g plain flour, plus extra for dusting

FOR THE FILLING
30g unsalted butter
3 large Bramley apples, peeled, cored and chopped
2 tbsp Somerset apple brandy
75g caster sugar

FOR THE CRUMBLE TOPPING
80g plain flour
40g unsalted butter, diced small
60g caster sugar
20 or so cobnuts, shelled and chopped

SERVES 4–6

First make the pastry. Beat the egg yolks and butter together in a bowl until evenly blended, then beat in the sugar. Stir in the flour and knead together until well mixed. Gather the pastry into a ball, wrap in cling film and leave to rest in the fridge for an hour.

Lightly butter a 26cm tart tin or 4 individual ones. Roll out the pastry on a lightly floured surface to a 5mm thickness and use to line the tin(s). Trim the edges and refrigerate for 1 hour.

Meanwhile, make the filling. Melt the butter in a pan, tip in the apples and cook for 4–5 minutes until soft. Add the brandy and sugar, stir well until dissolved, then remove from the heat.

To make the crumble, briefly whiz the flour, butter and sugar together in a food processor or mixer until the mixture resembles coarse breadcrumbs, or place in a bowl and rub together with your fingertips. Fold in the cobnuts.

Preheat the oven to 190°C/gas mark 5. Line the tart(s) with greaseproof paper, fill with baking beans and bake for 10–15 minutes until the pastry is light golden. Lower the oven setting to 180°C/gas mark 4. Remove the beans and paper and fill with the apple mixture. Top with the crumble and bake for 20–30 minutes until the top is golden brown. Serve.

# PEAR AND APPLE COBBLER WITH BERRIES

1 medium cooking apple, peeled and cored
2 pears, peeled and cored
120g caster sugar
200g plums, quartered, stoned and roughly chopped
200g blueberries
200g blackberries
thick cream or custard, to serve

FOR THE COBBLER DOUGH
85g unsalted butter, softened
110g caster sugar
220g strong plain flour, plus extra for dusting
1 tsp baking powder
a good pinch of salt
100ml milk
1 small egg, beaten

SERVES 4–6

Roughly chop the apple and pears and place in a heavy-based saucepan with the sugar. Cook over a low heat for 5–6 minutes with the lid on, stirring every so often, until the apple begins to break down. Add the plums and continue to cook for another 5–6 minutes. Remove from the heat and leave to cool for about 10 minutes. Preheat the oven to 190°C/gas mark 5.

Meanwhile, make the dough. Cream the butter and sugar until very pale and fluffy. Sift the flour, baking powder and salt over the mixture and fold in, with a little of the milk, until well combined. Gradually add the rest of the milk to achieve a sticky dough.

Flour your hands and shape the dough into 16–20 small rough balls. Place them on a non-stick baking sheet, brush with the egg and bake in the oven for 6–7 minutes.

Stir the blueberries and blackberries into the fruit mixture and transfer to a large ovenproof serving dish. Arrange the cobbler balls on top of the fruit and bake for 35–40 minutes until golden in colour. Serve hot, with cream or custard.

This is pure comfort food – especially if you serve it with thick cream or custard. Vary the fruit according to what you have to hand but do try to include a few handfuls of berries to give some colour.

# INDIVIDUAL BRAMBLE PIES

FOR THE PASTRY
110g butter, softened, plus extra for greasing
135g caster sugar
225g strong plain flour, plus extra for dusting
a pinch of salt
½ tsp baking powder
125ml double cream
1 medium egg white, mixed with 1 tbsp caster sugar

FOR THE FILLING
800g blackberries
120g caster sugar
1 tsp arrowroot or cornflour, mixed with 1 tbsp
    cold water

TO SERVE
icing sugar
thick cream or crème fraîche

SERVES 4

First make the pastry. Cream the butter and sugar together until smooth. Sift the flour, salt and baking powder together and stir into the butter until evenly combined. Now slowly incorporate the cream until well mixed.

Knead the dough lightly, then divide into 2 portions, one slightly bigger than the other. Shape each into a ball, wrap in cling film and refrigerate for 30 minutes.

Lightly butter four 10cm individual tart tins, about 3cm deep. Roll out the slightly larger ball of pastry on a lightly floured surface to about a 3mm thickness. Using an 18cm plate as a guide, cut out 4 discs. Line the tart tins, leaving about 5mm of pastry overhanging the edge.

Roll out the other portion of pastry and cut out 4 discs, a little more than 10cm in diameter, for the pie lids. Place on a tray. Put the tart tins and pastry discs in the fridge and leave to rest for 1 hour.

Meanwhile, to make the filling, put 200g of the blackberries into a saucepan with the sugar and 1 tablespoon of water. Bring to a simmer and cook gently for 3–4 minutes. Add the blended arrowroot or cornflour and simmer for another 2–3 minutes, stirring occasionally. Strain through a fine-meshed sieve into a bowl and leave to cool a little, then mix in the rest of the blackberries.

Preheat the oven to 200°C/gas mark 6. Remove the pastry from the fridge. Using a slotted spoon, fill the pastry cases with the blackberry filling. Moisten with the juice from the fruit, but don't add too much or they will go soggy. Brush the pastry rim with water, then lay the pastry lids over the pies, pressing the edges together to seal.

Brush the tops with the egg white and sugar mix, then make a small slit in the centre with the point of a knife. Put the tart tins on a baking tray and bake in the oven for 20–25 minutes until golden, turning the oven down a little or covering loosely with foil if they appear to be colouring too quickly.

Leave the pies to rest for about 15 minutes, then remove from the tart tins and transfer to serving plates. Dust with icing sugar and serve with a generous spoonful of cream or crème fraîche.

If you are a forager you're unlikely to miss out on making the most of our autumn abundance of blackberries – or brambles. You can add other fruits, such as blueberries or elderberries if you wish, or stick to the traditional blackberry and apple combination. You can also use frozen blackberries.

# AUTUMN FRUIT CRUMBLE

a good knob of butter

3 large Bramley apples, peeled, cored and roughly
    chopped

75g caster sugar

150g blackberries and/or any other wild berries,
    such as blueberries or elderberries

clotted cream or custard, to serve

FOR THE CRUMBLE TOPPING

40g cold unsalted butter, cut into small pieces

30g ground almonds

60g caster sugar

80g plain flour

SERVES 4–6

Preheat the oven to 190°C/gas mark 5.

Melt the butter in a pan, add the apples and sugar, and cook for 6–7 minutes, stirring occasionally until they are beginning to break down but are not too soft. Remove from the heat and stir in the blackberries and any other berries. Transfer to a large ovenproof pie dish or individual pie dishes.

Mix all the topping ingredients in a food processor or mixer, or rub between your fingers until they look like breadcrumbs.

Sprinkle the crumble topping over the top of the filling and bake in the oven for 30–40 minutes, until the top is golden brown.

Serve with clotted cream or custard.

# AUTUMN BERRY PUDDING

125g butter, softened, plus extra for greasing

185g caster sugar

2 medium eggs, at room temperature and beaten

125g self-raising flour, sifted

80ml milk

300g mixed autumn berries, such as blackberries,
    blueberries, elderberries, tayberries

150ml port

thick Jersey cream or custard, to serve

SERVES 4

Preheat the oven to 190°C/gas mark 5. Butter 4 individual heatproof pudding bowls or pots.

Beat the butter and 125g of the sugar in a bowl until light and fluffy, then beat in the eggs a little at a time. Carefully fold tablespoons of the flour into the mixture, alternately with the milk, until smooth.

Divide about a third of the berries evenly between the prepared moulds, then spoon the batter over them to three-quarters fill the pudding bowls. Cover each with a piece of foil, pleated in the middle, to allow room for expansion. Secure tightly under the rim with string.

Stand the pudding moulds in a deepish baking tray or ovenproof dish and surround with enough boiling water to come about halfway up the sides of the moulds. Cook in the oven for 35-40 minutes until the puddings are springy to the touch.

Meanwhile, place the remaining 60g of sugar and port in a pan over a medium-low heat and bring to the boil. Add the rest of the berries and heat until just warmed through, stirring them carefully.

To serve, run a knife around the puddings, then turn out onto warm serving plates and spoon the berries and sauce over them. Serve with cream or custard.

It doesn't need to be deep midwinter to appreciate a steamed fruit pudding. When there is an abundance of our autumnal soft fruits around, I like making puddings like this, using dark autumnal fruits that are plentiful in the hedgerows – like blackberries, blueberries, tayberries, loganberries, and perhaps even a few elderberries.

# AUTUMN FRUITS WITH SLOE GIN AND CREAMY RICE PUDDING

FOR THE RICE PUDDING

50g pudding rice

25g caster sugar

a pinch of freshly grated nutmeg

300ml milk

75ml evaporated milk

75ml thick Jersey or double cream

FOR THE FRUITS

1 vanilla pod

4 cloves

1 bay leaf

120g brown sugar

a few pared strips of orange zest

100ml sloe gin, or to taste

200–250g blackberries, elderberries or blueberries

4 ripe plums, quartered and stoned

SERVES 4

For the pudding, put the rice, sugar, nutmeg and milk in a pan and bring to the boil. Lower the heat and simmer for 20 minutes until the rice is tender, stirring from time to time. Add the evaporated milk, bring back to the boil and simmer gently for another 10 minutes. Transfer to a bowl and leave to cool.

Once cold, stir in the cream. Cover and leave in the fridge to set.

For the fruits, pour 200ml water into a pan. Split the vanilla pod lengthways, scrape out the seeds with a knife and add the seeds and pod to the water with the cloves, bay leaf, brown sugar and orange zest. Bring to the boil. Lower the heat and simmer gently for 7–8 minutes, then tip into a bowl and set aside to infuse and cool.

When the syrup is cold, drain the liquid through a colander and into a bowl. Add the sloe gin to taste, then add the fruits. Cover and leave for at least 2 hours, stirring occasionally.

Serve the fruits at room temperature, with the rice pudding.

" Here sloe gin is used rather like mulled wine, and you can add as little or as much as you wish. The choice of fruit is up to you – any plums will work, even greengages, and you can add pears, peeled and cut into wedges if you like. The more the merrier. "

If you haven't any sloe gin, then substitute with a fruity full-bodied red wine, using 300ml in place of the water and gin.

# GOOSEBERRY AND ELDERFLOWER MERINGUE PIE

FOR THE PASTRY
2 medium egg yolks
225g unsalted butter, softened
1 tbsp caster sugar
275g plain flour, plus extra for dusting
melted butter, for brushing

FOR THE FILLING
200g gooseberries
60ml elderflower syrup
60g caster sugar

FOR THE MERINGUE
2 egg whites
40g caster sugar

SERVES 4

**"** Some people find the sourness of gooseberries a bit off-putting, but they make really great desserts. With the exception of the red dessert variety, these berries need to be cooked with sugar. The elderflower gives them a complementary summery fragrance. **"**

To make the pastry, beat the egg yolks and butter together in a bowl until evenly blended, then beat in the sugar. Stir in the flour and knead together until well mixed. Wrap the pastry in cling film, flatten and leave to rest in the fridge for an hour before use.

Meanwhile, make the filling. Put the gooseberries, elderflower syrup and sugar in a pan over a medium heat. Cook, stirring every so often, for 5-6 minutes until the gooseberries have softened and the liquid has evaporated. Remove from the heat, cover with a lid or cling film and set aside.

Preheat the oven to 190°C/gas mark 5. Lightly brush 4 individual tart tins, 8-10cm in diameter and 3cm deep, with melted butter (or one large 20-23cm tart tin, about 4cm deep). Roll out the pastry on a lightly floured surface to a 3mm thickness. Cut out 4 discs (or one big one), large enough to line the tart tin(s).

Line the tin(s) with the pastry, trimming away the excess just above the rims. This pastry is delicate but forgiving, so if it starts to break just patch it up, moulding the pastry back together with your fingers. Crimp the edge for a neat finish, by pinching it between your thumb and forefinger all the way round. Leave to rest in the fridge for 1 hour.

Line the pastry case(s) with greaseproof paper discs, fill with baking beans and bake blind for 10-15 minutes until the pastry is lightly golden. Rest for 5 minutes, then remove the beans and paper. Turn the oven setting up to 200°C/gas mark 6.

Place the egg whites in a clean, dry bowl, making sure it is free from any trace of grease. Whisk, using an electric whisk, until stiff. Add half of the sugar and whisk for 2-3 minutes until the mixture is really stiff, then add the rest of the sugar and continue whisking until the meringue is very stiff and shiny.

To assemble, spoon the gooseberries into the tart case(s), then either pipe or spoon the meringue on top to cover completely. Place on a baking tray and bake in the oven for 3-5 minutes until the meringue just starts to colour. Serve hot or warm.

## CRANACHAN WITH RASPBERRIES

60g medium oatmeal
150g raspberries
600ml double cream
4 tbsp runny honey
4 tbsp malt whisky

SERVES 4

Preheat the oven to 150°C/gas mark 2 or heat a grill to medium. Scatter the oatmeal on a baking tray and toast in a low oven or under the grill until golden. You'll have to watch closely or it may burn.

Blend 50g of the raspberries in a liquidiser until smooth. Whip the double cream until stiff, then stir in the honey and whisky, and whisk well but do not over-whip. Fold in 50g of the oatmeal, then carefully fold in the raspberry purée to form a rippled effect.

Spoon the mixture into glass coupes or a serving dish, then scatter the rest of the raspberries and oatmeal on top.

## PEARS IN PERRY

4 firm pears
500ml perry
4 cloves
a small piece of a cinnamon stick
6 black peppercorns
2 tbsp caster sugar
a couple of handfuls of blackberries (optional)
clotted cream or ice cream, to serve

SERVES 4

Peel the pears, leaving the stalks intact, and cut a thin sliver off the base of each one so that they will stand upright.

Put the perry, cloves, cinnamon, peppercorns and sugar into a heavy-based saucepan and add the pears. Lay a piece of greaseproof paper over the fruit. Bring to a simmer and poach gently for about 45 minutes until the pears are soft and tender but still holding their shape.

Lift out the poached pears, using a slotted spoon, and set aside on a plate.

Continue to simmer the liquor in the pan until it has thickened and reduced by about two-thirds. Return the pears to the liquor and leave to cool.

To serve, stand each pear in a deep serving plate and spoon over some of the reduced liquor. Add a few blackberries, if using, and a scoop of cream or ice cream.

“Poaching pears in their own alcohol, perry, makes sense – I'm not sure why I didn't think of it before Matthew Fort gave me the idea. You can serve the pears with clotted cream or ice cream, or with blackberries and blackberry rippled cream as I have here.”

"Is this delicious dessert French or English in origin? It's difficult to say, as burnt cream seems to have been around for as long as *crème brûlée*. This creamy pudding is often called Trinity pudding, or Trinity cream, after the Cambridge college, although there is a story that the recipe came from an Aberdeenshire country house and was offered to the college back in the 1860s by an undergraduate. Earlier recipe books of the 1700s refer to a similar pudding as well, but I suppose at the end of the day it's just a good simple way to use up excess cream."

# TRINITY BURNT CREAM

600ml thick Jersey or double cream
8 egg yolks
75g caster sugar

SERVES 4

The day before you want to serve, bring the cream to the boil and reduce by one-third.

Meanwhile, mix the egg yolks with 1 tablespoon of the sugar in a heatproof bowl. Pour the slightly cooled reduced cream on to the egg yolk mixture and mix well.

Return the mixture to the pan and cook over a low heat, stirring constantly and without allowing it to boil, until the mixture coats the back of a spoon. Remove from the heat.

Pour into 1 large or 4 individual heatproof gratin dish(es), like ramekins, and leave to cool overnight in the fridge.

An hour before serving, sprinkle an even layer of the sugar over the top of the cream and caramelise either under a preheated very hot grill or with a chef's blowtorch.

# ELDERFLOWER ICE CREAM

300ml creamy milk, such as Guernsey or Jersey
6 egg yolks
100g caster sugar
300ml Jersey cream or clotted cream, or a mixture
200ml elderflower syrup, or more to taste

MAKES ABOUT 750ML

Pour the milk into a saucepan and bring to the boil, then remove from the heat.

Whisk the egg yolks and sugar together in a bowl, then pour on the milk, whisking as you do so. Return to the pan and place over a low heat. Cook, stirring constantly, using a whisk, for about 5 minutes until the custard has thickened lightly, but don't let it boil.

Pour the custard into a bowl and whisk in the cream and elderflower syrup. Leave to cool, then churn in an ice-cream machine until thickened. Scoop into glass bowls and serve, with summer berries if you like.

# ELDERFLOWER AND BUTTERMILK PUDDING WITH SUMMER FRUITS

12g leaf gelatine (4 sheets)
350ml buttermilk
50g caster sugar
250ml double cream
100ml elderflower syrup

FOR THE SUMMER FRUITS
100g strawberries, hulled
30g caster sugar
50g raspberries
50g blueberries
50g redcurrants

SERVES 4

66 This smooth, creamy pudding is rather like an Italian pannacotta. We don't use buttermilk that much, although in Ireland it's a fairly commonplace ingredient. You can get hold of it in good supermarkets and dairy shops; otherwise just use Jersey milk. 99

Soak the gelatine in a bowl of cold water for a few minutes to soften. Meanwhile, pour 100ml of the buttermilk into a saucepan, add the sugar and bring to the boil over a medium-low heat, stirring occasionally to encourage the sugar to dissolve.

Squeeze the gelatine leaves to remove the excess water. Remove the buttermilk from the heat, add the gelatine and stir until dissolved. Leave to cool until barely warm.

Whisk the cream, elderflower syrup and the rest of the buttermilk into the mixture. Pour into dariole moulds, ramekins or coffee cups and place in the fridge for 2–3 hours or overnight to set.

In the meantime, put the strawberries and sugar into a saucepan over a low heat and simmer very gently for about 5 minutes until the strawberries have turned to a mush. Strain through a fine-meshed sieve into a bowl, pushing down on the pulp with the back of a spoon to extract as much juice as possible. Leave to cool.

To serve, briefly dip the pudding moulds in hot water, then invert onto serving plates and shake gently to turn out. Scatter the raspberries, blueberries and redcurrants around the puddings and spoon the strawberry sauce over the top of the fruit.

You can introduce different fruits here as they come into season; in winter a compote of dried fruits or preserved fruits in alcohol works well.

# STRAWBERRY SUNDAE

300–350g strawberries, hulled
120ml clotted cream
400ml good-quality vanilla ice cream

**SERVES 4**

Whiz about half of the strawberries in a blender until smooth, then strain the purée through a fine sieve to remove the seeds if you wish.

Slice the rest of the strawberries. Put a few strawberry slices in the bottom of four tall glasses and spoon in some of the purée and clotted cream. Pile three small balls of ice cream into the glasses, scattering in more strawberry slices as you do so. Spoon on the rest of the strawberry purée and clotted cream, then top with the remaining strawberry slices to serve.

66 Fruit sundaes and knickerbocker glories conjure up memories of traditional British seaside holidays, although you rarely see them on menus these days. You're more likely to come across bought-in ice creams in every flavour under the sun. This seaside classic can be made with whatever fruit is in season at the time, but good-quality vanilla ice cream is crucial, whether it is homemade or bought. 99

# BLUEBERRY CHEESECAKE

450g blueberries, hulled
200g caster sugar
20g cornflour

FOR THE BASE
250g digestive biscuits or Hobnobs
80g butter, melted

FOR THE FILLING
300ml double cream
100g caster sugar
500g cream cheese
finely grated zest of 1 lemon
1 tsp vanilla extract

SERVES 4

66 A truly comforting dessert. I've used blueberries here, but you could substitute raspberries, blackcurrants or strawberries, making sure to adjust the sweetness accordingly. 99

Put 200g of the (softer) blueberries into a pan with the sugar and 175ml of water. Heat slowly to dissolve the sugar, then simmer for 7–8 minutes. Mix the cornflour with 25ml of water and stir into the mixture. Simmer, stirring, for 2–3 minutes. Strain through a fine sieve into a bowl, pressing the berries in the sieve to extract as much juice as possible. Leave to cool.

Line a 17–18cm springform cake tin with greaseproof paper. Crush the biscuits in a food processor to coarse crumbs. (Or put in a plastic bag and smash with a rolling pin.) Mix with the butter and pack into the cake tin to make a firm base using the back of a spoon.

Whip the cream and sugar together until fairly stiff. In another bowl, beat the cream cheese to soften, then fold in the cream with the lemon zest and vanilla extract. Lightly fold through half of the blueberry syrup to create a rippled effect. Spoon the mix onto the biscuit base and place in the fridge for 2–3 hours until firm.

Mix the rest of the fruit with the remaining blueberry syrup. To unmould the cheesecake, run a hot knife around the edge, then release the side of the tin and slide the cheesecake onto a board. Cut into slices and serve each one topped with a generous spoonful of blueberry sauce.

# CHRISTMAS MESS

40–50 fresh or vacuum-packed chestnuts
2 tbsp icing sugar
500ml double cream
80g caster sugar
150–200g meringue

FOR THE CRANBERRY SAUCE
200g fresh cranberries
90g sugar
1 small cinnamon stick
juice of 1 orange

SERVES 8

" Cranberries, in the form of a sauce or jelly, are synonymous with Christmas dinner, though these tart red berries are worthy of more than being just an adjunct to the turkey. Like chestnuts, they lend themselves to a host of savoury dishes and interesting desserts, such as this lovely meringue concoction, which is loosely based on an Italian *monte bianco*. You don't need to go to the trouble of making fresh meringues, there are plenty of good ready-made meringues on the market that are suitable for this dish. "

Preheat the oven to 200°C/gas mark 6. If using fresh chestnuts, make an incision in the top of each with a small sharp knife and place them on a baking tray. Bake in the oven for about 20 minutes, then remove and leave to cool.

Meanwhile for the sauce, put the cranberries, sugar, cinnamon and orange juice into a heavy-based saucepan. Stir over a low heat until the sugar has dissolved, then simmer gently for about 20-25 minutes until the cranberries have softened. Discard the cinnamon. Taste the sauce and add a little more sugar if necessary. Leave to cool.

Peel the chestnuts, removing as much of the brown skin as you possibly can. Place the cooked or vacuum-packed nuts on a foil-lined baking tray and dust with icing sugar. Bake in the oven for 20 minutes, turning them every so often. Remove and set aside to cool.

Whip the cream and caster sugar together in a bowl until very thick, using an electric whisk if you wish.

To assemble, break the meringue into pieces and fold into the cream with about two-thirds of the cold cranberry sauce and two-thirds of the chestnuts. Pile onto the centre of individual serving plates. Scatter the remaining chestnuts on top and spoon the rest of the cranberry sauce over. Serve at once.

## SLOE GIN JELLY SHOTS

1 tbsp caster sugar
6g leaf gelatine (2 sheets)
400ml sloe gin
thick Jersey cream, to serve (optional)

MAKES 16–20

Bring 200ml water to the boil in a saucepan, add the sugar and stir until dissolved, then remove from the heat.

Soak the gelatine leaves in a shallow bowl of cold water for a minute or so until soft. Squeeze out the excess water, then add to the sugar syrup and stir until melted. Stir in the sloe gin.

Pour into shot glasses and place in the fridge for a couple of hours or so until the jelly is set. Serve topped with a spoonful of thick cream if you like.

**❝** If you make your own sloe gin then this is a fun way to show it off at a party and it's a great talking point. Otherwise, it's not difficult to find good-quality sloe gin in the shops. Depending on how strong you want your jellies to be, you can up the gin and use less water. **❞**

I've got a thing about jellies, which I think goes back to my discovering that jelly was not the packeted rubbery stuff you buy in shops and dissolve in hot water. Grown-up jellies are great and you can have really great easy fun creating different versions throughout the year.

## APPLE AND BLACKBERRY JELLY

500ml clear apple juice
100g caster sugar (or less if the juice is sweet)
12g leaf gelatine (4 sheets)
120g blackberries
thick Jersey cream, to serve (optional)

SERVES 4

Bring 100ml of the apple juice to the boil. Add the sugar and stir until dissolved.

Meanwhile, soak the gelatine leaves in a shallow bowl of cold water for a minute or so until soft. Squeeze out the water, add the gelatine to the hot apple juice and stir until dissolved. Add the rest of juice, stir well and put the jelly somewhere cool, but do not let it set.

Fill individual jelly moulds or glasses, or one large mould, with half the berries, then pour in half of the cooled jelly. Put in the fridge for an hour or so to set, then top up with the rest of the berries and unset jelly. This allows the berries to stay suspended and not float to the top. Return to the fridge to set.

To serve, turn out and offer thick Jersey cream to go with the jelly.

You can buy various apple juices in the shops, from the highly pasteurised stuff in the shops that doesn't really resemble apples, to the quality stuff, like those produced by Chegworth Valley. Ideally, a clear juice is more suitable than a really cloudy one, so you can see the blackberries suspended in the jelly, but flavour is what we are really after here.

# MULLED PORT JELLY

9g leaf gelatine (3 sheets)
600ml port
2 cloves
1 cinnamon stick
65g caster sugar

MAKES ABOUT 600ML

Soak the gelatine leaves in cold water. Meanwhile, in a saucepan, bring half the port to the boil, together with the cloves, cinnamon and sugar.

Squeeze out any excess water from the gelatine leaves and dissolve them in the hot liquid. Add the rest of the port, pass through a fine sieve and leave to cool and set. Store in a sealed jar in the fridge.

66 Everyone has the odd bottle of port knocking around at Christmas time, and a great way to use it up is as a jelly to go with the obligatory lump of Stilton. 99

# STRAWBERRY AND SPARKLING WINE JELLY

12g leaf gelatine (4 sheets)
700ml fine-quality sparkling wine, such as
    Nyetimber, Chapel Down, Prosecco or Champagne
50g caster sugar
120g strawberries, hulled
thick Jersey cream, to serve

SERVES 4

Soak the gelatine leaves in a bowl of cold water for a few minutes to soften. Meanwhile, pour 200ml of the sparkling wine into a saucepan, add the sugar and bring to the boil over a medium-low heat, stirring occasionally to encourage the sugar to dissolve. Take off the heat.

Squeeze the gelatine to remove the excess water, then add to the wine syrup and stir until fully dissolved. Now stir in the rest of the wine. Leave to cool until barely warm, but don't allow to set.

Divide half of the strawberries between individual jelly moulds or attractive Martini glasses, then carefully pour in half of the cooled jelly, ensuring the berries are evenly distributed. Place in the fridge for an hour or so until set. Keep the rest of the jelly at room temperature, making sure it does not set.

Once the jellies have set, arrange the rest of the strawberries on top and pour on the rest of the jelly. (Setting the jelly in two stages allows the berries to stay suspended so that they don't float to the surface.) Return the jellies to the fridge to set.

To serve, briefly dip the pudding moulds, if using, in hot water, then invert onto serving plates and shake gently to turn out. Or set the Martini glasses on plates. Serve with thick Jersey cream.

This is a pretty posh jelly and not that cheap to make, but if you pick or buy wild or homegrown strawberries, then it's worth splashing out on Champagne or, better still, Nyetimber – the best sparkling wine produced in the UK. For a non-alcoholic version, use elderflower cordial, diluted with water or apple juice.

# ROAST PLUMS WITH COBNUTS AND CLOTTED CREAM

12–18 Victoria or other plums, depending on size
6 tbsp caster sugar
clotted cream or thick Jersey cream, to serve

FOR THE TOPPING
2 tbsp plain flour
40g hard butter, chopped into small pieces
½ tbsp brown sugar
4 tbsp oats
24–30 cobnuts, shelled and roughly chopped

SERVES 4

Preheat the oven to 200°C/gas mark 6. First make the topping: put the flour and butter into a bowl and rub together with your fingers until a breadcrumb-like consistency. Stir in the brown sugar, then mix in the oats and cobnuts. Spread out on a baking tray.

Halve the plums, remove the stones and place cut-side up on another baking tray. Sprinkle with the caster sugar.

Place both of the trays in the oven and bake for 15–20 minutes until the plums are lightly coloured and softened and the topping is golden; you may need to take the topping out before the plums.

Leave the plums to cool slightly, then transfer them to individual serving bowls and spoon over the cooking juices. Scatter over the cobnut topping and top with a generous dollop of cream.

We have lots of varieties of plums in the UK, from large Victorias to small greengages. You can use any variety for this dish, or a mixture. Cobnut trees are pretty specific to Kent; if you are unable to get hold of any cobnuts, use hazelnuts instead.

# SUSSEX POND PUDDING

250g self-raising flour
125g shredded beef suet
150ml milk
300g unsalted butter, softened, plus extra for greasing
200g soft light brown sugar
1 large unwaxed lemon

SERVES 4–6

**"** This unusual pudding is steamed with a whole lemon inside that serves two purposes: one to hold the pudding up and secondly to permeate the rich buttery sauce with a delicate lemony flavour as it cooks. Once the pud is turned out on to the serving dish, it will be sitting in a pond of delicious sweet lemony sauce. **"**

Mix the flour and suet together in a bowl, then gradually mix in the milk to form a dough. The dough should be soft but firm enough to roll out.

Roll out the dough to a circle large enough to line a 1.5 litre pudding basin. Cut a quarter out of the circle for the lid and to ease the lining of the bowl. Butter the pudding basin well, drop the pastry into it and join up the edges where the quarter was removed.

Mix the sugar and butter together and put into the lined basin. With a roasting fork or skewer, prick the whole lemon all over as much as you can so that the juices can escape during cooking, then push it into the butter mixture.

Remould the pastry for the top and roll it out to the correct size. Lay it on top of the filling and press the edges together to seal in the filling. Cover the top of the basin with a generous piece of foil, making a pleat down the middle to allow for expansion. Secure in place under the rim with string, making a string handle so it can be lifted easily.

Lower the pudding into a pan containing enough boiling water to come about halfway up the side of the basin. Cover and simmer for 4 hours, topping up with more boiling water as necessary.

To serve, use the string to lift out the basin and allow to stand for about 30 minutes, then remove the foil and loosen the sides with a small sharp knife. Put a deep serving dish over the basin and quickly turn the whole thing upside down – it may collapse a little but the flavour will be incredible.

# STICKY TOFFEE PUDDING

150g pitted dates
65g unsalted butter, softened, plus extra for greasing
175g soft dark brown sugar
2 medium eggs, lightly beaten
225g self-raising flour
ice cream, soured cream or crème fraîche, to serve

FOR THE TOFFEE SAUCE
600ml double cream
350g caster sugar
90g unsalted butter

SERVES 4–6

Put the dates into a pan with 250ml water and simmer over a low heat for 10-15 minutes or until the dates are soft and the water has almost evaporated. Whiz in a blender until smooth. The purée should be a good spoonable consistency; if too thick, thin with a little water. Leave to cool.

Preheat the oven to 180°C/gas mark 4. Grease a baking tin, measuring about 15cm × 12cm × 6cm, with butter and line with greaseproof paper.

To make the sponge, cream the butter and sugar together until light and fluffy. Add the eggs slowly, taking care that the mixture does not separate. If the mixture does start to curdle, add a little of the flour to rebind and continue adding the egg. Gently fold in the flour, with a large metal spoon, until evenly mixed. Finally, fold in the date purée.

Pour the mixture into the baking tin, spread out and bake for about 50-60 minutes or until the sponge is firm to the touch. Allow to cool in the tin for 10 minutes or so. Keep the oven on.

Meanwhile, make the toffee sauce. Pour half of the cream into a heavy-based pan and add the sugar and butter. Bring to the boil, stirring, and continue to boil until the sauce is golden brown, 8-10 minutes or even longer. Allow to cool for about 10 minutes, then whisk in the remaining cream.

Remove the sponge from the tin, trim the edges to neaten, then cut horizontally into 4 even layers. Re-line the tin with fresh greaseproof paper. Reassemble the sponge in the tin, spreading two thirds of the warm sauce in between the layers. Reheat the pudding in the oven for 15-20 minutes.

To serve, cut the pudding into 4-6 portions, place in warm bowls and top with the remaining toffee sauce. Serve with ice cream, soured cream or crème fraîche.

"To be successful, this addictive pudding must live up to its name. It's got to be sticky and gooey, and for that you need plenty of sauce between the layers to soak through and moisten them."

# WILTSHIRE LARDY CAKE

200g lard, softened, plus more for greasing
50g butter, softened
200g mixed dried fruit
75g mixed candied peel
200g granulated sugar

FOR THE BREAD DOUGH
650g strong white bread flour, plus extra for dusting
2 tsp salt
1 tsp caster sugar, plus more to sprinkle
7g sachet of easy-bake yeast

MAKES ABOUT 12 SLICES

First make the bread dough: in a warm bowl, mix the flour, salt, sugar and yeast. Add 400ml warm water and mix to a soft dough. Knead by stretching it and folding it for about 10 minutes on a lightly floured surface.

Mix the lard, butter, fruit, peel and sugar together and divide the mixture into 3 equal parts.

On a lightly floured surface, roll out the bread dough to a rectangular shape roughly three times as long as it is wide, and spread two-thirds of its length with one-third of the lard mixture, then fold both long ends of the dough into the centre and firmly press the edges with your fingers or the rolling pin. Repeat this process twice more, using up the remaining lard mixture, then roll it out to its original size.

Turn the dough over and place it in a shallow baking tin lined with lightly oiled greaseproof or silicone paper, with enough room for it to rise again. Leave to prove in a warm place for about 30 minutes, or until it has almost doubled in volume.

Meanwhile, preheat the oven to 190°C/gas mark 5. Bake the cake for about 45 minutes. Turn it out upside down on to another tray or large dish and leave to cool a little. Sprinkle the cake generously with caster sugar.

The lardy cake is best served warm, just as it is.

"This cake is just what its name suggests – lardy, but not as bad and fatty as it may sound. It's sort of based on a puff pastry-type recipe, layering the dough with fat and then folding and rolling. These days you don't get many recipes recommending the use of lard, but here it makes the cake deliciously gooey. It is rather filling, though, so you don't need too much. Lardy cake is traditionally from Wiltshire, although you find it in bakeries throughout the South West, and I remember eating it as a kid just out of the oven at Leakers bakery in Bridport."

## CHOCOLATE-DIPPED WALNUTS

24 walnuts in the shell or 150g good-quality shelled
    walnuts
200g good-quality dark chocolate
60–70g good-quality cocoa powder

MAKES ABOUT 48 PIECES

Shell the walnuts if you've bought them in their
shells. Break the chocolate into a heatproof bowl
and place over a pan of simmering water until
melted, making sure the bowl does not touch the
water. Sift the cocoa powder onto a shallow tray and
have another tray ready.

Dip the walnuts into the melted chocolate a few at
a time, then remove with a fork, tapping it on the
side of the bowl to encourage the excess chocolate
to run back into the bowl. Now drop them into the
cocoa, turning the walnuts with a clean fork and
shaking the tray so they are well coated. Place on
the clean tray. Repeat with the rest of the walnuts.

Store the coated nuts in an airtight container in a
cool place and use within a week.

## CHOCOLATE MOUSSE

250g good-quality dark chocolate, about 70% cocoa
    solids, broken into small pieces
50g unsalted butter, softened
6 very fresh medium eggs, separated, plus 3 extra
    egg whites
40g caster sugar
chocolate curls (shaved from a block of chocolate with
    a peeler), to serve

SERVES 4–6

Melt the chocolate in a heatproof bowl over a pan
of simmering water, stirring every so often and
making sure the bowl isn't touching the water.
Remove from the heat and beat in the butter, using
a whisk or spoon, until smooth. Beat the egg yolks
in another bowl and set aside.

In a clean, grease-free bowl, whisk the egg whites
until frothy but not stiff, using a mixer or an electric
whisk on a medium-high speed. Add half the sugar
and continue whisking on a low setting until stiff.
Add the rest of the sugar and whisk until the egg
whites stiffen up further. Now fold in the beaten
egg yolks using a metal spoon.

Carefully stir half of this into the chocolate mixture,
using a whisk, then fold in the rest with a large
spoon until evenly combined. Pour into a large
serving dish and leave to set for a couple of hours,
or overnight.

To serve, scoop a portion of mousse onto each
serving plate and finish with chocolate curls.

"Of all the chocolate mousse recipes that I have used over the years, this one is the simplest and yields the best results by far. It's wonderfully indulgent and always comforting."

## VENEZUELAN BLACK AND CIDER BRANDY TRUFFLES

650g good-quality dark chocolate, finely chopped
400ml double cream
50g Venezuelan black chocolate
200g unsalted butter, softened
100ml Somerset cider brandy
60g good-quality cocoa powder

MAKES ABOUT 30

Set aside 250g of the dark chocolate. Bring the cream to the boil in a pan, then remove from the heat and gradually add the 400g dark chocolate and the black chocolate, stirring with a whisk until melted and the mixture is smooth. Stir in the butter and cider brandy. Transfer to a bowl and leave to cool, then chill for 1–1½ hours or until the mixture is firm enough to spoon into rough shapes.

Spoon the mixture onto a tray lined with cling film in rough mounds. Leave in the fridge until firm.

Melt the reserved chocolate in a bowl over a pan of simmering water, making sure the bowl does not touch the water. Take off the heat and let cool for a few minutes. Sift the cocoa powder onto a tray; have another clean tray ready for the finished truffles.

Using a thin skewer or cocktail stick, dip each truffle quickly into the melted chocolate, allow the excess to drain off, then drop into the cocoa powder, shaking the tray so that the truffle becomes coated. When half of the truffles are coated, shake off the excess cocoa and lay on the clean tray. Repeat with the remaining truffles.

Store the truffles in a sealed plastic container lined with kitchen paper in the fridge (no longer than a month... as if). Bring them to room temperature about 30 minutes before serving.

" Time to celebrate two excellent West Country artisan products: Willie Harcourt-Cooze's 100% cacao black chocolate, made from Venezuelan cacao pods in Devon, and Julian Temperley's Somerset cider brandy. "

## HIX OYSTER ALE CAKE

60g sultanas
225g cold butter, cut into small cubes, plus extra for greasing
450g self-raising flour
a good pinch of salt
a good pinch of freshly grated nutmeg
a good pinch of mixed spice
a good pinch of ground cinnamon
225g molasses sugar
finely grated zest of 2 oranges
finely grated zest of 1 lemon
1 large egg, beaten
200ml Hix Oyster Ale

SERVES 8–10

Put the sultanas into a bowl, pour over enough boiling water to cover and leave to soak overnight.

The next day, preheat the oven to 160°C/gas mark 3. Line a 20cm × 10cm × 6cm loaf tin with buttered greaseproof paper. Drain the sultanas.

Sift the flour, salt and spices together into a bowl and stir in the sugar. Rub in the butter with your fingertips until the mixture resembles breadcrumbs. Stir in the orange and lemon zests, then gently mix in the egg, sultanas and ale.

Transfer the mixture to the prepared tin, spreading it evenly. Bake in the oven for 1½–1¾ hours or until golden and firm to the touch. To test, insert a fine skewer in the centre; it should come out clean.

Leave in the tin for 5 minutes or so, then turn out onto a wire rack and let cool before serving.

This is a nice, rich teatime cake that is also very good served with cheese. If you can't find my dark Oyster Ale, I'll allow you to use Guinness, stout or even a porter.

## BAKEWELL PUDDING

150g ready-made all-butter puff pastry
250g butter, melted
1 egg, beaten, plus 7 extra egg yolks
250g caster sugar
1 tbsp ground almonds
3 tbsp raspberry jam
cream, to serve (optional)

**MAKES ONE 20CM PUDDING**

Preheat the oven to 190°C/gas mark 5. Roll the pastry out to a thickness of about 5mm and prick it all over with a fork to prevent it from rising, then use to line a 20cm diameter, 3cm deep, preferably sloping-sided, tart tin (I use an ovenproof non-stick frying pan, as this seems to be as close to the original as you can get). Leave to rest for 1 hour in the fridge.

Meanwhile, in a heatproof mixing bowl, mix the butter, egg and extra yolks with the sugar and almonds, and stir over a pan of simmering water for 3–4 minutes until it reaches a honey-like consistency, without letting it touch the water.

Spoon the raspberry jam evenly over the bottom of the chilled pastry case, then pour the almond filling into the pastry case and bake the pudding for 45 minutes, or until the top is golden and the filling has just set. If it's browning too much, turn the oven down halfway through.

Serve the pudding warm or at room temperature, with or without some cream.

## CHERRY BATTER PUDDING

25g butter, melted, plus more for greasing
50g plain flour
50g caster sugar
2 eggs, beaten
250ml single cream, warmed
1 tbsp cherry brandy
a few drops of vanilla extract
450g ripe red or black cherries, stoned
icing sugar, for dusting
thick cream, to serve

**SERVES 4**

Preheat the oven to 200°C/gas mark 6 and grease a round ovenproof dish or tart tin or, better still, a non-stick one.

Sieve the flour into a bowl and stir in the sugar. Mix in the eggs and slowly whisk in the cream to form a light batter. Stir in the cherry brandy, vanilla extract and butter.

Scatter the cherries over the prepared dish or tin and pour in the batter. Bake for 20 minutes, then turn the oven down to 190°C/gas mark 5 and cook for a further 20 minutes, or until the batter has risen and is golden on top, but still creamy inside.

Dust with icing sugar and serve hot or warm from the dish, with thick cream.

"If you know your international puddings, then you may just recognise this one from across the water in France: yes, it's a kind of clafoutis – in fact, it is clafoutis and, inevitably, the old question is raised, who originated it? Well, this one is definitely Kentish and a simple dessert to use up just some of those excess summer cherries."

# A SHIPWRECKED TART

FOR THE PASTRY
225g unsalted butter, softened, plus extra for greasing
2 medium egg yolks
1 tbsp caster sugar
275g plain flour, plus extra for dusting

FOR THE FILLING
3 medium eggs, beaten
200g soft brown sugar
220g golden syrup
120ml cider brandy (ideally Shipwreck, see below)
100g unsalted butter, melted
1 tsp vanilla extract
a pinch of salt
100g walnuts, roughly chopped
100g hazelnuts, roughly chopped
100g shelled roasted chestnuts, roughly chopped

TO SERVE
vanilla ice cream, crème fraîche or double cream

SERVES 8–10

To make the pastry, beat the butter and egg yolks together until smooth, then beat in the sugar. Mix in the flour until evenly combined, but don't overwork. Knead the dough lightly and shape into a ball. Wrap in cling film and refrigerate for 30 minutes.

Butter a 25cm loose-based tart tin. Roll out the pastry on a floured surface to a large circle, 3–4mm thick, and use to line the tin. Trim the edges and refrigerate for 1 hour.

Preheat the oven to 180ºC/gas mark 4. To make the filling, blitz all the ingredients, except the nuts, in a food processor until smooth. Transfer to a bowl and fold in the nuts until evenly combined.

Fill the tart case with the nut mixture and bake for 20–25 minutes until golden brown. Serve with vanilla ice cream, crème fraîche or some double cream.

"This tart was inspired by Julian Temperley's 10-year-old Shipwreck Somerset cider brandy, which is aged in oak barrels washed up on Branscombe beach in Devon from the shipwrecked Napoli, hence the title."

# NORFOLK TREACLE TART

FOR THE SWEET PASTRY

110g butter, softened

135g caster sugar

1 tsp baking powder

225g strong flour, plus extra for dusting

a pinch of salt

125ml double cream

FOR THE FILLING

225g golden syrup

50g dark treacle

220ml double cream

75g oatmeal or fresh white breadcrumbs

2 eggs, beaten

1 tbsp lemon juice

extra-thick or clotted cream, to serve

SERVES 8–10

Make the pastry a couple of hours ahead: cream the butter and sugar together, then sieve the baking powder and flour together and stir into the butter mixture with the salt. Slowly pour in the cream until well mixed. Wrap in cling film and chill for 30 minutes before rolling.

On a floured table, roll out the pastry to about 5mm thick. Use to line a 26cm tart tin, about 3–4cm deep, and leave to rest in the fridge for 1 hour.

Preheat the oven to 160ºC/gas mark 3. Meanwhile, make the filling by mixing the golden syrup, treacle, double cream, oatmeal and eggs together, then stir in the lemon juice. Fill the tart tin with the mixture and bake for 40–50 minutes, then leave to cool.

Serve warm with some good extra-thick or clotted cream.

I have come across so many treacle tart recipes in my time, and all of them differing slightly from one another – some with cream, some with lemon and oats, or breadcrumbs to hold it all together. My preference is the deeper, lighter tart version, with that subtle hint of lemon.

# CORNISH SAFFRON CUSTARD TARTS

# PARKIN

250–300g ready-made all-butter puff pastry
plain flour, for dusting
300ml single cream
a good pinch of saffron strands
4 medium egg yolks
50g caster sugar
1½ tsp cornflour

MAKES 10–12 MINI TARTS

Roll out the pastry on a lightly floured surface to a 3mm thickness and prick it thoroughly all over with a fork. Loosely fold into three, wrap in cling film and leave to rest in the fridge for 30-40 minutes.

Have ready a 12-hole muffin tray. Unfold the pastry and cut out circles, using a 9-10cm cutter. Use to line the muffin tins, pushing the pastry into the corners and trimming the tops with a sharp knife. Line with discs of greaseproof paper and baking beans and rest in the fridge for 15 minutes.

Preheat the oven to 180°C/gas mark 4. Bake the tart cases for 10-15 minutes until they begin to colour, then remove the paper and beans and leave to cool for a few minutes.

Meanwhile, put the cream and saffron into a small saucepan and bring to the boil. Take off the heat and leave to infuse for 10 minutes.

In a bowl, mix together the egg yolks, sugar and cornflour. Pour the infused cream onto the egg mixture, stirring well with a whisk. Return to the pan and cook over a low heat for several minutes, stirring constantly with a wooden spoon until the custard thickens; don't let it boil. Pour into a jug.

Pour the saffron custard into the tart cases and bake for 10-12 minutes until set. Leave to cool a little, then loosen the tarts with a small knife and carefully remove from the tin. Serve warm or cold.

This is a nod to past Cornish saffron growing. Some traditional Cornish cakes are still made with saffron, but these days it is imported, mostly from Iran and Spain.

115g butter, plus extra for greasing
225g plain flour
1 tsp bicarbonate of soda
2 tsp ground ginger
1 tsp ground cinnamon
1 tsp mixed spice
1 tsp salt
110g coarse (pinhead) oatmeal
175g dark muscovado sugar
3 tbsp golden syrup
115g black treacle
150ml milk
1 large egg, beaten

MAKES 1 LOAF

Preheat the oven to 180°C/gas mark 4 and grease a (preferably non-stick) loaf tin with butter. Sift the flour, bicarbonate of soda, spices and salt into a bowl. Stir in the oatmeal and sugar and make a well in the centre.

Melt the butter, syrup and treacle in a pan over a low heat, whisking to emulsify. Remove from the heat and let cool.

When cooler, mix into the flour mixture with a wooden spoon, then beat the milk and egg together and stir into the mixture until well mixed.

Pour into the loaf tin and bake for 45-50 minutes, until still slightly soft to the touch. Leave to cool for 30 minutes or so before turning out.

"I've never been too much of a cake person, but there is something warming about the parkin, hence the old association in the North with eating it on Guy Fawke's Night. It probably doesn't get served on that particular night much these days and on the nights I've attended bonfire parties with my daughters, Ellie and Lydia, there wasn't a slice of parkin in sight."

# STOCKS
# AND SAUCES

# VEGETABLE STOCK

3 onions, peeled and roughly chopped
3 garlic cloves, peeled and roughly chopped
1 small head of celery, roughly chopped
3 leeks, well rinsed and roughly chopped
5 carrots, peeled and roughly chopped
2 bay leaves
a few sprigs of thyme
20 black peppercorns
a small bunch of flat-leaf parsley
1 tsp fennel seeds

MAKES 1–1.5 LITRES

Place all of the ingredients in a large saucepan and add enough cold water to cover. Bring to the boil, skim and simmer for 30-40 minutes.

Strain the liquor through a fine sieve. Taste and if the flavour isn't strong enough, boil to reduce the stock down a little.

# DARK MEAT STOCK

2kg chopped beef, veal, lamb or chicken bones, or a mixture
3 onions, peeled and roughly chopped
5 carrots, peeled and roughly chopped
3 celery stalks, roughly chopped
2 leeks, well rinsed and roughly chopped
½ head of garlic
1½ tbsp tomato purée
10 black peppercorns
a few sprigs of thyme
1 bay leaf

MAKES 1–1.5 LITRES

Raw bones make a better stock than leftover cooked ones, so ask your butcher to keep some for you – they'll need to be chopped up. If you want to make this into a sauce, reduce the stock until starting to thicken and add a little cornflour mixed with water to achieve the consistency required.

Preheat the oven to 200°C/gas mark 6. Put the chopped meat bones in a roasting tin with the vegetables and garlic and roast for about 15-20 minutes until golden brown, stirring every so often. Stir in the tomato purée and roast for another 10 minutes.

Tip the bones and vegetables into a large saucepan, cover with cold water and add the black peppercorns, thyme sprigs and bay leaf. Bring to the boil, simmer for 3-4 hours, skimming occasionally and topping up with water as necessary to keep the ingredients completely covered.

Strain through a fine sieve, then skim off any fat. Taste and, if the flavour isn't strong enough, boil to reduce down.

## CHICKEN STOCK

2kg chicken bones, rinsed and chopped
3 leeks, well rinsed and roughly chopped
3 onions, peeled and roughly chopped
3 celery stalks, roughly chopped
1 bay leaf
a few sprigs of thyme
2 garlic cloves, peeled and chopped
10 black peppercorns

MAKES 1–1.5 LITRES

Place all of the ingredients in a large saucepan and add enough cold water to cover. Bring to the boil and simmer for 2 hours, topping up with water and skimming as necessary.

Strain the liquor through a fine sieve. Taste and if the flavour isn't strong enough, boil to reduce the stock down a little.

## FISH STOCK

2kg white fish bones, such as sole, brill, etc., rinsed
2 leeks, well rinsed and roughly chopped
2 onions, peeled and roughly chopped
½ head of celery, roughly chopped
½ lemon
1 tsp fennel seeds
20 black peppercorns
1 bay leaf
a few sprigs of thyme
a handful of flat-leaf parsley

MAKES 1–1.5 LITRES

Place all of the ingredients in a large saucepan and add enough cold water to cover. Bring to the boil, then lower the heat and simmer for 20 minutes, skimming occasionally.

Strain the liquor through a fine sieve. Taste the stock and boil to reduce if the flavour isn't strong enough.

Don't overcook this stock or it will lose its freshness and may have a bitter taste.

# BASIC GRAVY

2kg beef, veal, lamb or chicken bones, or a mixture,
    chopped into small pieces
3 onions, peeled and roughly chopped
5 carrots, peeled and roughly chopped
3 celery stalks, roughly chopped
3 leeks, well rinsed and roughly chopped
½ bulb of garlic
1 tbsp tomato purée
2 tbsp plain flour
3–4 litres dark meat stock (see page 292)
10 black peppercorns
a few sprigs of thyme
1 bay leaf
1–2 tsp cornflour, mixed with a little water (optional)
sea salt and freshly ground black pepper

MAKES 2 LITRES

Preheat the oven to 200°C/gas mark 6. Put the chopped
bones in a roasting tin with the vegetables and garlic and
roast for about 15-20 minutes until golden brown, stirring
every so often. Stir in the tomato purée, then sprinkle in the
flour and stir well. Roast for another 10 minutes.

Put the roasting tin on the hob, add a little of the stock
and stir over a low heat, scraping up the sediment from the
bottom. Transfer everything to a large saucepan and pour
in the rest of the stock to cover. Add the black peppercorns,
thyme sprigs and bay leaf. Bring to the boil and skim, then
simmer for 2 hours, topping up with water to keep the
ingredients covered and skimming occasionally as required.

Strain through a fine-meshed sieve into a bowl and remove
any fat from the surface. Taste to check the strength and
boil to reduce and concentrate the flavour if necessary. If the
gravy is not thick enough, stir in the blended cornflour and
simmer, stirring, for a few minutes. Check the seasoning
before serving.

# POULTRY GRAVY

500g chicken, goose or duck bones, or a mixture, chopped into
    small pieces, plus the giblets from the birds
1 large onion, peeled and roughly chopped
2 medium carrots, peeled and roughly chopped
1 celery stalk, roughly chopped
1 leek, well rinsed and roughly chopped
2 garlic cloves, peeled and chopped
1 tsp tomato purée
1 tbsp plain flour
2 litres chicken stock (see page 293)
6 black peppercorns
a few sprigs of thyme
1 bay leaf
1–2 tsp cornflour, mixed with a little water (optional)

MAKES 1 LITRE

Preheat the oven to 200°C/gas mark 6. Put the poultry
bones, giblets, vegetables and garlic in a roasting tray and
roast for about 15-20 minutes until lightly coloured, giving
them a good stir every so often. When the bones are golden
brown, stir in the tomato purée and flour and stir well.
Return to the oven for another 10 minutes.

Transfer the roasting tray to the hob. Add a little of the stock
and stir over a low heat, scraping up the sediment from the
bottom of the tray. This will start the thickening process.

Tip everything into a large saucepan and pour on the rest of
the stock. If the stock doesn't quite cover the bones, top up
with some cold water. Add the peppercorns, thyme and bay
leaf. Bring to the boil and skim. Lower the heat and simmer
for 2 hours, topping up with boiling water as necessary to
keep the ingredients covered. Skim occasionally as required.

Strain through a fine sieve into a clean pan and remove any
surface fat. Taste and, if necessary, simmer to reduce and
concentrate the flavour. If it is not thick enough, mix in the
blended cornflour and simmer, stirring, for a few minutes.

## MAYONNAISE

100ml olive oil
200ml vegetable oil
2 egg yolks, at room temperature
2 tsp white wine vinegar
1 tsp English mustard
2 tsp Dijon mustard
½ tsp salt
freshly ground white pepper
a little lemon juice

MAKES ABOUT 300ML

Mix the olive and vegetable oils in a jug and set aside. Put the egg yolks, white wine vinegar, both mustards, salt and some pepper into a non-reactive bowl (aluminium will make the mayonnaise go grey) and set on a damp cloth to stop it from slipping. Mix well with a whisk, then gradually trickle the oil mix into the bowl, whisking continuously. If the mayonnaise gets too thick, add a few drops of water and continue whisking. When all the oil is incorporated, taste and adjust the seasoning, and add a little lemon juice.

## TARTARE SAUCE

25g gherkins, finely chopped
25g capers, rinsed and finely chopped
½ tbsp chopped flat-leaf parsley
4 tbsp mayonnaise (see left)
a little lemon juice
sea salt and freshly ground black pepper

MAKES ENOUGH FOR 4

Mix the gherkins and capers together with the parsley and mayonnaise. Season to taste with lemon juice, salt and freshly ground black pepper.

## AIOLI

6–8 garlic cloves, peeled
sea salt and freshly ground white pepper
2 egg yolks
300ml olive oil
a little lemon juice

MAKES ABOUT 300ML

Crush the garlic cloves in a little salt with the flat of a knife. In a bowl, mix the garlic, egg yolks and a good pinch of salt. While beating the mixture with a whisk, gradually trickle in the olive oil, stopping if it gets too thick and adding a teaspoon of water to prevent it from separating. When you have added nearly all of the oil, season with white pepper, add lemon juice to taste, then add the rest of the oil. Adjust the seasoning again if necessary. The consistency can also be adjusted with more water.

" A little Dijon mustard sometimes helps, or a touch of wine vinegar, to give the aioli that more savoury, mayonnaise-like flavour. If you don't want such a full-on olive oil taste, then cut it with vegetable or corn oil as per your preference. "

# BEARNAISE SAUCE

1 tbsp white wine or cider vinegar
1 small shallot, peeled and roughly chopped
a few sprigs of tarragon, leaves picked and stalks reserved
a few sprigs of chervil, leaves picked and stalks reserved
5 black peppercorns
200g unsalted butter
3 small egg yolks
sea salt and freshly ground white pepper
a little lemon juice (optional)

MAKES ENOUGH FOR 4–6

Put the vinegar, shallot, herb stalks, peppercorns and 2 tablespoons of water in a pan and simmer for 1 minute or until reduced to 2 teaspoonfuls. Strain and leave to cool.

Melt the butter in a saucepan over a low heat and let bubble very gently for 3–4 minutes. Remove from the heat, leave to cool a little, then pour off the pure liquid butter into a bowl, leaving the milky whey behind. Discard the whey. (Clarifying the butter in this way helps to keep the sauce thick.)

Put the egg yolks into a small heatproof bowl (or a double boiler if you have one) with half of the vinegar reduction and set over a pan of gently simmering water. Whisk the mixture until it begins to thicken and become frothy. Slowly trickle in two-thirds of the clarified butter, whisking continuously – preferably using an electric hand whisk. If the butter is added too quickly, the sauce is liable to separate.

Taste the sauce and add a little more, or all if it needs it, of the remaining vinegar reduction. Whisk in the rest of the butter. The vinegar should just cut the oiliness of the butter sauce; don't add too much. Season with salt and pepper to taste. Cover the bowl and leave in a warm, not hot, place until needed, but no longer than 20 minutes.

To serve, chop the tarragon and chervil leaves and stir into the sauce. Check the seasoning and add a squeeze of lemon juice, to taste. Whisk lightly.

# SEAFOOD SAUCE

3 tbsp tomato ketchup
2 tbsp freshly grated horseradish
a little lemon juice

MAKES ENOUGH FOR 4

Mix the ketchup and horseradish together. Season to taste with a little lemon juice. Serve with some oysters, raw clams or cold lobster.

# SHALLOT VINEGAR

4 shallots, peeled and finely chopped
100ml good-quality red wine vinegar

MAKES ENOUGH FOR 4

Place the shallots in the vinegar and leave to infuse for at least 1 hour before serving.

# SAUCE NANTUA

shells of 20–24 crayfish tails
4 shallots, peeled and roughly chopped
1 garlic clove, peeled and chopped
vegetable oil, for frying
1 tbsp plain flour
a good pinch of saffron strands
a few sprigs of tarragon
1–2 tbsp tomato purée
4 tbsp white wine
300ml fish stock (see page 293)
350ml double cream

MAKES ENOUGH FOR 4

In a large pan, fry the shells, shallots and garlic in oil for 6–7 minutes, until lightly coloured. Add the flour and stir. Add the saffron, tarragon and purée; stir well. Gradually stir in the wine and stock, bring to the boil and simmer for 10 minutes until reduced by half. Add the cream, bring to the boil and simmer for 30 minutes until reduced by half and a thick consistency. Strain through a colander into a bowl. Remove about half a cupful of shells and blend with the sauce in a liquidizer. Use a fine-meshed sieve to strain.

## SIMPLE FISH MARINADE

4 tbsp olive oil
1 tsp chopped thyme leaves
1 tsp finely grated lemon zest
sea salt and freshly ground black pepper

MAKES ENOUGH FOR 4

Mix all of the ingredients together in a bowl. Rub the mixture all over firm-fleshed fish like turbot, brill, swordfish or tuna just before grilling.

## SHELLFISH-INFUSED OIL

200g crab (or other crustacea) shells
1 litre oil, such as a mixture of rapeseed and vegetable or corn oil
1 tsp fennel seeds
12 black peppercorns
a small pinch of saffron strands
a good pinch of sea salt
a few sprigs of thyme

MAKES 1 LITRE

Place all of the ingredients in a large saucepan. Slowly bring to a simmer. Continue to simmer very gently over the lowest possible heat for about 15 minutes, to infuse the oil with the flavours from the shells and aromatics.

Remove the pan from the heat and set aside to infuse for 2–3 hours. Strain the infused oil through a muslin-lined sieve and store in sterilised bottles in the fridge. Once opened, use within 2–3 weeks.

"This is a good way to get the best out of tasty crab, lobster or crayfish carcasses, or even prawn shells. Keep it in the fridge and use for dressing salads or fish."

# WILD GARLIC SAUCE

2–3 handfuls of wild garlic leaves, washed and dried
1–2 tsp Tewkesbury or English mustard
100–150ml cold-pressed rapeseed oil
sea salt and freshly ground black pepper

MAKES ENOUGH FOR 4

Put the wild garlic leaves, mustard and 100ml of rapeseed oil into a blender and process as smoothly or as coarsely as you wish. Season with salt and pepper to taste. Add as much of the extra oil as you need to get the desired consistency.

❝Delicious served with grilled meats, roast poultry and game. When wild garlic is in season, purée some in a blender with a little oil and store it in a sealed jar in the fridge topped with oil. Alternatively, blend it with a little water and freeze it in ice cube trays.❞

# BAKED NEW SEASON GARLIC SAUCE

4 heads of new season garlic
a few sprigs of curly parsley
½ tbsp Dijon mustard, or more to taste
70g fresh white breadcrumbs
2–3 tbsp duck fat, warmed, or the pan juices from a roast chicken
a little milk, to mix
sea salt and freshly ground black pepper

MAKES ENOUGH FOR 4

Preheat the oven to 200°C/gas mark 6. Wrap the garlic bulbs in foil and bake them in the oven for 1 hour. Unwrap and leave until cool enough to handle, then peel away any tough outer skin.

Put the garlic into a blender with the parsley, mustard, breadcrumbs and warm duck fat or chicken juices and blend until smooth. Add enough milk to give the sauce a thick pouring consistency and season with salt and pepper to taste. Serve with roast chicken.

# CHOP HOUSE SAUCE

a couple of knobs of butter
1 small onion, peeled and finely chopped
1 garlic clove, peeled and crushed
a good pinch of cayenne pepper
1 tsp plain flour
½ tsp tomato purée
1 tbsp cider vinegar
1 tsp redcurrant jelly
1 tsp English mustard
250ml dark meat stock (see page 292)
sea salt and freshly ground black pepper
1 large dill pickle or a few gherkins, finely diced

MAKES ENOUGH FOR 4

Melt the butter in a heavy-based pan and add the onion, garlic and cayenne pepper. Cook gently for 2–3 minutes to soften, then stir in the flour, followed by the tomato purée, cider vinegar, redcurrant jelly and mustard.

Gradually whisk in the stock, bring to the boil and season lightly. Simmer very gently for about 15 minutes (a simmer plate or heat-diffuser mat is useful here). Add the dill pickle or gherkins and re-season if necessary. The sauce should be quite thick; if not continue simmering a little longer.

❝This slightly piquant sauce goes really well with simple grilled pork, bacon or veal.❞

# CHOP HOUSE BUTTER

1 tbsp cold-pressed rapeseed oil
1 red onion, peeled and finely chopped
1 garlic clove, peeled and crushed
1 tsp coarsely ground black pepper
½ tbsp chopped thyme leaves
½ tbsp freshly grated horseradish
100ml red wine
250g butter, softened
1 tbsp Henderson's Relish or Worcestershire sauce
1 tbsp HP sauce
1 tbsp Tewkesbury or English mustard
1 tsp Gentleman's Relish
2 tbsp chopped flat-leaf parsley
½ tbsp chopped tarragon

MAKES 300G

Heat the rapeseed oil in a pan and add the onion, garlic and black pepper. Cook gently for 2–3 minutes or until softened, then tip into a bowl. Add all of the other ingredients and mix until well combined.

Spoon the butter onto a sheet of cling film or greaseproof paper and shape into a cylinder, about 3cm in diameter, sealing it well. Refrigerate or freeze until needed, cutting off slices as necessary. Serve directly on steaks and chops.

# HERB BUTTER

250g butter, softened
a little lemon juice (optional)
sea salt and freshly ground white pepper
2 tbsp chopped flat-leaf parsley, chervil, chives or dill

MAKES 250G

Mix the softened butter with the lemon juice, if using, a little salt and pepper and the chopped herbs of your choice. Spoon the butter onto a sheet of cling film or greaseproof paper and shape it into a cylinder, about 3cm in diameter. Seal well.

Refrigerate or freeze until needed, cutting off slices as necessary. Pop them on top of fish or meat before serving.

You can vary the flavourings of this herb butter, which is a great way to dress grilled, griddled or barbecued fish, in lots of ways – adding chopped deseeded chillies or a good pinch of cayenne pepper or a few drops of Tabasco sauce. Alternatively, add some chopped shallots that have been sautéed in a little butter..

## BLUE CHEESE DRESSING

1 tbsp cider vinegar
½ tsp Tewkesbury mustard
20g blue cheese, broken into pieces
2 tbsp cold-pressed rapeseed oil
2 tbsp vegetable or corn oil
sea salt and freshly ground black pepper

MAKES ENOUGH FOR 4–6

Blend the cider vinegar, mustard, blue cheese and oils
together in a blender and season with salt and pepper to
taste. If the dressing is too thick, thin it with a little water.

66 This is a useful way to use up little bits
of blue cheese and can transform a salad
into something rather special. It is ideal
with robust leaves like Little Gem lettuce
and chicory, but I wouldn't try it on more
delicate leaves as it will overpower them. 99

## BRAMBLE DRESSING

6–8 blackberries
1 tbsp cider vinegar
4 tbsp cold-pressed rapeseed oil
sea salt and freshly ground black pepper

MAKES ENOUGH FOR 4–6

Crush the blackberries in a bowl using a fork, then whisk
in the cider vinegar and rapeseed oil. Season with salt and
pepper to taste. Leave to stand for about 30 minutes, then
push through a sieve with the back of a spoon into a bowl
and re-season the dressing if necessary.

The lovely deep mauve colour and the
combination of sweet and acidic flavours
make this dressing the perfect match for
game salads. I haven't used much in the
way of fruity dressings since the eighties,
but this one makes great use of an
abundant supply of wild blackberries.

## PICKLED WALNUT DRESSING

2–3 good-quality pickled walnuts, chopped, plus
    2 tbsp of their juice
4–5 tbsp cold-pressed rapeseed oil
sea salt and freshly ground black pepper

MAKES ENOUGH FOR 4–6

Whisk all of the ingredients together in a bowl or shake in a
screw-topped jar or bottle, seasoning to taste.

66 Pickled walnuts are one of those old-
fashioned, almost forgotten British
condiments. Their sweet, acidic taste
works brilliantly in a dressing. This one
goes really well with beetroot or cheese-
based salads, though once you've tasted
it you'll probably want to put it on
everything. 99

# HONEY AND MUSTARD DRESSING

2 tbsp cider vinegar
1 tbsp clear runny honey
1 tbsp grain mustard
3 tbsp cold-pressed rapeseed oil
2–3 tbsp vegetable or corn oil
sea salt and freshly ground black pepper

MAKES ENOUGH FOR 4–6

Whisk the cider vinegar, honey, mustard and oils together in a bowl or shake in a screw-topped jar or bottle. Season to taste. Use to dress bitter leaves like dandelion or chicory, or with a ham hock and pea salad (see page 80).

# TEWKESBURY MUSTARD DRESSING

1 tbsp cider vinegar
1 tbsp Tewkesbury mustard
4 tbsp cold-pressed rapeseed oil
sea salt and freshly ground black pepper

MAKES ENOUGH FOR 4–6

Whisk the cider vinegar, mustard and rapeseed oil together in a bowl or shake in a screw-topped jar or bottle. Season with salt and pepper to taste.

66 Tewkesbury mustard is a blend of mustard and horseradish with a clean taste and sharp bite, which dates back to Shakespearean times. It's perfect to use in place of Dijon mustard in dressings to give a truly British taste. 99

# MIMOSA DRESSING

½ tbsp cider vinegar
juice of ½ small lemon
1 garlic clove, peeled and halved
2 sprigs of tarragon
2 tbsp vegetable or corn oil
2–3 tbsp cold-pressed rapeseed oil
sea salt and freshly ground black pepper

MAKES ENOUGH FOR 4–6

Whisk the cider vinegar, lemon juice, garlic, tarragon and oils together or shake in a screw-topped jar or bottle. Season with salt and pepper to taste. Leave to infuse overnight and strain before using.

66 We developed this years ago – for the classic salad that is topped with grated egg to give the look of a mimosa flower. However, I use this dressing in many other salads. 99

# TARRAGON DRESSING

1 tbsp cider vinegar
1 tsp English or Tewkesbury mustard
1 garlic clove, peeled
a few sprigs of tarragon
2 tbsp cold-pressed rapeseed oil
3 tbsp vegetable or corn oil
sea salt and freshly ground black pepper

MAKES ABOUT 100ML

Put all the ingredients into a clean bottle or jar. Shake well and leave to infuse for at least an hour, preferably overnight, at room temperature. Strain before using to dress your salad.

# DRINKS

# HIX FIX

2 morello cherries in Somerset eau-de-vie
250ml Nyetimber sparkling wine

MAKES 2

Place a cherry with a teaspoon or two of the cherry liqueur in the bottom of 2 champagne glasses, preferably saucers.

Top up with 125ml of sparkling wine or Champagne.

66 Well this has certainly been the biggest selling cocktail in all of the restaurants. It all started when I gave our manager in Lyme Regis a jar of Julian Temperley's morello cherries steeped in eau-de-vie made from his cider brandy. On my next visit to Lyme I noticed scribed up on the windows 'Hix Fix'. As I glanced around the room almost every table had one. I consequently bought some old fashioned Champagne saucers for it and the Hix Fix took off. Keith Floyd had a couple before his last lunch at the Fish House before he sadly passed away. 99

We serve these in the restaurants with British sparkling wine Nyetimber so it is 100% British, but you can use Champagne or Prosecco instead. Perry also works well.

# BERGAMEISTER

100ml gin
juice of 2 bergamot oranges
50ml rhubarb syrup (see below)
1 egg white
2 morello cherries in Somerset eau-de-vie

FOR THE RHUBARB SYRUP
250g rhubarb, trimmed and chopped into small chunks
250g caster sugar
1 vanilla pod, split lengthways

MAKES 2

For the rhubarb syrup, put the rhubarb and 375ml hot water in a saucepan and simmer until the rhubarb starts to break down. Pass the rhubarb through a sieve into a bowl and add the sugar and vanilla pod. Allow this to cool so that the vanilla infuses the rhubarb. Once cool, strain into an airtight container until needed.

Pour the gin, orange juice, rhubarb syrup and egg white into a shaker, and shake (this dry shake without ice allows the egg white to emulsify). Fill the shaker with cubed ice and shake briskly to produce a thick foam. Strain the drink into sour glasses and garnish each with a morello cherry and a splash of the eau-de-vie they are steeped in.

66 A friend of mine Louise Wachtmeister and I were having cocktails in Mark's Bar one night at the beginning of the bergamot season and our bar consultant Nick Strangeway came up with this little gem. 99

## SOPHIA'S SLING

150ml white port
400ml Fever-Tree tonic water
a couple of good squeezes and a few wedges of lemon

MAKES 2

Place a few ice cubes in two highball glasses and
add the port, tonic and lemon juice. Garnish each
with a lemon wedge to finish.

"This cocktail is named after Sophia Bergqvist, who
owns the Quinta de la Rosa winery in the Douro
valley, Portugal. She serves this on arrival to visitors
to the vineyard and for pre-dinner drinks. We do a
twist on this at the Hix Oyster & Fish House where
we add a couple of tablespoons of Tonnix red wine,
which floats on the top."

## BLOODY HOT BLACK COW

400–500ml good-quality canned or chilled
  tomato juice
6 whole pickled chillies (guindillas are best)
150–250ml Black Cow vodka
a few drops of Tabasco sauce
a couple of good pinches of sweet Spanish paprika

SERVES 4

Pour the tomato juice into a muslin-lined sieve
set over a large bowl or a jelly bag. Transfer to the
fridge and leave overnight to strain and extract a
clear juice. Gently squeeze the sieve if you want to
add a little of the pulps colour to the clear juice.

Use a pestle and mortar or the end of a rolling pin
to bash up two of the chillies, then add to a jug with
the vodka, Tabasco and strained tomato juice and
mix together well.

Place one ice sphere or cube into 4 chilled martini
glasses and sprinkle the ice with the paprika. Strain
the liquid into the glasses, garnish each with a
whole chilli and serve.

"I don't really like messing with
classic drinks like a Bloody Mary but
sometimes a pre-dinner drink requires
a lighter touch so you can fit a second
one in! How much heat you want in this
drink is up to you, so feel free to spice it
up with more chillies and Tabasco."

## QUINCE PRINCE

150ml quince gin (see below)
150ml sugar syrup
juice of 1 lemon
1 egg white

FOR THE QUINCE GIN
500g quinces, coarsely grated
1 litre gin
50g sugar

MAKES 2

To make the quince gin, mix the quince, gin and sugar together and store in a sterilised airtight container such as a kilner jar for 3-4 weeks. Strain through a fine sieve and store in airtight bottles until required.

To make the cocktail, half fill a cocktail shaker with ice, then add the quince gin, sugar syrup, lemon juice and egg white and shake vigorously for 10-15 seconds. Strain into serving glasses such as tumblers or large stemmed glasses.

❝I named this cocktail after the Princes – as in the food writer Rose and her husband Dominic – who regularly bring me quinces from their Dorset home. This infusion makes a litre of quince gin, which lasts well and can be used for all sorts of drinks.❞

## SOMERSET TEMPERLEY SOUR

50–60ml Somerset cider brandy
1 tbsp Kingston Black aperitif
4 tbsp apple syrup (see below)
juice of 1 lemon
1 egg white
2 morello cherries in Somerset eau-de-vie

FOR THE APPLE SYRUP
200g crab apples, Bramley apples or sharp dessert
    apples, roughly chopped
2 tbsp caster sugar, plus extra to taste

MAKES 2

To make the apple syrup, put the apples into a saucepan with the sugar and a cup of water, bring to the boil and simmer gently over a low heat for about 8-10 minutes, or until the apples are soft. Strain through a fine-meshed sieve, pushing a little of the apple pulp through the sieve. The syrup should be quite sweet but still taste of apple – add a little more sugar to taste, stirring, if necessary. Leave to cool.

To serve, half fill a cocktail shaker with ice cubes. Add the cider brandy, Kingston Black, apple syrup, lemon juice and egg white and shake well for 20 seconds. Strain into a couple of glasses, garnishing each with a cherry to finish.

❝I first created this with a few handfuls of crab apples I had to hand at my house in Dorset. If you can't find crab apples, you can use Bramley or even normal dessert. The cherries can be bought online or at the restaurants or substituted for cherries soaked in another liqueur.❞

## THE KING'S JEWELS

a couple of strips of clementine rind
100ml gin
10ml King's Ginger liqueur

FOR THE PINEAPPLE SYRUP
the flesh of ½ small pineapple, chopped into
    small pieces
100ml sweet vermouth

MAKES 2

To make the pineapple syrup, place the pineapple in a non-reactive bowl and pour over the vermouth. Cover with cling film and leave at room temperature for 2 days. Strain and set aside.

To serve, rub the clementine rind around the inside of 2 chilled or frozen martini glasses and divide between the glasses. Half fill a cocktail shaker with ice. Add the gin, King's Ginger and all of the strained pineapple syrup. Stir for 10-15 seconds before straining into the glasses.

" A few years back I was sent a bottle of King's Ginger from Berry Bros which was formulated by them in 1930 for King Edward VII. The liqueur was created to stimulate and revive his majesty during his morning rides in his new horseless carriage. I often take King's Ginger on a shoot or fishing trip to warm the cockles. "

## MAGGIE STRIKES BLACK

80ml Black Cow vodka
40ml Blue Curaçao liqueur
juice of 1 lemon
40ml Somerset morello cherry brandy liqueur
a couple of pre-made ice spheres or cubed ice
2 lemon twists

MAKES 2

Half fill a cocktail shaker with ice, add the vodka, Curaçao, lemon juice and cherry liqueur and shake for approximately 10 seconds.

Place a few ice spheres or cubes in 2 tumblers and strain over the liquid. Serve garnished with a twist of lemon.

" I created this cocktail to celebrate the life of Maggie Thatcher. The Curaçao gives it a lovely blue colour that I'm sure she would have appreciated. "

Ice spheres help to avoid the rapid dilution that can occur with crushed or cubed ice. Sphere moulds can be bought from good retailers and can be made in advance and stored in bags in the freezer for all sorts of drinks.

## PEATINI

a couple of handfuls of pea shoots, washed
50ml Plymouth gin
20ml sugar syrup
juice of ½ lemon
2 pea pods, to serve

MAKES 2

Place the pea shoots in a liquidiser with 2 tablespoons of water and blend together to make a smooth purée.

Half fill a cocktail shaker with ice cubes. Add the gin, pea shoot purée, sugar syrup and lemon juice and shake for 10-15 seconds. Strain into 2 chilled martini or coupé glasses. Split the peas in their pods and push on to the side of the glasses to serve.

66 The idea for this came after a pea-shoot lunch that we held at Hix Oyster & Chop House a few years ago. 99

## TARTAN TIPPLE

60ml Chivas Regal 12 year old blended Scotch whiskey
40ml Somerset Pomona
dash of Bitterman's Celery bitters
20ml good-quality blood orange marmalade
2 twisted strips of orange zest, to serve

MAKES 2

Fill a mixing glass with some ice cubes. Put the whiskey, Somerset Pomona, bitters and marmalade into the mixing glass. Stir for approximately 10 seconds. Place a large cube of ice into each tumbler. Strain the liquid over the ice. Place the rind over the surface of the drink and serve.

66 Marmalade isn't an obvious ingredient for a cocktail, but it really gives this drink a great breakfast feel. Good at any time of the day. 99

## CHOCOLATE MARTINIS

50g good-quality dark chocolate
100ml vodka or gin
20ml orange liqueur (Cointreau is good)
20ml crème de cacao
long strips of orange zest, cut with a canelle knife,
    or a peeler, and shredded
1 cinnamon stick, broken up into shards
1 tbsp grated chocolate or a cocoa stick

MAKES 2

Melt the chocolate in a bowl over a pan of simmering water, giving it an occasional stir. Remove from the heat and whisk in the vodka or gin. This is the base for your martini and you can mix as much or as little of it with the other liqueurs to suit your friends' tastes.

Put the chocolate mixture into a cocktail shaker, add both liqueurs and fill it with ice. (You may need to do this in two batches, depending on the size of your cocktail shaker.) Pour the mix into chilled martini glasses and garnish with the orange zest, cinnamon and grated chocolate.

"Years ago when I lived in Shoreditch I would have the occasional fridge clearing party. At some stage of the evening these would always appear..."

## YORKSHIRE SHRUBARB

50ml rhubarb shrub (see below)
50ml gin
50ml Manzanilla sherry
2 strips of orange zest

FOR THE RHUBARB SHRUB
150g Yorkshire rhubarb, roughly chopped
150g caster sugar
150ml Somerset cider vinegar

MAKES 2

For the rhubarb shrub, mix the rhubarb and sugar together, place in a non-reactive container, cover and store in the fridge for 24 hours. Stir in the vinegar, cover and let it sit in the fridge for another 72 hours. Strain through a fine meshed sieve into a sterilised bottle or container and store in the fridge until required.

To serve, half fill a cocktail shaker with ice, add the rhubarb shrub, gin and sherry and stir for approximately 15 seconds. Strain the mixture into chilled coupé glasses. Rub the orange rind around the rim and place in a glass filled with ice.

"This cocktail was created for Mother's Day by one of our bartenders at Hix Oyster & Chop House. The recipe makes more of the rhubarb shrub than you need but it will keep in the fridge for 1 month in an airtight container or preserving jar."

# INDEX

# ACKNOWLEDGEMENTS

Putting together a compendium of recipes isn't as straightforward as it may seem, so a big thanks needs to go to Jo Harris, for her meticulous checking and her eye for detail.

Art plays a big part in how my restaurants look so it was great to be able to represent that within this book. I'd like to thank Tracey Emin, Caragh Thuring, Michael Landy, Michael Craig-Martin, Polly Morgan, Sarah Lucas, Laura Quick, Gary Webb, Mat Collishaw, Sue Webster and Tim Noble for letting me feature their work within these pages. Long may our relationship continue.

Thanks to all at Quadrille Publishing, especially Publishing Director Jane O'Shea and the team who have worked on this book. And to Jason Lowe, my long time food photographer and friend.

And finally, a very special thank you to the staff, suppliers and customers who have all helped to make the restaurants such a huge success.

# ARTWORK CREDITS

**2** HIX © Tracey Emin, 2009 (neon); **8–9** *Lunch with the FT* © Caragh Thuring, 2013 (newsprint on paper); **59** *Pineapple Weed* © Michael Landy, 2002 (originally published by Paragon Press); **88–89** *Knife, Fork, and Spoon Column* (detail) © Michael Craig-Martin, 2011; **117** *Endless Plains* © Polly Morgan, 2012 (photo courtesy Tessa Angus) ; **150** *Chicken Soup* © Tracey Emin, 2008, (21 × 14.7cm, pen on paper); **178–179** *Pie Mobile (I said kiddley diddley eye)* © Sarah Lucas, 2002 (tinned Fray Bentos Pies, mobile, electric motor); **217** *Fat Welsh Asparagus* © Laura Quick, 2013; **249** *Pies and Pavlovas* © Gary Webb, 2009 (cast resin wood and aluminium); **291** *Last Meal on Death Row: Allen Lee Davis* © Mat Collishaw, 2012 (digital transfer print on goatskin parchment edition; 520 × 412.2mm; originally published by Other Criteria and Dark Matter); **303** *Mark's Finger* © Tim Noble and Sue Webster, 2009 (900 × 311mm; 4 Sections of neon, electronic timer)